HEARING HEALING
HOPE

HEARING HEALING HOPE

The Ministry of Service in
Challenging Times

Edited by Gabrielle McMullen, Patrice Scales and
Denis Fitzgerald

Connor Court Publishing

Connor Court Publishing Pty Ltd

PO Box 7257
Redland Bay QLD 4165
sales@connorcourt.com
www.connorcourt.com

ISBN: 9781925826210

Cover Artwork: St Vincent's Health Australia Reconciliation Action Plan Collaborative Art Project.

Artists: Bianca Beetson, Vicki Couzens and Jeffrey Samuels in collaboration with 48 St Vincent's Health Australia staff members.

Title: *Reconciliation: Towards excellent health, happiness and equality, 2016.*

Medium: Silkscreen on magnani paper, 3 panels, edition of 55, 100 x 73cm each.

Printed in Australia

CONTENTS

Hope – Our Engagement with the Challenges

Preface

Archbishop Mark Coleridge

There has never been room for complacency in a Church that seeks to be at the service of humanity. The challenge of the Second Vatican Council to "read the signs of the times and interpret them in light of the Gospel" needs to be taken up in every part of the Church, in every age. One reason for this is that society changes around us.

Today in Australia we find ourselves in a world that has never been wealthier, but where more people are seeking refuge than at any time since the Second World War. We are the heirs to more than 25 years of national economic growth, but with rising job insecurity, entrenched long-term unemployment and high levels of youth underemployment. We have a ground-breaking National Disability Insurance Scheme but are left with many unanswered questions about its impact on individuals and families and on those who seek to serve them.

The mission of the Church remains to preach the Gospel of Jesus Christ, but so much around that core is in flux and that can blur the focus. Pope Francis reminds us of the joy that we should radiate as we seek to serve people where the need is greatest. But this can be a real challenge in the shadow of child sexual abuse and its cover-up, and after the very public humiliation by the Royal Commission into Institutional Responses to Child Sexual Abuse which turned the spotlight on this darkness. Exciting innovation and commitment in the delivery of services and in work for justice sit alongside a continuing drift away from regular Church attendance.

In such a moment, there is an evident need for dialogue and

cooperation among those who lead and inspire the response of the Church to those in need. Such leaders are today overwhelmingly lay, predominantly female, achieving excellence in their professional careers, and doing this with a critical but deep commitment to the call of the Gospel.

It was this group that gathered at the national Catholic Social Services conference in Melbourne in February 2018. Together, they offered insight into and shed light upon the challenges of the day, as we see in the pages of this book.

Hearing, Healing, Hope gathers up the fruit of the conference. It brings the work together as a basis for further reflection and makes it available to a wider readership – to people gathered around a board table, for example, or to an executive team, or a group of staff new to an organisation.

May this book help the whole Church to move more joyfully along the path of hearing, healing and hope in service of a world which, for all its horrors, is deeply loved by God.

Introduction

Gabrielle McMullen AM, Patrice Scales and Denis Fitzgerald

Introduction

The 2018 national conference entitled *Hearing, Healing, Hope* was held on 21-23 February at the Catholic Leadership Centre in East Melbourne. This volume captures the essence of that gathering which was a most successful collaboration of Catholic Social Services Australia and Catholic Social Services Victoria. The theme of the conference – *Hearing, Healing, Hope* – emerged from reflection on many aspects of the environment in which social services and other Church ministries operate in Australia today.

Hearing

As conference planning was underway in 2017, the Royal Commission into Institutional Responses to Child Sexual Abuse was nearing conclusion – key for all parts of the Church was hearing both the voices of survivors of abuse and the confronting findings of the Royal Commission. Other voices were also seeking to be heard – those of victims of family violence, the homeless, refugees and asylum seekers, those with disability dealing with the new National Disability Insurance Scheme (NDIS), Indigenous Australians and countless others experiencing disadvantage. The Church as a whole must be attuned to their needs and those in Catholic social services and other Church ministries ask themselves not only what Jesus would hear in the contemporary Australian "field hospital", to use the terminology of Pope Francis,[1] but also how they can most effectively

---

[1] Fr Antonio Spadaro, 2013. Interview with Pope Francis; see w2.vatican.va/content/francesco/en/speeches/2013/september.index.html.

respond. Furthermore, Pope Francis had put out to us the challenge "to hear both the cry of the earth and the cry of the poor".[2]

Healing

There is much healing to be done. In his 'field hospital' interview, Pope Francis emphasised the centrality of healing for the mission of Church in the modern world:

> The thing the church needs most today is the ability to heal wounds and to warm the hearts of the faithful; it needs nearness, proximity. I see the church as a field hospital after battle. It is useless to ask a seriously injured person if he has high cholesterol and about the level of his blood sugars! You have to heal his wounds. Then we can talk about everything else. Heal the wounds, heal the wounds ... And you have to start from the ground up.[3]

This 'healing' ministry then extends to the causes of marginalisation and disadvantage, where a deeper healing is required. And in Australia today, this work must be accompanied by healing within the Church, lest the aftermath of sexual abuse somehow limits the ministry of the Church and its agencies in service and work for justice.

Hope

There are countless Catholic ministries across Australia – alongside many other people and organisations – serving at the margins, healing wounds, transforming lives and strengthening families and communities. Many dedicated staff go the extra mile, with a vocational commitment to service of the vulnerable. There is much innovation, and inspiring professional competence. All of this is a source of great hope, and gives confidence that the issues and changes

---

[2] Pope Francis, 2015. Encyclical Letter, *Laudato Si': On Care for Our Common Home*, n. 49. Vatican City: Vatican, accessed at w2.vatican.va/.
[3] A. Spadaro, op. cit.

within Australian society today can be effectively addressed, as social services and other Church ministries, faithful to the mission of Jesus, truly "heal the wounds". Such hope was reflected in feedback on the conference from an emerging leader participant who wrote: "I walked away having a real sense of optimism for the future of Catholic Social Services".

The conference made a major national contribution this year to the ongoing formation that is critical for mission. It brought together truly engaging speakers together with 250 delegates from key governance, executive and leadership roles in Catholic social services across the country and from other Church agencies. Participants valued hearing the presenters' insights on the opportunities and challenges facing society, service agencies and the Church and its ministries, but they also valued the dialogue with one another, enriched by delegates' wide-ranging expertise and experiences.

This book now makes available to a wider audience the keynote addresses, forums and workshop presentations of the conference, as well as reflections on the conference themes and feedback from commentators and conference participants. In doing so, it joins publications arising from earlier Catholic Social Services conferences in 2012,[4] 2014[5] and 2016.[6] This collection is part of a literature that reflects back to the sector and to the wider Church and society a dialogue around foundations and directions that will be strengthened by the engagement of a broad readership.

At the 2018 Ozanam Conversation, broadcaster Geraldine Doogue AO, in conversation with Bishop Vincent Long OFM Conv

---

[4] John Warhurst, 2012. *Charity and Justice: St Mary MacKillop and Australian Society*, Catholic Social Justice Series No. 72. Alexandria, NSW: Australian Catholic Social Justice Council.
[5] Gabrielle McMullen and John Warhurst (eds), 2014. *Listening, Learning, Leading: The Impact of Catholic Identity and Mission*. Ballarat: Connor Court.
[6] Gabrielle McMullen, Patrice Scales and Denis Fitzgerald (eds), 2016. *Review, Reimaging, Renew: Mission Making a Difference in a Changing World*. Redland Bay, Qld: Connor Court.

of Parramatta, spoke about the good works of the Catholic community as exemplified by the St Vincent de Paul Society, noting:

> The expression of charity, and Jesus' words, are being enacted but the words often aren't there to describe it ... we have got the actions. I think, strangely enough, we haven't got the words to restate ... this great tradition that we've inherited ... in a way, it is the antithesis of "all talk, no action" ... I want a bit more talk and reflection on why we do what we do because I think that is the way to rescue the Catholic brand.[7]

Importantly, this book and its chapters, which are summarised below, seek to capture in words some of the actions that are the "great tradition" of the social services of the Australian Church.

Hearing – Challenges of Contemporary Church and Society

This first section of the book provides stimulating reading and sometimes disturbing reflections on the challenges that our contemporary Church and society are facing. The chapters are diverse, sometimes offering very personal reflections, at other times drawing to our attention the realities of living in a political and economic world that seems not to be able to close the gap of disadvantage.

Phil Glendenning's chapter looks across many levels at the challenges, the opportunities and hopes of serving those who are at the heart of the mission of the Church. Glendenning reflects on the "unfinished business" of reconciliation with our Indigenous brothers and sisters, on the need for a fundamental change in power relations in the Church, and on the challenge not to be silent when we hear the cries of people seeking asylum. He points to the hope of a "People's

---

[7] Geraldine Doogue, 26 April 2018. St Vincent de Paul Society's 2018 Ozanam Conversation: 'What it Means to be a Catholic Organisation in a Post-Royal Commission World', Catholic Leadership Centre, Melbourne; see www.vinnies.org.au/page/Publications/VICTORIA/.

Movement" that takes Gospel values into the public debate, and to the possibilities of the 2020 Plenary Council that will be infused with the lived experience of those at the margins.

The chapter based on the conference forum on economics draws on three interesting and divergent views presented by Joe Zabar, John Roskam and Clare O'Neil MP. Zabar's "'Thou shalt not" to an Economy of Exclusion and Inequality' is a sobering assessment of contemporary Australian inequality, of an economy that is not adequately addressing the unnecessary hardship suffered by many Australians. Roskam and Lane in 'The Importance of the Dignity of Work' argue that mandated minimum wages operate to exclude the most vulnerable from experiencing the dignity of work and from sharing in prosperity. Roskam and Lane argue further that caring about people includes a preferential option for those without work. In 'Inequality in the Digital Economy', O'Neil reminds us that while Australia is one of the wealthiest countries in the world, inequality is a feature of Australian life and, she fears, this will continue. O'Neil argues that we must protect people who are at the bottom of the labour market, and that investment in education and skills for the new economy is vital.

In 'Moving Justice and Solidarity from the Dictionary to the Workplace of Catholic Social Services', Fr Frank Brennan SJ AO takes the reader on a journey of human rights with some powerful observations. He reflects on Pope Francis and his trip to Myanmar, and the criticism that ensued when Francis did not, as it might have been expected, openly criticise the Myanmar administration's treatment of the Rohingya people. Francis' method was much more subtle, argues Brennan, and in the end Brennan's assessment is that Francis did well. Turning to Australia, Brennan says that we all need to remain vigilant if we are to be a truly inclusive nation ensuring peace and security for all. He then reflects further on the same-sex marriage debate and the continuing episcopal discussion around Pope Francis' exhortation *Amoris Laetitia*. Finally, Brennan challenges us to take the words 'justice' and 'solidarity' out of the dictionary, and work with them so they become a reality.

Geraldine Doogue AO delivered the Mary MacKillop Oration at the *Hearing, Healing, Hope* conference dinner, and her personal reflections focused on the state of the Catholic Church and her own struggle in understanding what the future of the Church will be. She called it her "Holy Saturday thinking" and her contribution to this book will resonate with many people, as it did with guests at the dinner. Doogue, quite surprisingly, as she admits, turns to the experiences of Germany and to Judaism and the Jewish people as examples of peoples who have re-built and re-created their culture, and can provide Catholics with sources of hope and energy. Ultimately, Doogue reflects, the way forward for a thriving Catholic Church in Australia is as an institution with much more collaboration, power- and influence-sharing, and mutual respect between clergy and laity.

The title of Maria Harries' chapter, 'Responding to Abuse, Ensuring Safety and Dedication to Service', as well as being that of a forum at the conference, sums up the breadth of the issues that face the Catholic community. Harries draws on her own experience as a member of the Truth Justice and Healing Council and the wisdom and insights of Robert Fitzgerald AM, a Commissioner on the Royal Commission into Institutional Responses to Child Sexual Abuse, and of Sheree Limbrick, the CEO of the newly established Catholic Professional Standards Ltd. This chapter is essential reading for the Catholic community. Whether in social services, health, education or parishes, we must face the reality of the Church's dire handling of child abuse, and humbly care for victims and look to a future that puts the safety of children in our care first – this is compelling reading.

Healing – Communities with which we Work

This section of the book examines some of the practical, and often inspiring, ways in which Catholic social service organisations, in the face of many challenges, carry out the mission of the Church to care for and empower the disadvantaged in our community. Social housing, asylum seekers, people with disability, and family violence are just some of the topics that were covered in conference workshops. The chapters in this section draw on the presentations made at the conference with a particular focus on healing.

In 'Effective Advocacy of Public Policy', Patrice Scales draws on the presentations made at the workshop by Sally Parnell of Jesuit Social Services, Karen Lococo of Sacred Heart Mission and Phil Glendenning, representing both the Edmund Rice Centre and the Refugee Council of Australia. As this chapter shows, advocacy work in the youth justice system, with people who are homeless, Indigenous people and asylum seekers is ongoing, often difficult, and sometimes successful. The final part of this chapter offers guidance for organisations wishing to improve their advocacy and public campaigns.

The plight of asylum seekers and new migrants is the focus of the insights from the workshop 'Support for Asylum Seekers: Sharing Information and Insights from around the Country'. Adrian Foley, in bringing together the learnings of this workshop, argues that we, as Christians and part of the Catholic Church, carry an even greater responsibility than non-faith aligned organisations, to support and help newcomers to our country. Great effort is already being made through parishes, Catholic social service agencies and schools to support asylum seekers and new migrants but this work needs to continue and grow. The chapter challenges us as Australians to extend mercy, compassion and a welcome to those who, for many reasons, are displaced or forced to leave their birth countries.

The shared experience of three speakers working closely with the issue and impact of family violence are presented in Fiona Basile's chapter, 'Church Leadership in Preventing and Responding to Family Violence : Sharing Resources and Insights from around the Country'. Di Swan, Jocelyn Bignold and Charlie King offered thought-provoking insights into the work they and their organisations do to support victims and survivors of family abuse, how we as a community can work to prevent family abuse, and the impact that early intervention programs in the sporting environment in the Northern Territory has had on reducing the incidence of family abuse. The chapter finishes with a number of recommendations that Catholic social services and the wider Church must take up if family violence is to be stopped.

Darlene Dreise begins the chapter, 'It's Time – Working for Wellness and Empowerment for Our Aboriginal and Torres Strait Islander Brothers and Sisters', with a powerful, personal story – a parable – of hope and possibility. The importance to Indigenous peoples, of story-telling and re-telling, of art and dance, as ways of preserving heritage and lessons for living, is a thread throughout this chapter. Dreise reflects on the deep impact of holistic wellness for Indigenous groups and the important role that people working in ministries of care have in the empowerment and flourishing of our First Peoples. Her reflections in 'Looking Forward, Looking Back' remind the reader that despite the unceasing challenges facing Indigenous wellbeing, we can look to the First Peoples' resilience, influence, wisdom and intellectual insights as optimistic signposts for the future.

The National Disability Insurance Scheme (NDIS) is one of the most ambitious social reforms in Australian political history. Two workshops held at the conference addressed both the ideal and the reality of the Scheme as it is brought to full implementation. The chapter, 'The National Disability Insurance Scheme: Opportunities and Challenges for Mission-based Agencies', by Ingrid Hatfield brings together the collective wisdom, experience and insights of key players in its implementation. The first workshop explored areas of convergence and tension between NDIS policies and practices and the mission of Catholic agencies. The second workshop provided an opportunity for agencies to connect with the collective expertise of Catholic agencies delivering services through the NDIS.

May Lam in the chapter, 'Social Housing: Exploring Opportunities for Affordable Housing Initiatives', reports on the efforts of a number of Catholic social service organisations which are working to provide affordable housing options for the increasing number of people who are long-term homeless and people who are falling into homelessness. The reporting from the workshop explores the challenges of responding to social housing needs faced by two specific agencies, Centacare Ballarat and CatholicCare Tasmania, and the implementation of solutions that they have delivered. The chapter also reports on two housing action networks in Sydney and Victoria as they, too, examine options for how the wider Church can play a significant role in tackling this continuing social problem that Australia, despite its wealth, is failing to address effectively.

Robyn Miller, CEO of MacKillop Family Services and a child protection practitioner for over 30 years, in the chapter, 'Excellence in Caring for Vulnerable Clients: Going beyond the Rhetoric and Compliance to Explore Excellence in Care', maintains that current mainstream systems of child protection have not worked, and that what is really needed are relationally-based and long-term solutions to support families, to prevent harm and to prevent children coming into care. In the past decade, the number of children and young people in care in Australia has increased by 82 per cent – it is obviously time for new approaches. Miller details MacKillop's implementation of the Sanctuary Model with its focus on trauma-informed care and explains the impact that the Sanctuary Model has had on her organisation's approach to caring for the most vulnerable children, young people and families in our community.

Hope – Our Engagement with the Challenges

While a sense of hope imbues many elements of the previous chapters, the following chapters of this book examine some of the broader structural and societal topics with which Catholic social service agencies, and to some extent the wider Church, is engaged and which are a source of inspiration and hope. From the environment, to governance, to the empowering work of parishes, there is much in these chapters to illustrate that the mission of serving the most disadvantaged in our community remains strong despite the challenges that face Church agencies.

'A Healthy Earth for a Flourishing Society: Implementing *Laudato Si'* is a report from Mark Monahan of the forum that led into the conference. This forum aimed to challenge all within the Catholic social services community to consider how they could respond to the call of Pope Francis in *Laudato Si'* to care for "our common home". As well as Jacqui Remond's overview of *Laudato Si'*, this chapter gives a moving report on the words – and the silence – of Dr Miriam-Rose Ungunmerr-Baumann AO about the rich wisdom of Australia's First Peoples. The report also relates practical examples of two organisations, Jesuit Social Services and the St Vincent de Paul Society, which are working on different aspects of eco-social justice both in the workplace and with those who are vulnerable.

In 'Emerging Issues in Not-for-profit Governance', Elizabeth Proust AO covers a range of pressing issues for boards of governance of both for profit and not-for-profit organisations. Trust, culture, increased accountability, financial viability and advocacy – as Proust puts it, "a tsunami of change" – cannot be ignored, yet also offer opportunities to achieve great outcomes for organisations and their beneficiaries, and deliver on mission. The comments and discussion reported from the interactive workshop illustrate the breadth of governance issues that are causing concern to organisations.

In a chapter on the second of the conference's governance workshops, Gabrielle McMullen AM and Des Powell AM address 'Priorities in Governance of Catholic Organisations', focusing not only on civil governance but also on mission in decision-making and stewardship of ministries. Board directors and trustees, argue McMullen and Powell, carry significant responsibilities on behalf of the Church, and therefore must make an unequivocal commitment to formation. Case studies around three themes – deeper understanding of the identity of a Catholic ministry, authenticity of a Catholic ministry and managing risk – illustrate the challenges faced by many contemporary ministries.

Catholic parishes might be thought to be leaders in providing 'grass-roots' social services and welfare activities within their local communities. But with declining attendees at Mass, and a younger cohort turning away from traditional religious activities, can parishes make claim to being active in this area of community service? In the chapter, 'Love of Neighbour – What are our Parishes Doing?', Bob Dixon draws on the conference presentations by Bob Dixon, Bernadette Dennis and Terry Kean that present very encouraging evidence that there is a wide range of welfare services and social justice activities happening in parishes across Australia. Drawing on data from the National Church Life Survey, and examples of support services for the most marginalised and disadvantaged in parishes across Australia, including work being done for international aid projects, and local support for asylum seekers and refugees, the answer is 'yes' – the parish environment remains a robust and active source of service and social justice.

In the next chapter of this section focused on hope, Paul Bongiorno AM, veteran journalist and columnist, in his reflective piece, shares observations from his viewpoint as conference facilitator. It is interesting to note that his original expectations of the conference, in the context of the Royal Commission, and his final observations were quite different. The conference did not shirk from facing up to the challenges that the Church now has before it. He reflects on the contribution of many of the keynote and other presentations, and finally notes that in coming together participants were able "to take heart from their fellow labourers in the vineyard of the Lord".

Denis Fitzgerald follows with a reflection on the various liturgies and spiritual elements of the conference, and their integration into the hearing, healing and hope that was the program for the gathering.

The closing forum of the Catholic Social Services conference focused on 'Bringing Healing and Hope to the World'. It offered an opportunity for participants to reflect on the previous elements of the conference and contextualise their learnings in participants' ministries. The session, facilitated by Fr Frank Brennan SJ AO, invited participants to "grapple together with some of the challenges that face us as a sector, as a church, as a community in this challenging and changing environment of Australia". In the concluding chapter of the book, Gabrielle McMullen has captured "examples of renewal and energy shared" at this forum, which offered an "opportunity to 'account for the hope within us' on hearing all that is happening".

Conclusion

The Second Vatican Council challenged all parts of the Church to engage fully with the world:

> The joys and the hopes, the griefs and the anxieties of the people of this age, especially those who are poor or in any way afflicted, these are the joys and the hopes, the griefs and the anxieties of the followers of Christ.[8]

This book, and the conference from which it emerged, are part of an ongoing dialogue about that engagement, a dialogue that must

---

[8] Pope Paul VI, 1965. *Pastoral Constitution on the Church in the Modern World: Gaudium et Spes*, n. 1, accessed at www.vatican.va.

be rich and robust if hearing, healing and hope are to be dominant features of this work.

As the Church in Australia is moving towards the Plenary Council 2020, we are called to "listen to what the Spirit is saying" and "to engage in an open and inclusive process of listening, dialogue and discernment about the future of the Catholic Church in Australia".[9] The 2018 Catholic Social Services conference contributed to this process through its dialogical focus and broad national representation. A key message from the conference was that Catholic social services together with health, aged care, education and other ministries of the Church are vibrantly engaged in bringing Christ's healing ministry to Australian society today, even as they address the many challenges that they face in doing so.

---

[9] Information on the Plenary Council 2020 can be accessed at plenarycouncil.catholic. org.au/.

Hearing – Challenges of Contemporary Church and Society

1

Catholic Social Services as Agents of Hearing, Healing and Hope

Phil Glendenning AM

This chapter had its basis in the opening keynote address at the 2018 Catholic Social Services national conference held in Melbourne. Let me begin, as I did at the conference, by acknowledging the traditional custodians of this land, the Wurundjeri people of the Kulin nation. At the same time, I acknowledge the traditional custodians of all those other lands where readers of this chapter reside and pay my respects to their elders past and present.

I do not make that acknowledgment lightly. I do it because history happened in those places, and much of that history remains unfinished business, unreconciled. And as the old saying goes, if we do not learn from the sins of our history, we are bound to repeat them. And as a nation, repeat them we have, for too long and too often, and not just with regard to our Aboriginal and Torres Strait Islander peoples, our First Peoples, but also to the last to arrive, people seeking asylum and refugees. There are linkages in the way Australia has treated the First Peoples and the last to arrive, and some key learnings for us.

I want to start by affirming the wonderful work of Catholic Social Services, which is a profound source of hope in this world of fake news, 24/7 news cycles and reality TV (which is really '*escape* from reality' TV). There is a crisis in leadership across the world from Donald Trump to Brexit to the shenanigans of local politicians.

The conference was timely as we explore the barriers, challenges, hopes and opportunities we face in serving those who are at the heart of the mission of the Church. It canvassed environmental conversion, economic paradigms, human rights challenges, the NDIS (National Disability Insurance Scheme), housing, refugees and Indigenous peoples' rights. It was a big agenda. In particular, it considered the implications of the outcomes and learnings from the Royal Commission into Institutional Responses to Child Sexual Abuse. And that was a good thing. I believe that this post-Royal Commission time offers a real opportunity for liberation and redemption for the Church in Australia. The truth sets us free, and this ugly truth had been hidden for too long.

One of the biggest challenges we face is to reflect on the leadership required to address the need for root and branch reform in the Church, and in our wider society, to ensure that what we have heard over the past five years can never happen again. It is easy to become cynical when we consider the state of the world and, with the notable exception of Pope Francis, the state of the world's leadership. But I have always held that cynicism is just an elegant form of surrender, and the one thing we must not do in the light of challenges we face is surrender. And yes, there are plenty of challenges, but there is also plenty of hope.

The ongoing work of Catholic Social Services right across this nation is a clear example of where we have to look to find that hope. And this work is not just about 'us' doing good to others. If we get it right, then we can find ourselves in a situation of mutuality, of learning from each other.

The week before the conference marked the 10th anniversary of Kevin Rudd's National Apology to Australia's Indigenous Peoples,[1] though you had to look hard to find much mention of it in the midst of vindictive political 'barneys'.

---

[1] The apology can be accessed at www.australia.gov.au/about-australia/our-country/our-people/apology-to-australias-indigenous-peoples.

Indeed, even on the political junkies' Sunday morning hangover cure, ABC TV's *Insiders*, it took 50 minutes until it was even mentioned, briefly. On the anniversary day itself, the Prime Minister walked out of a launch of the *Close the Gap* report for another commitment – Father of Reconciliation and now Senator Patrick Dodson referred to this as "indicative of the deafness, of the absolute derision and contempt this Government is meting out to Aboriginal people".[2] This Government, of course, does not have that on its own. All Governments, with some noticeable exceptions, have failed to listen to Indigenous Australians. The recent rejection of the Uluru *Statement from the Heart*,[3] is but another example. We are living in difficult, hardening times, reflected by:

- the situation of Manus and Nauru with their offshore detainees,
- worldwide 65 million people displaced and 24 million refugees,
- the recent suicide attempt at Homebush of a young Sri Lankan.

Calculated cruelty works best when it is accompanied by silence, by deafness and an unwillingness to hear.

This deafness is nothing new. This inability to hear is often how the powerful in society and, as the Royal Commission has found, in the Church have walked away from responsibility to those broken by 'the system' that excludes them, or by a toxic culture. Yet real active intense listening is the key to finding hope, not just for the Church but across society.

Over 20 years ago at a Let's Talk Reconciliation Conference in

---

[2] Senator Dodson's comments can be accessed at patrickdodson.com.au/doorstop-closing-the-gap/.

[3] For a copy of the statement, see www.referendumcouncil.org.au/final-report#toc-anchor-ulurustatement-from-the-heart.

Northern Ireland, Aboriginal leader Olga Havnen was asked by the Sinn Fein Mayor of Belfast what would need to happen for a reconciled Australia to become a reality. She said that there were five steps:

- recognition of Aboriginal and Torres Strait Islanders as the First Peoples of Australia,
- acknowledgment of the unique rights to land, culture, language and spirituality that flows from that recognition,
- a commitment to social justice that is both formal and substantive
- negotiations in good faith, and
- a fundamental change in power relations.[4]

When the issue about a change in power relations was mentioned, some of the politicians on the stage went demonstrably pale. However, a few short years later, that was what was delivered in the Good Friday Agreement that put an end to the Irish Troubles and ushered in a new era of peace in Northern Ireland. Power was shared. The guns were put down.

Reconciliation here remains a fundamental plank in the unfinished business of this country. However, Havnen's very wise five steps of *recognition, acknowledgment, commitment to justice, good faith negotiations leading to a change in power relations* could provide us with a template for learning from the Royal Commission and to build something new.

I agree with the view of Francis Sullivan, CEO of the Church's Truth Justice and Healing Council,[5] that it is not enough for the Church to get its house in order, the house has to be re-built. I would like to take this opportunity to pay tribute to Sullivan for his leadership

---

[4] Olga Havnen, September 1999. Speech given at Let's Talk Reconciliation Conference, Belfast.

[5] For Sullivan's speech, see www.tjhcouncil.org.au/media/132927/170310-SPEECH-Catalyst-for-Renewal-Hunters-Hill-Francis-Sullivan.pdf.

and witness of behalf of all of us in attending the Royal Commission for every day of its sittings. We owe him a great debt.

This is not a time to put the wagons in a circle. There needs to be an honest and open recognition of the history that happened, of the abuses and systematic cover-ups; an acknowledgment of the hurt and pain to the victims, their families, and to the Catholic people; and an acknowledgment of the criminal culpability of a culture that allowed this to happen and be covered up. There needs to be a commitment to justice that is formal and substantial. Victims must be heard and listened to and compensated properly. In many instances, of course, this has been happening. It needs to continue. It needs to continue for a long time.

However, there must also be a fundamental change in power relations in the Church. The culture of secrecy and of unquestioning deference to the hierarchy must change. As the Royal Commission concluded: There was "a catastrophic failure in the leadership … and ultimately in the structure and culture of the Church over decades to effectively respond to the sexual abuse of children by its priests …. That harm could have been avoided if the Church had acted in the interests of children rather than in its own interests".[6] Here lie the seeds for the future, in putting this right.

Those of us involved in Catholic Social Services and the 'punters' in the Church need to see the outcomes of the Royal Commission as an opportunity for liberation and redemption. The child abuse scandal and crimes represent a sordid truth that was hidden. The fact that the truth is out now, as horrific as it is, is far preferable to keeping it hidden.

Last year should not be seen as the Catholic Church's *annus horribilis*, as has been suggested, because of the outcomes of the

---

[6] Royal Commission into Institutional Responses to Child Sexual Abuse, 2017. *Report of Case Study No. 28: Catholic Church Authorities in Ballarat*, 403, accessed at www.childabuse-royalcommission.gov.au/.

Royal Commission and the same sex marriage plebiscite. Last year was, however, an *annus horribilis* for Behrooz Boochani and the other hundreds of men trapped on Manus island for up to five years; it certainly was for Fatima, an asylum seeker on Nauru who is facing imminent death from heart disease who will not leave Nauru for hospitalisation in Australia because the Australian Government have banned her 17-year-old son from accompanying her. It has been one *annus horribilis* after another for the victims of child sexual abuse and their families.

If the truth sets us free then we need to embrace this opportunity to act in the interests of the other, rather than in the interests of the institutional Church. There is no room here for the 'yes, but' response – that admitting that terrible things happened but "hey, we run great schools, hospitals and social services". That will not do any longer. It is like saying to Indigenous Australians, sorry about the Stolen Generations but look at the money the Government spends. That completely misses the point.

Acting in service to others is something that all Catholic Social Services aspire to do, and do in reality, working alongside the poor, the disabled, the homeless, the Indigenous, the refugee and the broken every day. It is in this work, the spirituality that drives it, and the compassion that sustains it, that we find the hope to face the future.

The late great Columban Fr Cyril Hally used to say to me that you will not hear the Gospel at the centre, but you will hear it at the edges. As Pope Francis says, "Go to the fringes". This is where our social services are based. It is where Jesus went.

Jose Comblin writes of his deep concern for the fate of Christianity in the West and its adherence to what he sees as the Religious Pole as opposed to the Gospel Pole. They, of course, do not have to be mutually exclusive, but Comblin warns of a Western Church that focusses too much on the Religious Pole which he says requires a tight hierarchical caste system, with a focus on rules and regulations, tightening and straightening, judgments of who is in and who is out, hell-bent on defending the institution. The Gospel Pole, however, takes us back to the social reality, to engagement with the poor. It takes us to places that are messy, chaotic, heroic, painful and joyful, the ups and downs of life, where lives are lived. These are the places where Jesus hung out and the people with whom he hung out.[7]

Royal Commissions of themselves do not necessarily deliver lasting change. Sadly, 27 years after the Royal Commission into Aboriginal Deaths in Custody, the situation concerning Indigenous incarceration rates is worse now in 2018 than when the Royal Commission made its recommendations. Change will only come when it is demanded and made a priority. That task is up to all of us.

For the future, unquestioning loyalty to the institutional Church should no longer be espoused as a fine Catholic attribute: it has led to deep institutional failure with catastrophic results for many families and vulnerable children. As Fr Frank Brennan SJ has written: "We Catholics all need to get better in our firm, respectful, and demanding encounters with our hierarchy".[8] Indeed, to question *is* to care. Not enough questions were asked in the past. That was the culture and that is the culture that has to change.

So, we need to work for change, building on the great work that is being done by Catholic Social Services' organisations. This work is not only important in the life of the Church, it is essential for our society that we engage with the factors that limit the possibility of the living of a fully human life – environmental destruction, poverty, racism, discrimination, an economic order that reduces people to servants of an economy rather than equal citizens in a society.

This notion of *the citizen* is one we have to defend, especially in

[7] See, for example, José Comblin, 2010. The March 2010 UCA Lecture, accessed at iglesia-descalza.blogspot.com.au/2010/11/jose-comblin-march-2010-uca-lecture.html.
[8] Frank Brennan SJ, 14 December 2017. "A Catholic Reflection on the Royal Commission as the Curtain Closes on Act One", accessed at johnmenadue.com/.

these days where it often seems that we all live together in an *economy* rather than a *society*. This is significant because the people who live in a society are *citizens*, and they have *rights* and they have *responsibilities*. However, those who reside in an economy are *customers* or *consumers*, with *choices*, dependent on how much wealth they have access to.

This paradigm shift from a society to an economy has been accompanied by a shift in language: people who travel in planes are no longer referred to as *passengers*, now they are *customers* – listen to the boarding announcement next time you are at an airport. Banks no longer provide *services*, they sell *products*. I remember recently renegotiating my mortgage and was told by the bank manager how "we have some great new products for you". And those *who* reside in the care of a psychiatric institution in NSW are no longer *patients* or *residents*, everyone is a *client* – what are they purchasing?

Moreover, those who live in a society are valued inherently for *who they are*, as human beings with inalienable rights. In an economy we value people for *what they can do*, for their utility or production value. And once we base our relationships and interactions on economics primarily rather than humanity, it becomes easier to treat people in inhuman ways. Welcome to the Northern Territory's Don Dale youth detention centre and its treatment of Aboriginal youth! Welcome to Nauru and Manus Island!

If we are not attentive to the words we use and the assumptions and values they represent, this enables and emboldens "an ideological creep back to bigotry and to racism". Patrick Dodson explains: "It is fine if you sit in some leafy suburb and never rub shoulders with people who are battling to interpret and navigate their way through modernity in this land of Australia, with its highly-sophisticated culture and its complexities of protocols and procedures and social ethos".[9]

---

[9] Patrick Dodson, 24 November 2016. 'Racial Discrimination Law Amendment (Free Speech) Bill 2016', accessed at parlinfo.aph.gov.au/.

David Ervine, a Northern Irish Unionist politician who became great mates with Dodson, the former Aboriginal Catholic priest with Indigenous and some Irish ancestry, summed this up when he visited Australia in 2002 to speak at the Treaty Conference, reflecting on the state of race relations in Australia: "I can smell racism. It doesn't grow wild in a field. It is tended in a window box". He went on to suggest that the then Prime Minister had a very green thumb![10] The point here is simple: words count, language matters.

In his 2016 speech in the Senate calling for Section 18c of the Racial Discrimination Act not to be watered down, Dodson said: "If this nation cannot stand up for the weakest, the poorest and those who are most vulnerable because of their race, their ethnicity or their beliefs, then we have become a very sad replication of what democracy is about".[11]

In the same way, if the Catholic Church in Australia cannot stand up for, *and be seen to stand up for*, the weakest, the poorest and those who are most vulnerable because of their race, ethnicity, beliefs or health, then we would be a sad replication of the Church Jesus wants us to be. This is the work of Catholic Social Services; Catholic Social Services do this, not just in the Church, but in Australian society. Australian society needs to hear this. So, we cannot be silent. Martin Luther King once famously said that silence is betrayal, and that we begin to die the day we are silent.

The 24 million refugees worldwide, the population of Australia, are not just numbers. They are human beings. They are brothers, fathers, sisters, mothers, friends. They are children – more than half are children.

---

[10] David Ervine, 27 August 2002. Opening Plenary Address, National Treaty Conference, co-hosted by the Aboriginal and Torres Strait Islander Commission, Australians for Native Title and Reconciliation and the Australian Institute for Aboriginal and Torres Strait Islander Studies, National Convention Centre, Canberra.

[11] P. Dodson, op. cit.

Emmanuel Kant was right when he proclaimed that human beings should never be used as a means to an end. They are an end in themselves. The wrong done to them must be righted, the cruelty to refugees and people seeking asylum must stop and this sorry chapter in Australian history must be closed.

This generation has a challenge on its hands. All of us, unless you are an Aboriginal or Torres Strait Island person, are descended from someone who came from somewhere else by boat. Even in recent times the vast majority of people seeking asylum in this country arrived by plane, not by boat. There remains something about us and boats. Ask an Aboriginal person.

Given events in the Federal Parliament in February 2018, with an end to bi-partisan commitment to constitutional recognition of Aboriginal and Torres Strait Islander peoples in the Constitution, there is an opportunity for all of us to put on the record our support for the unfinished business of Australian history, to be taken seriously and not used for partisan political point-scoring. The Uluru Statement is a conservative proposal with no legislative power. The "nothing about us without us" notion has been rejected again. We cannot accept that; we must not accept that.

Part of the theme of both the Catholic Social Services conference and this book, calls for Hearing. Over the many years I have spent in this work, it is the voices of the people that point the way forward to Healing and to Hope, the other elements of the theme.

Consider a poem penned by a young Iranian asylum seeker who spent a number of years in mandatory detention, after arriving in Australia by boat:

I do not know
what will happen after I die
I do not want to know.
But I would like the Potter

to make a whistle
From the clay of my throat.
May this whistle fall into the hands
Of a naughty child
and the child blow hard on the whistle continuously
with all the suppressed and silent air of his lungs
and disrupt the sleep
of those who seem dead to my cries.

We must proclaim to that asylum seeker, and all others who seek protection only to be met by cruelty, that we are not dead to their cries; and we must never be dead to these cries, no matter what the limits or blindfolds of the domestic political debate.

The work of Catholic Social Services is testament that the Church is not blind. But this work also needs to be proclaimed – loudly – not just to the members of the Church but to all of society. The cry of this young man seeking asylum is echoed in the voices of Indigenous people, the homeless, the disabled, the lonely, the invisible people, the very people Catholic Social Services encounter on a daily basis. These people matter.

In particular, we cannot be dead to the cry of the Indigenous peoples of this country seeking fairness, equality and recognition *in their own land*. Again, as Martin Luther King famously said, we begin to die the day we are silent about the things that matter. Today, the first and last peoples of this nation must not have their cries met with the deadening silence of indifference. They matter.

In recent times we have heard that the biggest threat to our way of life is immigration, with the narrative proclaiming that migrants take our jobs, and the Minister for Immigration and Border Protection Peter Dutton MP claiming that refugees not only take jobs but clog up unemployment queues at the same time. This is despite the fact that all the research indicates that Australians are more inclined to employ other Australians than any other group. And we hear that in Melbourne people are scared to go to a restaurant for fear of being accosted by African gangs. This is blind populism straight from the Donald Trump playbook.

The words of British journalist, Laurie Penny, writing for the *New Statesman* three years ago about Europe, seem ever more apt today, not just for the European continent but also for Australia:

> The greatest threat to our 'way of life' is not migration. Migration does change society, although far less so than, for example, technology, economic austerity, escalating inequality, globalisation or climate change. But the greatest threat to our "way of life", if there has ever been such a thing on this vast and varied continent, is not that someday you or I might be sitting on a bus and hear someone speaking Pashto or Tigrinya. The threat is that we will swallow the public narrative that immigrants, people from non-European countries are less human than the rest of us, that they think and feel **less**, that they matter **less**. Europeans are quite capable of sitting calmly in the bubbling water of cultural bigotry until it boils away every shred of compassion we have left. That's the real threat to our 'way of life'.[12]

That's the real threat in Australia as well. I often say to young people, never let someone tell you that compassion for others is a form of weakness. In fact, it is our greatest civilising strength.

Healing requires that we reclaim the values that enable people to have life and have life to the full. We must reclaim the language, and fundamentally put humanity and the planet back in the picture. The language we use matters, because when we strip back the language we

---

[12] Laurie Penny, 14 August 2015. "Europe Shouldn't Worry About Migrants", *New Statesman*, accessed at www.newstatesman.com/, emphasis added.

reveal the *assumptions* underpinning decisions, and when we strip back the assumptions underpinning decisions we reveal the *values* on which decisions are based.

As we have learnt in the refugee sector, we have to advocate *for* something not just *against* something. We need to work together with those we seek to serve to *create the space* where the authentic voice of people with lived experience can be heard. Ours is not to speak on their behalf but to work with people – we then liberate each other together. We will need not to be afraid to raise our voices because, and I quote Martin Luther King again, "We begin to die the day we are silent about the things that matter".

There is a need in Australia for an articulate, cohesive and clear voice of Catholics talking about our issues, and not just within the Church. We need a Peoples' Movement that takes Gospel values into the public debate. In the lead-up to the 2020 Plenary Council,[13] we need to infuse it with the lived experience of those at the margins. Catholic Social Services will have a key role to play.

For me, the Plenary Council can go a long way towards rebuilding and renewing the Church, if it follows the aspirations of Bishop Vincent Long OFM Conv of Parramatta – that is, if it aspires to a Church that is:

- less an enclosure for the virtuous but more an oasis for the weary and the downtrodden,

- less an experience of exclusion and elitism and more an encounter of radical love, inclusiveness and solidarity,

- less an attitude of 'we are right, and you are wrong' and more of an openness to truth wherever and from whoever it is to be found,

- less a leadership of control and clericalism but more a

---

[13] The Australian Catholic Church plans to host a Plenary Council in 2020-2021; see www.plenarycouncil.catholic.org.au/.

diakonia of a humble servant exemplified by Christ at the Last Supper,

- less a language of condemnation, and
- less a preoccupation for its own maintenance but more a concern for the Kingdom and the people of God.[14]

We are indeed on the threshold of renewal and transformation, and a new paradigm based on mutuality not exclusion, service not clericalism, engagement with the world not flight from or hostility against it. To achieve this renewal and transformation, we will need to maintain our passion and enthusiasm. This can often be difficult to do. We must remain close to the people, listening.

For me, maintaining hope and optimism comes down to a simple decision – to Choose Life! Maintain the faith in the Christian 'craziness' (as Jon Sobrino suggests) that it is still possible to live on this planet like a human being.

Look to history – *change happens*. It does so particularly through Peoples' Movements, where people coalesce to take joint action around shared values, inspired by a mobilising vision – for example:

- the environment movement,
- the women's movement,
- the anti-apartheid movement,
- the movement for disability rights,
- the peace movement,
- the fall of the Soviet Union and the Berlin Wall,
- the independence of East Timor and South Africa.

Now is not the time for putting the wagons in a circle. We need a 'Peoples' Movement' in the Church, including significant lay leadership

---

[14] Vincent Long OFM Conv, 2016. Ann D Clark Lecture, accessed at catholicoutlook. org/.

in partnership, of course, with bishops, clergy, religious and people of goodwill. All in. We will need to be brave in our pursuit of justice in words and deeds as we seek change: justice for those who have been hurt by the Church and those in our community who have been left behind by poor Government policy or through an economy that fails to value them as people. We seek to build a world reflective of Jesus' love where:

- the needs of the poor take priority over the wants of the rich,

- the freedom of the weak takes priority over the liberty of the powerful, and

- the access of marginalised groups in society takes priority over an order which excludes them.

In the words of Seamus Heaney, some will often say it is futile to hope "on this side of the grave" but occasionally in the lives of people and nations the great tide of justice rises up and "hope and history rhyme".[15]

As we go about this task we do more than hope, but work and live *in expectation* that the change is 'gonna' come. Time to start blowing on those clay whistles and go and change history!

---

[15] Seamus Heaney, 1991. *The Cure at Troy.*

2

Economics for a Flourishing Society

Joe Zabar, John Roskam, Aaron Lane and Clare O'Neil MP

Pope Francis has sent a powerful message to Catholics and the global community that our current economic paradigm must change. Too many people continue to be excluded from meaningful participation in our society due to an economy that gives priority to assets and markets over people. The Catholic Church in Australia is seeking to respond, including through the Australian Catholic Bishops' 2017-2018 Social Justice Statement 'Everyone's Business – Developing an Inclusive and Sustainable Economy'.

The 2018 Catholic Social Services national conference also addressed Pope Francis' challenge with a forum on economics for a flourishing society. The keynote speaker was Joe Zabar of Catholic Social Services Australia. John Roskam of the Institute of Public Affairs and Clare O'Neil, Federal Member of Parliament, responded to his paper. This chapter brings together the input and the insights of the three presenters, each of them coming from personal and contrasting perspectives, and each of them thought-provoking. It demonstrates the complexity of the economic and political environment in which Catholic Social Services and other agencies serving the marginalised and disadvantaged have to operate. In a time of globalisation, marketisation and insecure employment, it explores economics for a flourishing society.

"Thou shalt not" to an Economy of Exclusion and Inequality

Joe Zabar

Just as the commandment "Thou shalt not kill" sets a clear limit in order to safeguard the value of human life, today we also have to say, "thou shalt not" to an economy of exclusion and inequality. Such an economy kills.[1]

Introduction

Pope Francis' statement is not one merely for theological or academic contemplation. It is in effect Pope Francis' call to establish a new benchmark for our economy, one where exclusion and inequality are no longer a natural and accepted consequence of its operation.

There can be no doubt that our modern global economy has created unprecedented economic growth and lifted billions of people out of poverty. The proportion of people living in extreme poverty globally has reduced from 41.91 per cent in 1981 to 10.67 per cent in 2013.[2]

Global gross domestic product (GDP) has grown almost 9-fold since 1980 and by 2022 is expected to be around $US103,000 billion. Emerging and developing countries will account for 44 per cent of global GDP in 2022 up from 24 per cent in 1980.[3]

Since 1980 Australia's GDP has grown from $US163 billion reaching $US1,390 billion in 2017. Two of Asia's fastest growing econo-

---

[1] Pope Francis, 2013. Apostolic Exhortation: *Evangelii Gaudium*. Vatican City: Vatican, n. 53, accessed at w2.vatican.va.

[2] World Bank, 2016. World Development Indicators, Share of the Population Living in Extreme Poverty, accessed at data.worldbank.org/indicator.

[3] International Monetary Fund, 2017. World Economic Outlook, DataMapper, accessed at www.imf.org/en/Publications/WEO/Issues/2017/09/19/world-economic-outlook-october-2017.

mies, namely China and India, have seen exceptional GDP growth over this same period. China's GDP is now almost 40 times larger than in 1980 reaching a staggering $US11,940 billion while India's GDP has increased 13-fold hitting $2,440 billion in 2017.

Today, these two countries are global economic powerhouses, and have helped Australia achieve an unprecedented period of economic growth. While Australia's fortunes have waned slightly post the Global Financial Crisis (GFC), our economy continues to grow.

On 6 December 2017 the Treasurer, Scott Morrison, released the National Accounts for the September quarter 2017.[4] In his release, the Treasurer stated:

> Today's national accounts is another encouraging set of numbers, reinforcing an economic strategy that is based on driving growth through increased investment to secure better days ahead.
>
> The September quarter created more than 100,000 jobs. That's more than 1,000 jobs every day. So far this year we have experienced the strongest jobs growth in forty years, with four out of five jobs being full time.

The Treasurer also noted that the September quarter saw increased economic growth to 2.8 per cent through the year, which places Australia towards the top of the major advanced economies, with profits also rising in the quarter by 1.2 per cent, delivering through the year growth of 16.7 per cent. The Treasurer rightly points to these economic indicators as proof positive that the Australian economy is doing well.

Our latest national economic statistics might be comforting for the Government, but they hide the lived reality of:

---

[4] The Hon. Scott Morrison MP, 6 December 2017. National Accounts – September Quarter 2017, media statement, accessed at www.scottmorrison.com.au/news/national-accounts-september-quarter/.

- three million Australians, including more than 730,000 children, living in poverty,[5]
- more than 700,000 people unable to find suitable work,[6]
- 160,000 long-term unemployed,[7] and
- 1.1 million people looking to increase their hours of work in order to improve their financial wellbeing.[8]

Leaving Too Many People Behind

Despite the positive economic numbers, our economy is leaving too many people behind. The reality is that our economy is not adequately addressing the unnecessary hardship suffered by many Australians. Significantly, our current economic policy settings, which give primacy to markets and competition, are increasing inequality in Australia.

We are becoming a nation divided, with the spoils of economic growth becoming ever more concentrated. In the recent briefing paper, 'Growing Gulf between Work and Wealth', Oxfam Australia's CEO Dr Helen Szoke said:

> Over the decade since the Global Financial Crisis, the wealth of Australian billionaires has increased by almost 140 per cent. Yet over the same time, the average wages of ordinary Australians have increased by just 36 per cent and average household wealth grew by 12 per cent.[9]

[5] Australian Council of Social Services (ACOSS), 2016. *Poverty in Australia 2016*. Sydney: ACOSS and Social Policy Research Centre, UNSW, 8, accessed at www.acoss.org.au/wp-content/uploads/2016/10/Poverty-in-Australia-2016.pdf.

[6] Australian Bureau of Statistics, November 2017. 6202.0 *Labour Force, Australia*, accessed at www.abs.gov.au.

[7] Australian Bureau of Statistics, December 2017. 6291.0.55.001 *Labour Force, Australia, Detailed – Electronic Delivery*, Table 14b 'Unemployed persons by Duration of job search and Sex – Trend, Seasonally Adjusted, and Original', accessed at www.abs.gov.au.

[8] Australian Bureau of Statistics, November 2016. 6202.0 *Labour Force, Australia*, accessed at www.abs.gov.au.

[9] Helen Szoke, 22 January 2018. *Australia's Inequality Crisis: Oxfam Paper* media release, accessed at www.medianet.com.au/releases/152247/.

Sadly, rather than acknowledging the limitations of our economy and working to address them, many seek to demonise those that the economy leaves behind.

Failing to correct our current economic and social policy settings will only further entrench intergenerational disadvantage in Australia. Ignoring them altogether is both morally and economically fraught.

Today the concepts of 'merit' and 'fair go' can no longer be regarded as universal Australian values, because for too many young Australians their future prosperity is dependent on the wealth of their parents.[10] Unless this is addressed, we will see an ever-increasing level of inequality in Australia, consigning those families in poverty to intergenerational disadvantage simply because they were born in the wrong post code.

We are not all born equal. Circumstances, not of our own making, will factor heavily in the opportunities we have and the quality of the life we lead. As a society blessed with riches, we have witnessed rapid advances in technology, education and medicine giving hope and opportunity to people, who only decades earlier, might have been forgotten or ignored by everyone other than their family and friends. Activism, addressing issues of social inequality such as gender pay, disability employment and recognition of our First Peoples, has created a better and more inclusive society. While much more needs to be done, there is a ready acceptance by most Australians that policies which discriminate against a person based on gender, race, disability or religion are wrong.

However, when it comes to economic policies that favour one class or group of people ahead of another we seem less concerned. Economic inequality, whether deliberate or as a consequence of the operation of the market, seems somehow acceptable. While we

---

[10] Silvia Mendolia and Peter Siminski, 2015. *New Estimates of Intergenerational Mobility in Australia*. Bonn, Germany: IZA, Discussion Paper no. 9394.

might acknowledge the moral hazards of discrimination, we temper our concern for fear that it might interfere too much with how the economy works. It appears that we are all for fairness and equality as long as it does not impact too heavily on the economic 'bottom line'.

That said, governments have recognised that power imbalances exist in our market-based economy and have enacted legislative protections in areas such as the labour market. However, such laws only provide minimum safeguards.

Our legislators seem reticent to tackle the economic policies which create or entrench economic inequality. How is it that we:

- allow investors to leave units vacant in Docklands while young people struggle to access the housing market in Melbourne,

- force the employees of charities to bear the risk of government policies of marketisation and competition in the social services sector through the casualisation of their employment,

- require students to carry the burden of debt for undertaking tertiary studies while allowing multinational companies to construct their financial affairs to pay little or no tax in Australia, or

- permit the Government to provide tax relief to businesses while implementing cuts to welfare payments and supports?

We have given legislators a free pass when it comes to economic policies which discriminate against those without means. It is that free pass which creates systemic inequality in Australia and which needs to be addressed as a matter of urgency.

Contemporary Australian Inequality

Inequality was a hot issue in 2017 and I dare say it will be again at the time of the next federal election.

In July 2017, speaking at the Melbourne Institute, Opposition leader Bill Shorten said: "We need a new focus on the biggest threat to our health as an economy and our cohesion as a society: inequality".[11]

In doing so, Mr Shorten marked out his party's agenda to arrest inequality in all its forms, but with a particular emphasis on addressing inequality which stems from economic policies which give primacy to those with wealth at the expense of those without.

The Government would have none of this talk of inequality, with Treasurer Scott Morrison accusing Mr Shorten of "producing an economic program based on the narrow lens of envy".[12] In his speech to the Australian Industry Group in Adelaide in July 2017 Morrison backed his argument with the following points:

- between 2011 and 2014, the Gini coefficient for household disposable income decreased from 0.311 to 0.299,

- the HILDA survey has shown relatively little change in household income inequality between 2001 and 2014,

- analysis released in 2015 showed that while income inequality has risen in most Organisation for Economic Co-operation and Development (OECD) countries over the past three decades, in Australia it had increased by substantially less than in many comparable OECD countries, and

- the poorest 20 per cent of households, on average,

---

[11] The Hon Bill Shorten MP, 21 July 2017. 'Tackling Inequality: A Labor Mission', Melbourne Institute, accessed at www.billshorten.com.au/speech_tackling_inequality_a_labor_mission_melbourne_institute_friday_21_july_2017.

[12] Malcolm Farr, 27 July 2017. 'Treasurer in Savage Strike at "Politics of Envy" Ahead of Bill Shorten's Inequality Speech', accessed at news.com.au.

receive cash transfers and social services benefits worth more than eight times what they pay in taxes.[13]

Morrison ended his speech with a now all too familiar government catch cry, "grow our economy and ensure that all Australians get a fair go".

There are two clear propositions underpinning Treasurer Morrison's position: first, Australia does not have an inequality problem; and second, if there is an issue with inequality then we can rely on the trickle-down economics of the past 40 years to deliver everyone the prosperity they seek.

Pope Francis has a different view to that of the Treasurer about our current economic paradigm. He stated:

> ... some people continue to defend trickle-down theories which assume that economic growth, encouraged by a free market, will inevitably succeed in bringing about greater justice and inclusiveness in the world. This opinion, which has never been confirmed by the facts, expresses a crude and naïve trust in the goodness of those wielding economic power and in the sacralised workings of the prevailing economic system. Meanwhile, the excluded are still waiting.[14]

To deny the existence of economic inequality is to deny the lived experience of millions of Australians who struggle each day to put food on the table and to provide their families with safe and secure housing.

To state that the poorest 20 per cent of households, on average, receive cash transfers and social services benefits worth more than eight times what they pay in taxes, is to traverse a well-worn and

---

[13] The Hon Scott Morrison MP, 27 July 2017. 'Guaranteeing the Essentials – A Foundation for Fairness', address to the Australian Industry Group, Adelaide, accessed at sjm. ministers.treasury.gov.au/speech/019-2017/.
[14] Pope Francis, 2013, op. cit., n. 54.

offensive path that we are a society of lifters and leaners. It seems that our poor, our vulnerable, our sick and our aged have a place in our society and it is at the bottom of the pile. Their value is not measured in terms of human dignity and social contribution but in terms of financial cost, to be supported only if we can afford to do so.

Why Does Inequality Matter?

So why does addressing inequality matter? Besides our moral obligation, there are sound political and economic benefits in doing so.

Institutions such as the United Nations, International Monetary Fund (IMF) and OECD have examined this question carefully and have concluded that inequality can be a serious threat to social and political stability as well as economic growth. The issue of political stability is one which Australia should consider carefully in light of the experience in the United States of America.

Journalist James Walsh[15] writing for *The Guardian* examined why American voters were turning to Bernie Sanders in the last US presidential primaries. Walsh cites a deep vein of concern for the current state of American politics but also white-hot anger about the inequities of the USA's economic and political systems and the inability of generations of leaders to affect any kind of meaningful change.

Moisés Naím, a contributing editor at *The Atlantic* and a fellow at the Carnegie Endowment for International Peace, recently wrote:

> The conventional wisdom is that, in many places across the developed world, members of the middle class are railing against a stagnation or even decline in their standards of living. According to this view, a toxic mix of globalization,

---

[15] James Walsh, 13 February 2016. *The Guardian*, accessed at www.theguardian.com/us-news.

immigration, automation, inequality, nationalism, and racism can fuel the frustrations that encourage voters to punish "establishment" ideas and politicians.[16]

While Naím goes on to argue that prosperity does not necessarily buy greater political stability, he does highlight the implications of a political and economic system that fails to deliver improved living standards for its citizens.

Declining living standards is a challenge for our Government today. *The Australian's* Editorial on 6 January 2018 said:

> The household incomes of average Australians have fallen 1.6 per cent in the year to September, after taking into account inflation, interest and taxes. This represents a sustained fall in living standards not matched since the 1990-91 recession. In short, wages growth has not kept up with increased costs, especially in the energy, health and housing sectors, while any modest boost to incomes is often absorbed by bracket creep. The impact is being felt most in middle Australia, among people who are being squeezed and often struggle to pay their bills.[17]

Inequality and poverty have social, political and economic consequences, which our Parliament would be unwise to ignore.

The causes of poverty and economic inequality in Australia are complex. The 2015 study *Dropping Off The Edge*[18] by Catholic Social Services Australia (CSSA) and Jesuit Social Services found that low household income is a central factor in shaping life opportunities

---

[16] Moisés Naím, 25 August 2017. "The Uprising of the Global Middle Class", *The Atlantic*, accessed at carnegieendowment.org/2017/08/25/uprising-of-global-middle-class-pub-72924.

[17] "The Living Standard Challenge", 6 January 2018. *The Australian* (online), accessed www.theaustralian.com.au/.

[18] Tony Vinson and Margot Rawsthorne with Adrian Beavis and Matthew Ericson, 2015. *Dropping Off The Edge 2015: Persistent Communal Disadvantage in Australia*. Melbourne: Jesuit Social Services and Catholic Social Services Australia.

for individuals and their families. While not a surprising finding in itself, the correlation between income adequacy and disadvantage is so strong that it warrants closer attention.

In August 2017, the University of New South Wales' Social Policy Research Centre (SPRC) released its report *New Minimum Income for Healthy Living Budget Standards for Low-Paid and Unemployed Australians.*[19] The report, developed in partnership with CSSA, the Australian Council of Social Services (ACOSS) and United Voice, measured the basic costs associated with a minimally adequate standard of living, a level below which no-one should be allowed to fall.

The research found that the welfare payment system is failing and the settings for the minimum wage are beginning to fray. Those in the welfare system find themselves between $47 and $126 per week below the minimum budget standard. Low paid households on the minimum wage fared only slightly better. A family with two children on the minimum wage was some $88 per week below the minimum budget standard.

The inadequacy of income for low-income households is both real and ever growing. The latest Australian Bureau of Statistics data on *Household Income and Wealth*[20] showed that the share of household income of the lowest three quintiles combined was less than the highest quintile. Further, the aggregate share of household net worth for the highest quintile is 62.5 per cent which is almost double that of the combined net worth of all other households. Interestingly, the net wealth of households in the highest quintile has grown from 59 per cent in 2003-2004 to 62.5 per cent in 2015-2016 and yet over the same period net worth of all other quintiles has declined. Even

---

[19] Peter Saunders and Megan Bedford, 2017. *New Minimum Income for Healthy Living Budget Standards for Low-Paid and Unemployed Australians: Summary Report.* Sydney: SPRC, UNSW.

[20] Australian Bureau of Statistics, December 2017. 6523 *Household Income and Wealth, Australia, 2015-16,* Table 1.1 'Household Income and Income Distribution', accessed at www.abs.gov.au.

if we accept that economic inequality in Australia is only growing slightly, is it economically prudent and morally acceptable that the top 20 per cent of Australian households own more than 60 per cent of Australia's wealth?

While economic inequality may rail against our sense of fairness, it has an economic impact which, also if left unaddressed, could undermine our economy to the detriment of all. The IMF has found that income inequality has adverse effects on economic growth and sustainability. Analysis published by the IMF in 2015 found that if the share of income of the richest 20 per cent increases, GDP growth actually declines over the medium term.[21] As economist Joseph Stiglitz once said, "An economic system that only delivers for the very top is a failed economic system".[22]

The most compelling question, which must be asked, is this – if economic inequality is morally wrong, and politically and economically damaging, why does is it exist? The short answer is that we have allowed it to exist. And why have we allowed it? My sense is that up until the GFC most Australians were served well by the neo-liberal economic construct. However, our market-based capitalist system, post GFC, in particular, has failed to improve living standards for the middle class, all the while continuing to deliver for those with wealth. The impacts of economic inequality are now being felt by people other than the poor and this group is beginning to question the fairness of the system.

We can address this decline and keep the benefits of Australia's market-based capitalist system. However, this will require us to revisit

---

[21] Era Dabla-Norris, Kalpana Kochhar, Frantisek Ricka, Nujin Suphaphiphat and Evridi-ki Tsounta, 2015. *Causes and Consequences of Income Inequality: A Global Perspective*, IMF Staff Discussion Note SDN/15/13, accessed at www.imf.org/external/pubs/ft/sdn/2015/sdn1513.pdf.

[22] Joseph Stiglitz, 2014. "The Price of Inequality: How Today's Divided Society Endangers Our Future", *Sustainable Humanity, Sustainable Nature: Our Responsibility Pontifical Academy of Sciences*, Extra Series 41, Acta 19. Vatican City: Vatican, 1-21.

the underlying philosophy of our current economic policy settings, neo-liberalism.

Re-visiting Neo-liberalism

Neo-liberalism was the 'sugar hit' that our faltering global and national economy needed in the late 1970s and early 1980s. Introduced in Australia under the Hawke-Keating Governments and embraced by all subsequent governments, neo-liberalism has reshaped Australia socially, culturally and economically.

The application of neo-liberalism transformed the focus of society and the state towards improving economic efficiency. The market thus became the ideal to which education, health and welfare services were encouraged to conform in order to ensure national economic survival.[23]

At its most basic neo-liberalism is about redefining the relationship between the individual and the state. The policy consequence of this paradigm is one which is focussed on reducing government expenditure, cutting taxes, promoting deregulation and privatisation, and the state withdrawing from human services, or at least their delivery. Addressing inequality requires curbing the excesses of neo-liberalism. There is a need for political courage to address the limitations of our current economic policies and the harm they are doing to our society.

In October 2017, CSSA launched an occasional paper titled *An Economy that Works for All*. In his opening remarks, Emeritus Professor John Warhurst said: "CSSA has ventured deliberately into the government kitchen where policies are made and has not been afraid to feel the heat. This paper and today's launch is another one of those occasions". The paper makes several recommendations to enliven the principles outlined in the Bishops' 2017-2018 Social

---

[23] Mark Beeson and Ann Firth, November 1998. "Neoliberalism as a Political Rationality: Australian Public Policy since the 1980s", *Journal of Sociology*, 34, 221.

Justice Statement 'Everyone's Business – Developing an Inclusive and Sustainable Economy'.

Key amongst these recommendations is a call to build a new national accord between government, civil society and business working together for our economic common good. A focus on the common good need not be contrary to the neo-liberal ideal of individual interest. These can be held in healthy tension. To give purpose to this tension and harness the benefits of it, however, we must shift the issues affecting the poor and disadvantaged from the fringes of our economic policy thinking to the centre.

Thus, an accord would articulate the responsibilities of government, civil society and business in building a flourishing and just society with particular attention to the poor and disadvantaged. The first priority of the accord should be to examine government finances, how they are constructed, how income is collected, and how revenue is distributed. The accord must also consider the interrelationship between the three groups in the delivery of services and, more critically, the provision of adequate income, especially for those in need.

Revenue raised through the tax system must not be squandered on activities or policies that simply serve to entrench the *status quo* or enrich those with wealth. Instead, revenue should be used to enhance the wellbeing of society and those services that support that goal. Priority must be given to ensuring that those who need support through the transfer system receive the income and services they require to live with dignity.

Determining the level of pensions or welfare payments, whether through income support such as Newstart or Family Tax Benefit payments, should not be left to governments. CSSA has called on the government to establish an independent commission to develop evidence-based benchmarks to ensure that these payments are adequate to enable people to participate fully in our society and live with dignity.

For those in work, especially those on low incomes, we must give priority to recalibrating our industrial relations framework to address growing casualisation and insecure employment. This is an increasing problem for the social services sector driven primarily by government policy of marketising services such as aged care and disability services.

While casual employment has a role in our modern economy, its growing hold on the labour market brings with it heightened job insecurity. This, in turn, negatively impacts economic activity. Creating an American-style working poor is unacceptable both morally and economically.

The business community must not be so burdened with taxes and regulation as to undermine its capacity to grow and create secure and meaningful employment. In return, it must recognise government investment in the rule of law and social and capital infrastructure that enables it to trade with certainty and security. Businesses must operate on the principle that 'if you trade here, you pay here', refraining from practices that shift proceeds overseas to limit their tax contribution in Australia.

Businesses and regulatory institutions such as the Australian Securities and Investments Commission (ASIC) should be encouraged to work together in developing new performance metrics that promote 'patient capital' to encourage CEOs and their boards to invest for the medium to long term.

Finally, it is essential that we challenge the current orthodoxy regarding membership of boards of key state institutions, particularly economic institutions such as the Reserve Bank of Australia, to ensure that the voices of those impacted by their decisions are considered and understood.

Properly implemented these various measures and directions would have a positive impact on the economy and the society it serves.

However, like any change, it will be difficult. It will be especially difficult for those who have benefitted most from the current system. To those people I say, be patient: what might be lost in the short term will be repaid over time through improved economic activity and growth.

We have an opportunity to make our economy stronger, fairer and more inclusive. This will require a new way of thinking and a new way of working, where we give primacy to the common good. This is not a job for governments alone; it is a job for the society as whole. Success will be achieved when we hear the voices of those the economy now ignores, heal those that the economy has discarded, and give hope to those on the margins so that they too can flourish in a society and economy which gives them life with dignity.

The Importance of the Dignity of Work

John Roskam and *Aaron Lane*

The industrial revolution throughout the 19th century is a major signpost in the journey of human flourishing. Ordinary people experienced improvements to their income and standard of living at an unprecedented rate. However, this period of technological and economic progress was disruptive. The steam engine and other mechanical tools fundamentally changed how work was organised and the types of jobs that existed. For instance, the emergence of factories as a new locus of work displaced individual craft and trade workers but created new employment possibilities for others as production levels increased and trade horizons expanded. Today, we are approaching another signpost. Today's digital revolution threatens again to displace existing ways of working through automation, machine learning and the rise of digital platforms.

At the Institute of Public Affairs (IPA), we are very aware that economic policy must serve human needs. Narrow and sterile terms like 'economic productivity' and 'GNP' (Gross National Product) and 'the Gini coefficient'[24] do not capture the human dimension of individuals experiencing the dignity of work. The research activities of the IPA that would once have been labelled 'industrial relations policy' we now conceive of as 'The Dignity of Work Project'.

The Catholic Church has always been awake to changing circumstances and the "signs of the times".[25] In 1891, Pope Leo XIII's *Rerum Novarum* responded to the economic upheaval of the industrial revolution by rejecting the Marxist class war mentality and laying the foundations of the social doctrine of the Church. Fundamental to the social doctrine was the concept of the dignity of work. Just as the industrial revolution prompted the Catholic Church to examine the barriers to the dignity of work, today's digital revolution presents a new challenge for the Catholic Church, namely to re-ask the social question of how the dignity of work can be affirmed in today's economy.

The contribution in this chapter examines a key tension – centralised minimum wages – that needs to be rethought. Here, we argue that mandated minimum wages operate to exclude the most vulnerable from experiencing the dignity of work and from sharing in prosperity.

The Dignity of Work

What do we mean by the dignity of work? There are several overlapping dimensions. The starting point is the Christian understanding that humans have an inherent dignity because we are created in the image and likeness of God.[26] In other words, the value of work derives from

---

[24] The Gini coefficient is a commonly used measure of inequality; see www.oecd.org/social/income-distribution-database.htm.

[25] Pope Paul VI, 1965. *Pastoral Constitution on the Church in the Modern World: Gaudium et Spes*, n. 4, accessed at www.vatican.va.

[26] *Genesis* 1:27.

the value of the human person.[27] In this way, people are not merely 'factors of production'. Even the most routine and monotonous work should be valued.

Another dimension is vocational – the Bible calls humans to "till and keep" the garden.[28] In this way, we create something new through our labour. Thus, people often speak of work as providing us with a sense of purpose. Indeed, Pope St John Paul II spoke of a "spirituality of work".[29]

A further dimension is relational – there is a social aspect to work that helps us form a closer communion with each other. Work fulfils our worldly needs: Pope Leo XIII spoke about exerting oneself "for the sake of procuring what is necessary for the various purposes of life, and chief of all for self preservation".[30] At the same time, our work fulfils the needs of others which is why Pope St John Paul II described work as "an expression of love".[31] Putting these three aspects together, it is through work that we can truly flourish.

Minimum Wages as a Barrier

Too many young people in Australia today are without the dignity of work. Last year, the Brotherhood of St Laurence reported that approximately 50,500 young people between the ages of 15 and 24 years are long-term unemployed, three times more than a decade ago.[32] While the current national headline rate of youth unemployment

[27] Pope St John Paul II, 1981. Encyclical Letter on Human Work: *Laborem Exercens,* Section II, accessed at w2.vatican.va/.

[28] *Genesis* 2:15.

[29] Pope St John Paul II, 1981, op. cit., Section V.

[30] Pope Leo XIII, 1891. Encyclical on Capital and Labor: *Rerum Novarum,* n. 44, accessed at w2.vatican.va/.

[31] Pope St John Paul II, 1989. Apostolic Exhortation: *Redemptoris Custos,* Section IV, accessed at w2.vatican.va/.

[32] Brotherhood of St Laurence (BSL), December 2017. *Reality Bites: Australia's Youth Unemployment in a Millennial Era.* Melbourne: BSL, accessed at www.bsl.org.au/advocacy/youth-employment/.

is 12.2 per cent, the Brotherhood's previous research showed that a further 18 per cent of young people were underemployed.[33] In several regional centres youth unemployment rates exceed 20 per cent. Part of the cause is that entry level jobs are disappearing. The Brotherhood noted "a sharp decline in the number of entry-level jobs since 2006 – a reduction of more than 50 per cent – has contributed to the challenges that young jobseekers face".[34]

At the same time, some groups, including the Australian Catholic Bishops Conference, have lamented that the minimum wage no longer provides for a 'living wage'.[35] Australia's minimum wage is already one of the highest among OECD nations.[36] Traditionally the Catholic Church has rightly focused on the moral duty of employers to pay a 'just wage'.[37] What is 'just' will depend on individual circumstances and needs to be viewed in the dynamic context of a person's lifetime. In line with the principle of subsidiarity, there is no good reason that there should be a national minimum wage where the rate in inner city Sydney is the same as in outback Queensland. The moral issue is not at what rate the minimum wage should be set but ensuring that "the types of jobs available are such that people at different stages in their lives can find work that enables them to fulfil their lifetime plans and objectives".[38] But the higher the minimum wage, the more job opportunities that are excluded.

---

[33] Brotherhood of St Laurence, March 2017. *Generation Stalled: Young, Underemployed and Living Precariously in Australia.* Melbourne: BSL, accessed at www.bsl.org.au/advocacy/youth-employment/.

[34] Brotherhood of St Laurence, December 2017, op. cit.

[35] Australian Catholic Bishops Conference (ACBC), 2017. cf Ref 4, 180: 'Everyone's Business: Developing an Inclusive and Sustainable Economy', Social Justice Statement 2017-2018, Canberra: ACBC, accessed at www.socialjustice.catholic.org.au/publications/social-justice-statements.

[36] See Organisation for Economic Co-operation and Development, "Real Minimum Wages", accessed at stats.oecd.org/.

[37] See Pope John Paul II, 1981, op. cit. n. 19.

[38] Robin Klay and John Nunn, 2003. "Just Remuneration Over a Worker's Lifetime", *Journal of Markets and Morality*, 6(1), 177.

At a time of high youth unemployment and digital innovation over the horizon, those with an interest in promoting the dignity of work must be mindful of seemingly well-intentioned policy interventions that actually make a tough situation worse. Nobel laureate Milton Friedman once observed that "the real tragedy of minimum wage laws is that they are supported by well-meaning groups who want to reduce poverty. But the people who are hurt most by higher minimums are the most poverty stricken".[39] Economic theory is clear about the negative effect of the minimum wage on employment – this is confirmed by the balance of the empirical evidence.[40] While this may be in the form of job losses, it is more likely to be manifest in slower employment growth and the removal of low-skilled entry-level jobs over time.

Minimum wages might have a positive image, but they have an ugly history. They are designed to exclude people from the workforce. For example, when minimum wage laws were introduced in Victoria in 1896, the express intention of minimum wage laws was to exclude foreign workers – in Victoria, then mainly Chinese – and single women from the workforce because these people were willing to work for lower pay than white men.[41] In modern times there may not be the same discrimination based on race or gender, but there is exclusion based on the perception that some work should not be valued. Minimum wages effectively ban work, affecting the most marginalised in society.

The Gap between Welfare and Work

One of the enduring misconceptions about the minimum wage in the modern era is that it is a safety net. The truth is that the minimum

---

[39] Milton Friedman, 1966. 'The Minimum Wage Rate, Who Really Pays?': An Interview with Milton Friedman and Yale Brozen, Free Society Association background paper, 26-27.

[40] For a summary, see Aaron Lane and Mikayla Novak, March 2014. 'Submission to the Fair Work Commission: Annual Wage Review 2014', Institute of Public Affairs.

[41] Victoria Parliamentary Debates Session 1895, Hansard, 17 October 1895 (Alexander Peacock), 2637.

wage only applies to those people in a job. The unemployment benefit is the actual safety net. This is why the data show that increasing the minimum wage is a poor way to help those in poverty, as most people in poverty are already without work.[42] Minimum wage laws enact a perverse preference that some people remain unemployed at a much lower standard of living.

Low rates of unemployment benefits for young people are not necessarily problematic, because work should be encouraged. But the income gap between welfare and work is significant. For instance, the minimum wage is currently $22.86 per hour for a 21-year-old casual employee.[43] By contrast, most single unemployed people receive the equivalent of $7.09 per hour on Centrelink's Newstart allowance.[44] This equates to a welfare gap of almost $1,200 per fortnight. A push to 60 per cent of median wages to create a 'living wage' (for which the trade unions are lobbying) would increase the casual rate to over $30 an hour, prohibiting more work and further widening the gap. The truth is that a job opportunity paying $15 per hour, for example, would immediately improve the standard of living for a young person on welfare.

Because of our understanding of the dignity of work, we know that a job provides benefits beyond monetary reward. A part-time job for a young person could help pay for higher education or training, or it could be an experience to gain skills and enhance their future earning potential. Numerous studies have demonstrated the non-economic benefits to people from paid employment – greater happiness from 'earned success', increased social interaction, improved outcomes for mental and physical health.[45]

If it is acceptable for a young person to be on welfare of $7.09

---

[42] A. Lane and M. Novak, 2014, op. cit.

[43] Fair Work Commission, 2017. *Annual Wage Review 2016-17*, [2017] FWCFB 3500.

[44] This rate is based on a fortnightly payment of $538.80 averaged over a 38-hour working week.

[45] For a summary, see Arthur C. Brooks, 2015. *The Conservative Heart: How to Build a Fairer, Happier, and More Prosperous America*. New York: Harper Collins.

per hour, why is it illegal for the same person to work for $15 per hour? Here we are confronted with a moral choice. Do we want to make it illegal for an unemployed person to take a job to better their own position and enjoy the dignity of work, or do we want to make it easier for unemployed people to lift themselves out of poverty?

The Future of Work

The digital revolution is providing young people with new ways of working in the 'sharing economy'. Whether it is a ride-sharing platforms like Uber, accommodation sharing on Airbnb, or contracting work on Airtasker, there is a strong moral case for maximising the opportunities available for unemployed and underemployed workers to take advantage of sharing economy platforms. Importantly, these platforms are currently not subject to minimum wage laws because workers are independent contractors.[46] This has been good news for young people in an economy of inclusion. The majority of digital platform workers are not seeking traditional full-time work, instead they are taking advantage of new opportunities to top up their income or keep active between jobs. For example, a recent survey of 3,000 Uber drivers in Brisbane found that almost a third were unemployed prior to signing up, including many long-term unemployed, and the remainder appeared to be underemployed.[47]

The digital economy will continue to be disruptive to traditional industries and there are calls to extend barriers like exclusionary minimum wage laws to new ways of working. But caring about people includes a preferential option for those without work. As the digital revolution approaches, we must remain wary of regulatory interventions that will exclude some people – particularly young

---

[46] For a discussion of this issue, see Aaron Lane, December 2017. "A Platform to Work", *IPA Review*.
[47] Felicity Caldwell, 15 April 2017. "Almost a Third of Brisbane Uber Drivers Unemployed Before Signing up", *Brisbane Times*, accessed at www.brisbanetimes.com.au/.

and low-skilled workers – from the workforce. Public policy, in the creation of which we all participate, must have as its focus ensuring as many Australians as possible, particularly young Australians, have the opportunity to have the dignity of work.

Inequality in the Digital Economy

Clare O'Neil MP

Australia is one of the wealthiest countries in the world. It has achieved 26 years of uninterrupted economic growth, which, *The Economist* reliably reports, is the longest period of uninterrupted growth of any country in the world, ever.[48] Many in our country have contributed to and benefited from that growth. As the economic tide has risen in Australia, most boats have risen with it. The data clearly show us that Australian households right across the income spectrum have seen their incomes grow significantly over this 26 years – that does not mean every single Australian is better off, but on average, incomes have grown significantly even for those not earning very much. So, in a discussion about poverty and living standards, it is important that we recognise that Australia has been doing something right over that period of time.

Joe Zabar has described our economy as 'neo-liberal', and John Roskam has disputed that. On this issue I side with John Roskam. Yes, in general, Australian governments have tried to remove themselves from the functioning of the economy where they can, but that is not all that government does in Australia.

Australia has created incredible institutions, such as Medicare, which have ensured the benefits of our growing wealth have been shared by everyone. We have one of the best, most efficient welfare

---

[48] "How Australia Broke the Record for Economic Growth: Twenty-Six Years and Counting", 6 September 2017. *The Economist*, accessed at www.economist.com/blogs/economist-explains/2017/09/economist-explains-3.

systems in the world. We have mostly-free public schools. Australia's higher education system has enabled four in ten Australians to receive a university education, with a deferred payments system which means that growing up in a poor family generally does not deprive you of further education. While Prime Minister Hawke and Treasurer Keating are celebrated for floating the dollar, it was the fact that they increased Year 12 retention rates from roughly 40 to roughly 70 per cent that might be most worth celebrating.

Despite the successes, inequality has been a feature of Australian life and it will continue to be so unless we actively address it. The distribution of wealth is out of kilter with our national values. Today, the nine wealthiest Australians control as much wealth as do the poorest four and a half million. My goal as a Member of Parliament is to make sure that a child who is growing up in my community, in Noble Park or Springvale South, has just as good a chance of becoming a company CEO, running a non-profit organisation, or being a High Court judge, as someone who is growing up in the Prime Minister's electorate. Enabling each and every one of our children to reach their full potential, regardless of where they are born or where they live, is the foundation a flourishing society.

A flourishing society has to be an equal society. In a fair society, merit, individual capacity and effort should determine who ends up rich and less rich. But today, 90 per cent of Australia's billionaires are 'pale and male'. We also know that an Indigenous man in Australia is more likely to have a prison record than a university degree, and a four-year-old who is growing up in a disadvantaged community is twice as likely to be developmentally delayed than a child growing up in a very wealthy one.

Inequality cannot be a part of a flourishing society because inequality allows human potential to go to waste. One need only consider the areas of disadvantage outlined in the CSSA and Jesuit Social

Services' report *Dropping Off The Edge*[49] to understand the enormity of the problem in Australia. How many Howard Floreys, Pat Dodsons and Frank Brennans are we missing out on because a child was unfortunate enough to born into the wrong suburb?

The human cost of inequality is but one price we pay as a society. Inequality also has an economic cost. There is increasing concern from institutions like the International Monetary Fund (which is not exactly known for its left leaning) that inequality is actually bad for economic growth. While I think Australia has done a reasonably good job of making sure that most Australians have benefitted from economic growth, I am less convinced that will continue into the future, unless we change our current policy course.

Many people would be familiar with the mobile app called Instagram. Many would also remember the company, Kodak, a film and camera giant. At its peak, Kodak supplied 90 per cent of the photography market and directly employed 145,000 Americans. In around 2012, Kodak went bankrupt due to the digital revolution. A few months after that, Instagram was sold to Facebook for a billion dollars. At that time, Instagram had eleven employees. The point I make here is not so much about the changing business environment brought about by digital disruption but rather how digital technology and technology more generally are impacting upon our workforce.

As a Member of Parliament, I visit many factories and, while the factory floor will be absolutely humming, pumping out widgets at a great rate, there is an eeriness to the floor because of the absence of workers. There might be five or six people where once there may have been twenty or more. It is not just factory workers being replaced by technology, there are farm workers and even white-collar professions, such as paralegals, accountants and junior lawyers, who are beginning to be impacted upon by the technological revolution.

---

[49] T. Vinson and M. Rawsthorne, 2015, op. cit.

An Oxford University study in 2012 found that something like half of all the jobs that exist today are going to be gone in two decades. Anyone who read the *Financial Review* on 22 February 2018 would have seen a story about seek.com's report to the Parliament in which they state that, in their view, machines could do half of all the jobs they are advertising right now.

Think back to the Instagram example: the Instagram founders will likely be multimillionaires for the rest of their lives and so too their grandchildren. For the Kodak workers, it would be a different story: many might have found trouble gaining employment, and, for some, they may never have worked again.

The digital age is not only shaping the employment outcomes for current and future generations but also changing the way wealth is distributed. Technology is pushing the benefits of the economy up for those who are at the top of the labour market but keeping them down for those at the bottom. When you read the paper today, you can feel there are really two big stories happening in the economy. There is a good story for business. Every quarter we seem to read that the Commonwealth Bank has broken a new record for its business profits. But the same paper will tell us that household incomes in Australia are going backwards in real terms. The economy is in danger of becoming one that no longer serves the majority of people and, should that arise, we will have a really big problem on our hands.

Earlier I used the metaphor of the rising tide lifting boats to describe Australia's economy of the past. This lift to the economy and workers' income occurred through productivity gains being shared with workers through improved wages. Today, however, we are seeing a major break in the relationship between improved productivity and wages growth. In today's economy, productivity is growing but the economic gains from that productivity improvement are not generally making their way to workers – their wages are not growing. The rewards are increasingly being captured at the top.

If there is one statistic that really brings this all together, it is the performance of our economy over the last year. Over that period business profits rose by more than 20 per cent. That is huge growth, but the average Australian household went backwards. The concern I have is that technology is impacting on our economy in such a way as to disrupt the relationship between productivity and wages growth which was such a strong feature of our economy in years past. That is what helped lift all the boats. And if it breaks, this disruption will lead to much greater inequality in Australia.

Unions are a very important part of the equation. Australians are less likely to join a union today than they have ever been. We have less than 10 per cent union penetration in the private sector, and that is part of what is creating this problem. In an environment where the strong majority of workers are not union members, how can workers bargain together and demand their fair share of the productivity gains in the way to which they were accustomed?

As a Member of Parliament, it is my job to come up with solutions to some of these difficult problems. So first, I think we do need to change our approach to, as well as the policies and the systems for, sharing the benefits of economic growth in Australia. One of the things we should do better is to protect people who are at the bottom of the labour market. That means we must resist the increasing pressure to reduce minimum wages and take away social supports, and stop this endless attack on the welfare rights of young people. We must protect penalty rates, especially for our lowest paid workers. The decision to cut penalty rates is significant for the 700,000 people affected but also for our economy. We cannot afford to sit back and let them all take a pay cut in an environment where we know there is huge pressure on household incomes. Doing so will simply add to growing inequality in Australia.

We also need to fix some of the issues in our tax system. This is not a time where we want to give $65 billion in tax cuts to the biggest companies in this country. The proposed tax cut will not fix any of the problems that I have noted, indeed it has the potential to add to inequality in Australia.

There is one thing that we know is going to help us fix this problem and it is investment in education and skills for the new economy. When we look at who is winning and who is losing in the new economy, the people who are doing well have got off to a good start in their education, and stuck with it as long as they could. The big winners are the tertiary-educated, or at least the highly skilled. So, a key piece of the inequality puzzle is for government to ramp up support for young people, to invest in their future by ensuring they are skilled and supported to make the transition from education to work, so that they can enjoy the prosperity which comes with well-paying jobs.

Without a big change to how we do things in Canberra, we are going to see the problem of inequality get worse in the future. However, our values and commitment to a fair go should give us hope that together we can address the slide backwards and deliver a flourishing and more inclusive economy. We actually know what we need to do. We just need a government in charge that has the will to do it.

3

Moving Justice and Solidarity from the Dictionary to the Workplace of Catholic Social Services

Frank Brennan SJ AO

Since World War II, the language of human rights has helped people of all faiths and none to communicate and co-operate, seeking to satisfy the preconditions for everyone to achieve their full human flourishing in community. This language of human rights, when rightly used, allows us to strike the right balance when there are conflicting claims by individuals with different interests or with different world views. This year we mark the 70th anniversary of the United Nations Declaration of Human Rights (UNDHR) which has been fleshed out by a later series of UN conventions and declarations that have set up the international architecture for the protection of these rights.

The Centenary of *Pacem in Terris*

Pope John XXIII embraced the language of human rights in his 1963 encyclical *Pacem in Terris*. After a lifetime of diplomatic service in the Church, Pope John had no hesitation in giving papal approval to the United Nations and to highlighting the many points of agreement between the UNDHR and time-honoured principles of Catholic social teaching. Pope John wrote:

> We are, of course, aware that some of the points in the declaration did not meet with unqualified approval in some quarters; and there was justification for this. Nevertheless,

we think the document should be considered a step in the right direction, an approach toward the establishment of a juridical and political ordering of the world community. It is a solemn recognition of the personal dignity of every human being; an assertion of everyone's right to be free to seek out the truth, to follow moral principles, discharge the duties imposed by justice, and lead a fully human life.[1]

Pope John's successors have been justifiably wary when they think that some use of human rights language becomes skewed with the advocates being too focused on rugged individual autonomy rather than communal solidarity which always maintains care for the poor and marginalised. We always need to keep an eye on individual duties as well as individual rights, and we need to limit individual rights not only when they come into conflict with other rights, but also when they violate the common good or the public interest, when they disrupt public order or public morality.

It is fashionable nowadays to downplay any notion of public morality on the basis that there is no agreement in a pluralistic democratic society about what is right or wrong. This downplaying might help explain the public's loss of trust in institutions and in authority. But anyone who doubts the community's sense and commitment to public morality need only consider the visceral community reaction to child sexual abuse and to the failure of institutions to guard against it. Public morality is on display in all aspects of public life. When cricketers wearing 'the baggy green' are caught red-handed plotting to cheat by tampering with the ball, the community outrage points to a sense that there are some things which are just wrong, regardless of the consequences, and whether or not you are caught.

For Pope John and his successors, the human dignity of the poorest

---

[1] Pope John XXIII, 1963. Encyclical on Establishing Universal Peace in Truth, Justice, Charity and Liberty: *Pacem in Terris*. Vatican City: Vatican, n. 144, accessed at w2.vatican. va/.

and most marginalised has been a litmus test for the application of the language of human rights. At the commencement of his pontificate in 2013, Pope Francis marked the 50th anniversary of *Pacem in Terris* asking two questions:

> Looking at our current reality, I ask myself if the words justice and solidarity are only in our dictionary or if we all work so that they become a reality?
>
> *Pacem in Terris* draws a line that goes from the peace to be built in the hearts of men to reviewing our model of development and of action at all levels so that our world may become a world of peace. I ask myself, are we willing to accept this invitation?[2]

In Cairo just weeks after the terrorist bombing of Christian churches there, Pope Francis attended an international peace conference at the Al-Azhar Mosque and University with the Grand Imam Ahmed el-Tayeb. Pope Francis told the world that "three basic areas, if properly linked to one another, can assist in dialogue:

- the duty to respect one's own identity and that of others,
- the courage to accept differences, and
- sincerity of intentions".[3]

Seeking Dialogue Despite Difference

The language of human rights can help us when we are seeking dialogue despite a difference in world views, despite a difference in religious faith, despite a difference in class interests, and even despite a difference of views amongst members of the Catholic Church about how the Church should be structured and what it should teach. There

---

[2] Pope Francis, 3 October 2013. 'Address to Conference Sponsored by Pontifical Commission for Justice and Peace'. Vatican City: Vatican, n. 1, accessed at w2.vatican.va/.

[3] Pope Francis, 28 April 2017. 'Address to the Participants in the International Peace Conference', Al-Azhar Conference Centre, Cairo. Vatican City: Vatican, accessed at accessed at w2.vatican.va/.

is not necessarily any one right answer when it comes to resolving a conflict of rights or a clash between individual rights and the common good. When there is no one right answer, what is important is a process which brings all claimants or their perspectives to the table, where we can respect each other's identity, accept differences, thinking and advocating sincerely.

Pope Francis is the first pope we have known who does not hail from Europe. Having come from the global south, he does not equate Christendom and Europe. Having exercised Church leadership in a country where there was a dirty war orchestrated by corrupt military, he knows there are limits to what we can expect from the State when it comes to the protection of the human dignity of all persons. He does not expect to find true justice for all on this side of the grave. He is constantly emphasising the need for mercy as well as justice. He knows that all players, himself included, are sinners and that we must seek justice and peace in an imperfect world. Thus, the need for solidarity with those who suffer endemic inter-generational injustice when justice lies beyond their reach. Thus, the need for mercy when no government and no Church is able to build the perfect society.

Francis has a deep suspicion of those who trumpet individual rights as pre-eminent. In his apostolic exhortation *Evangelii Gaudium* he reached back to the teaching of Pope Paul VI, spelling out the need to ensure that the individual rights of the rich are not invoked to trample the needs of the poor. He wrote:

> Sometimes it is a matter of hearing the cry of entire peoples, the poorest peoples of the earth, since 'peace is founded not only on respect for human rights, but also on respect for the rights of peoples'. Sadly, even human rights can be used as a justification for an inordinate defence of individual rights or the rights of the richer peoples. With due respect for the autonomy and culture of every nation, we must never forget that the planet belongs to all mankind and is meant

49

for all mankind; the mere fact that some people are born in places with fewer resources or less development does not justify the fact that they are living with less dignity. It must be reiterated that 'the more fortunate should renounce some of their rights so as to place their goods more generously at the service of others'. To speak properly of our own rights, we need to broaden our perspective and to hear the plea of other peoples and other regions than those of our own country. We need to grow in a solidarity which 'would allow all peoples to become the artisans of their destiny, since every person is called to self-fulfilment'.[4]

In his encyclical *Laudato Si'* two years later, Francis calls everyone to engagement in an honest and open debate, respecting the competencies of all, and inspired by the vision of St Francis of Assisi who is the model of the inseparable bond "between concern for nature, justice for the poor, commitment to society, and interior peace".[5] In his words and in his actions, Francis demonstrates this meshing of the four strands which make up the authentic life: the relationship to nature, the poor, society and the inner self. He writes:

In the present condition of global society, where injustices abound and growing numbers of people are deprived of basic human rights and considered expendable, the principle of the common good immediately becomes, logically and inevitably, a summons to solidarity and a preferential option for the poorest of our brothers and sisters. This option entails recognising the implications of the universal destination of the world's goods. It demands before all else an appreciation of the immense dignity of the poor in the

<hr>

[4] Pope Francis, 2013. Apostolic Exhortation: *Evangelii Gaudium*. Vatican City: Vatican, n. 190, accessed at w2.vatican.va/. Pope Francis quotes in this passage from Pope Paul VI's *Populorum Progressio*.
[5] Pope Francis, 2015. Encyclical Letter: *Laudato Si'*. Vatican City: Vatican, n. 11, accessed at w2.vatican.va/.

light of our deepest convictions as believers. We need only look around us to see that, today, this option is in fact an ethical imperative.[6]

Like Francis, we are all called to respond to this ethical imperative by enunciating principles, engaging in respectful and sometimes confronting dialogue with decision makers, standing in solidarity with those who suffer ongoing injustice, and praying that the kingdom of justice and peace might come to be realised more urgently on this planet on this side of the grave. In situations of acute injustice where justice and peace will not be coming any time soon, this can be a difficult challenge.

Pope Francis' Visit to Myanmar

Let us consider the case study of Pope Francis's recent visit to Myanmar in the wake of the Rohingya crisis. This makes for a good case study because there was concerted criticism of Francis for the way he conducted himself. The critics included human rights advocates and western journalists who thought it was time to rule a line in the sand, putting the Myanmar leadership, including Aung San Suu Kyi, on notice that their treatment of the Rohingya, who had fled across the border in their hundreds of thousands, was completely unacceptable. The critics demanded that Francis mention the Rohingya by name in his public statements while in Myanmar. He did not, and this led to the suggestion that Francis lacked backbone or at least had feet of clay, being an advocate only for his own Catholic minority when things came to the crunch.

Francis, however, was more subtle, measured and strategic. He first stated a set of principles in public, in a manner which could not cause offence, or which at least could not attract public demurrer. Next he engaged in private discussions with Myanmar's leaders, applying the

---

[6] Ibid. n. 158.

principles to the case at hand. He then stood in solidarity with the Rohingya once he crossed the border to Bangladesh. Subsequently, he explained to the world what he had done. In the end, I think he did well. In fact, I think he did as well as any world leader could have, working so that justice and solidarity might become a reality there on either side of the border of Myanmar and Bangladesh.

Thus, initially he delivered an address to the civic leaders in Myanmar. At that time, the world did not know that the military leadership tried to steal the march by having their leader call on the Pope before he met with Aung San Suu Kyi. Francis denied the military any opportunity for photos, insisting on the strict protocol that he first meet with Aung San Suu Kyi. Then addressing all the government and military leaders, he said:

> The future of Myanmar must be peace, a peace based on respect for the dignity and rights of each member of society, respect for each ethnic group and its identity, respect for the rule of law, and respect for a democratic order that enables each individual and every group – none excluded – to offer its legitimate contribution to the common good.[7]

No-one could take exception to this statement of principles. No-one was left in any doubt about who was included in the reference to "none excluded". He had mentioned the Rohingya in all but name. They were clearly uppermost in the mind of the speaker and his listeners in Yangon and across the globe. He had laid the groundwork. Earlier in the day, he had delivered a speech to the religious leaders in Myanmar [8] and, then in addressing the officials, he stated the following in relation to religious communities:

[7] Pope Francis, 28 November 2017. 'Meeting with Government Authorities, the Civil Society and the Diplomatic Corps', International Convention Centre (Nay Pyi Taw), Myanmar, accessed at w2.vatican.va/.

[8] Pope Francis, 28 November 2017. 'Meeting with the Religious Leaders of Myanmar in the Refectory of the Archbishop's House', accessed at w2.vatican.va/.

In the great work of national reconciliation and integration, Myanmar's religious communities have a privileged role to play. Religious differences need not be a source of division and distrust, but rather a force for unity, forgiveness, tolerance and wise nation building. The religions can play a significant role in repairing the emotional, spiritual and psychological wounds of those who have suffered in the years of conflict. Drawing on deeply-held values, they can help to uproot the causes of conflict, build bridges of dialogue, seek justice and be a prophetic voice for all who suffer.[9]

Once again, no-one could take exception to this statement of principle. But here was the leader of the Catholic minority telling the Buddhist majority that the despised Muslim Rohingya minority had a place at the table of national reconciliation and integration.

It was an open secret that Myanmar's Cardinal Charles Maung Bo had strongly counselled the Pope that it would be counterproductive to mention the Rohingya specifically by name. Yes, this could make life more difficult for the Catholics once the Pope left the country. But also, it would make life more difficult for the Rohingya. There was room for prudential differences of opinion about the consequences of the Pope buying into this human rights catastrophe. Typical of the western criticism aimed at Francis was this report in *The Guardian* by Joanna Moorhead:

> The truth is, and this visit has made this abundantly clear, the primary role of the pope is as the leader of the Roman Catholic community.
>
> The Catholic church has many strengths, including in its humanitarian work – after all, it has representatives across the planet, and for all the bad apples we've become increasingly aware of, there are many good men and women

---

[9] Pope Francis, 28 November 2017. 'Meeting with Government Authorities, the Civil Society and the Diplomatic Corps', op. cit.

working tirelessly to improve the living conditions of people who live in challenged situations. But it has weaknesses too, including the fact that its leader, while he might look like a world peacemaker, must look out first and foremost for his own people. And that, it seems, is what has had to happen here.[10]

Undeterred and unbowed, Francis proceeded to Bangladesh where he addressed an ecumenical and interreligious meeting for peace, emphasising the need for trust and "a culture of encounter, dialogue and cooperation". He said:

It is a particularly gratifying sign of our times that believers and all people of good will feel increasingly called to cooperate in shaping a culture of encounter, dialogue and cooperation in the service of our human family. This entails more than mere tolerance. It challenges us to reach out to others in mutual trust and understanding, and so to build a unity that sees diversity not as a threat, but as a potential source of enrichment and growth. It challenges us to cultivate an openness of heart that views others as an avenue, not a barrier.[11]

Coming to the conclusion of his two-nation journey, Francis then prayed with other religious leaders while meeting with 16 Rohingya refugees at the residence of the Archbishop of Dhaka. The refugees travelled from Cox's Bazar in order to meet with the Pope. The original intention was that they would meet only the Pope and in silence. During the prayer meeting with the other religious leaders, Francis embraced some of the refugees saying:

Dear brothers and sisters, all of us are close to you. There is little that we can do because your tragedy is so great. But

[10] Joanna Moorhead, 29 November 2017. *The Guardian*, accessed at www.theguardian.com/commentisfree/2017/nov/28/pope-francis-catholics-rohingya.
[11] Pope Francis, 1 December 2017. 'Ecumenical and Interreligious Meeting for Peace', Garden of the Archbishops' Residence, Dhaka, accessed at w2.vatican.va/.

let us make room in our heart. In the name of everyone, of those who persecute you, of those who have wronged you, above all for the indifference of the world, I ask your forgiveness … Let us not close our hearts, or look the other way. The presence of God, today, is also called 'Rohingya'.[12]

Details about the meeting were sketchy until the Pope got on the plane back to Rome next day. In his usual style, he then gave a free-ranging press conference to the travelling press corps. He disclosed, "I knew that I would be meeting the Rohingya. I knew neither where nor how, but that this was a condition of the journey, for me, and the procedures were worked out".[13]

After he had greeted the Rohingya, he invited the other religious leaders to do the same. He told the journalists on the plane: "I thought that we were in an interreligious meeting, while the leaders of the other traditions were at a distance. [So I said:] 'No, you come too: these Rohingya are all of ours'. And they greeted them. I didn't know what more to say because I was looking at them, I greeted them … And I thought: 'We have all spoken, the religious leaders. But one of you, say a prayer, one from your group …'. And I think perhaps it was an imam, a 'cleric' of their religion, who offered that prayer, and they too prayed there with us".[14]

He had stated the principles. He had engaged in dialogue with the powerful. Then he had stood in solidarity and prayed with the poor and oppressed. Then, and only then, he explained to the world what he had attempted to do and what he had achieved. He had no intention of travelling to Myanmar and Bangladesh simply stating principles without meeting with the Rohingya.

---

[12] Pope Francis, 1 December 2017. 'Remarks of the Holy Father to the Group of Rohingya Refugees', Dhaka, accessed at w2.vatican.va/.

[13] Pope Francis, 2 December 2017. 'Press Conference on the Return Flight from Bangladesh', accessed at w2.vatican.va/.

[14] Ibid.

He also offered a common-sense lesson on working for justice and peace. He conceded to the critical press corps that he could have publicly read the 'Riot Act' to the Myanmar military leaders on his arrival in Yangon, but it would not have achieved anything other than his political neutering and praise from an impotent western media seeking simplistic pontifical declarations of right and wrong. He suggested that you could slam the door in the face of your listener with the result that the message never arrives. The alternative was to open the door to dialogue respectfully. Appealing to the journalists as fellow communicators in the public square, he said, "I haven't, let's say it this way, had the pleasure of slamming the door in a face, publicly, a denouncement, but I did have the satisfaction of dialoguing and letting the other speak and to say my part and in that way the message arrived and to such a point did it arrive that it continued and continued".[15]

A Pope for Our Times

With Pope Francis, it is not who is in or who is out that matters; it is not right or left that counts; it is not what is right or wrong that provides the ultimate lessons; it is not truth declared by authority that is trumps; it is not justice that provides all the answers to relationships and social questions. It is not that the Church is the perfect society, providing the clear answer to every pastoral problem and every social or political challenge. Francis is a pope for our times. He is a response and a complement to his immediate predecessors, Popes John Paul II and Benedict XVI. Under the leadership and example of Francis, accompaniment, discernment, conscience and mercy are given their due place alongside distinctive Catholic identity, moral certainty, definitive teaching, and notions of commutative, distributive and social justice. He sets out not to provide definitive answers or end points; rather he is a disrupter wanting to shake up everyone, in and out of Church, inviting them to question their starting points and their

---

[15] Ibid.

motivations, leading a Church which is more like a field hospital than a basilica, a Church which is a pointer to a crucified and resurrected Christ rather than a final destination with all the answers.

Understandably, those who see the Church as the clear teacher of moral doctrine in season and out of season can be troubled by the greyness and opaqueness of some of Francis's teachings. But his pastoral stance resonates strongly with the lived experience of so many people confronting the mess and complexity of modern life. He insists that "individual conscience needs to be better incorporated into the Church's praxis" and that

> [C]onscience can do more than recognise that a given situation does not correspond objectively to the overall demands of the Gospel. It can also recognise with sincerity and honesty what for now is the most generous response which can be given to God, and come to see with a certain moral security that it is what God himself is asking amid the concrete complexity of one's limits, while yet not fully the objective ideal.[16]

It is not simply a matter of applying universal rules to a particular situation nor of arguing casuistically to render one's situation as compliance with the rules. Rather it is a matter of "pastoral discernment" practised by friends in the Lord who accompany each other, engaging in spiritual conversation.

The Australian Context

All of us who have come to Australia, the great south land of the Holy Spirit, count our blessings. Our situation is very different from that in Myanmar. We live in a country which has welcomed people from every nation on the planet, people of every religion on earth. We are blessed to live in a country where peace and security are usually

---

[16] Pope Francis, 2016. Post-Synodal Apostolic Exhortation: *Amoris Laetitia*. Vatican City: Vatican, n. 303, accessed at w2.vatican.va/.

assured, and where the rule of law is strong and robust. Having chaired the National Human Rights Consultation for the Rudd Government in 2009, I am left in no doubt that the protection of human rights for minorities in Australia remains a demanding political task given that, unlike the United Kingdom, New Zealand, Canada and the United States of America, we do not have any bill of rights. When recourse to the courts is not possible here, as it would be in those countries, it is necessary for us to be more vigilant in our political processes and in our cultural perspectives ensuring respect for the dignity of every person, and at all stages of life. We are blessed to be citizens of a nation with resilient democratic institutions, a coherent separation of powers, a sensible separation of church and state, and an appropriate relationship between religion and politics. All these blessings contribute to an inclusive Australia where we can all feel at home, assured of our place in the sun.

But we all need to remain vigilant if we are to be a truly inclusive nation, ensuring peace and security for all, and an assured place of belonging for the one who is 'other'. The gap between the rich and poor is widening; inequality is becoming entrenched in the land of the fair go. Faith in public institutions, particularly amongst the young, is in decline. Notions of tradition, authority and community are readily replaced by the individualism of the age, presuming that each atomised individual can work out the meaning and pursue the good without the need for recourse to past learnings or to inclusive institutions which provide the space for reasoned compromise and practical idealism. Major Australian institutions, whether they be the larger political parties or mainstream Christian Churches, are being augmented by smaller niche parties and faith communities without 'the baggage' of the past.

Though we Australians accept people of all faiths and none, there is a growing tendency in the public square for secular atheism to be not only the default position, but the privileged perspective pushed by the self-selecting elites. The tell-tale of this tendency is the increasing prevalence in our media of those commentators who label all religions as irrational. There are many aspects of our religious beliefs, whatever they be, which are non-rational, in the sense that they cannot be proved or disproved just by the use of reason. But this does not make them irrational. There are many aspects of life, including mortality, suffering and sustained injustice which do not lend themselves only to rational analysis, when we come to reflect on the chasm beyond death, the mystery of suffering, and the grace of mercy which transcends even justice. These non-rational aspects of life have to be embraced by us all, whether we be religious believers or not. We have our different ways of embracing these non-rational, mysterious aspects of life. We may confront them as non-relational emptiness or as relational blessing.

There is no reason why the secular atheist should be able to define the terms or to limit the consideration of these aspects of life in the public square. Australia is not a theocratic state, and for that, I thank God, my fellow citizens and our forebears. But neither is Australia an atheistic state, and long may the *status quo* be maintained for the good of all Australians seeking a truly inclusive nation in which the state views religious faith and its absence equally and not preferentially. In Catholic social services we help and work with people of diverse faiths and none, affirming the blessing of life in an inclusive country where all world views are to be respected. We are able to affirm that our spiritual lives sustain and strengthen our public lives and the vitality of the *polis*. We know well the problems highlighted by Pope Francis in his apostolic exhortation *Evangelii Gaudium:*

> The process of secularisation tends to reduce the faith and the Church to the sphere of the private and personal. Furthermore, by completely rejecting the transcendent, it has produced a growing deterioration of ethics, a weakening of the sense of personal and collective sin, and a steady

increase in relativism. These have led to a general sense of disorientation.[17]

In the wake of the Royal Commission into Institutional Responses to Child Sexual Abuse, it is a brave representative of the Catholic Church who will put up his or her head in the public square agitating for justice and solidarity on contested moral and political issues. I take heart from the recent observation by ex-Prime Minister and unashamed Christian Kevin Rudd when he was speaking at the Australian Catholic University:

> You need folks out there who are professionally committed to the business of what I describe as focused, uncompromising Christian ethics, or in the case of the academy more broadly, public policy which in a given set of circumstances will deliver the goods minus politics of compromise. You need folks out there who are constantly holding up the ethical goal posts of our society. Because the nature of parliamentary democracy is that it will be a process of compromise south of that. And the day to day question, the week to week question, the year to year question, is how far south, a little bit, or a long way, or disappearing through the floor?[18]

The 2017 Same-sex Marriage Debate

I am one Catholic priest who has been speaking in the public square trying to set true north for those ethical goal posts for the last 30 years. Let me reflect on just one recent contested political issue in the public square. I voted 'yes' in last year's Australian Bureau of Statistics (ABS) survey on same sex marriage. As a priest, I was prepared to explain why I was voting 'yes' during the campaign. I voted 'yes', in part, because I thought that the outcome was inevitable. But also, I

[17] Pope Francis, 2013, Apostolic Exhortation, op. cit., n. 64.
[18] Kevin Rudd in Conversation with Greg Craven, 14 February 2018. Institute for Religion, Politics and Society, Australian Catholic University, accessed at www.acu.edu.au/1381114.

thought that full civil recognition of such relationships was an idea whose time had come. Considerations of the common good required that we consider the wellbeing of all persons affected by any change to law and policy, including the increasing number of children being brought up by same sex couples in stable loving relationships. What was needed was an outcome which helped to maintain respect for freedom of religion, the standing of the Churches, and the pastoral care and concern of everyone affected by such relationships, including this increasing number of children being brought up in households headed by same sex couples committed to each other and their children. I thought it appropriate that at least a handful of clergy should come out and, when asked, express their intention to vote 'yes'.

I am also the CEO of Catholic Social Services Australia (CSSA). At the time of the survey, CSSA published this statement:

> CSSA has no formal position on what enrolled voters should say in response to the voluntary survey being conducted by the ABS on whether the *Marriage Act* should be amended by the Australian Parliament to expand the definition of civil marriage to include a relationship between two persons of the same sex.
>
> CSSA and its members are employers and service providers who happily affirm the dignity, gifts and personal commitments of all our employees and those whom we are privileged to serve. We never discriminate against persons on the basis of their sexuality or marital status.
>
> Being a Catholic agency, CSSA operates under the auspices of the Catholic Bishops and accepts Church teaching on theological issues such as the sacramentality of marriage and the limits on what relationships are recognised by the Catholic Church as sacramental marriage.

Even though most Catholics who voted ended up voting 'yes', as

I did, I presume that the majority of our bishops voted 'no'. But I know that some bishops did vote 'yes'. In the lead up to the vote, a couple of bishops (and there were only a couple, though others may have been upset while deciding not to communicate directly with me) wrote to me taking strong exception to the position I had taken. One of these bishops claimed, "With regard to the current postal survey on legally redefining marriage to include same sex unions, a Catholic is morally obligated to vote 'no'. There is no option to claim that in good conscience that a Catholic can vote 'yes'".[19] I disagreed strongly with this bishop. I think I voted 'yes' in good conscience. I thought his argument was the 21st century equivalent of a bishop telling the flock that they had to vote for the Democratic Labour Party (DLP). I think those days have gone, and they have gone forever. During the plebiscite campaign I took heart from the very pastoral response from those bishops like Vincent Long who wrote:

> Throughout much of history, our gay and lesbian (or LGBTI) brothers and sisters have often not been treated with respect, sensitivity and compassion. Regrettably, the Church has not always been a place where they have felt welcomed, accepted and loved. Thus, regardless of the outcome of the survey, we must commit ourselves to the task of reaching out to our LGBTI brothers and sisters, affirming their dignity and accompanying them on our common journey towards the fullness of life and love in God.

> Let us pray, discern and act with the wisdom of the Holy Spirit. Catholics, in keeping with the tradition of the Church, are asked to exercise their consciences, ensuring that they are informed as they come to exercise their democratic rights in the coming postal survey.[20]

---

[19] Letter of a bishop to author, 8 November 2017.
[20] Bishop Vincent Long, 13 September 2017. 'Pastoral Letter on the Same-Sex Marriage Postal Survey', accessed at parralmf.org.au/2017/09/15/bishop-vincent-longs-pastoral-letter-on-the-same-sex-marriage-postal-survey/.

Archbishop Mark Coleridge, an accomplished scripture scholar and then Vice-President of the Australian Catholic Bishops Conference, got it right on how Catholics might vote when he was interviewed on national television during the plebiscite campaign. He told David Speers on *Sky News*:

> To think of a Catholic vote all going one way is just naïve. Of course, it's possible to vote 'yes'. It depends why you vote 'yes'. It's possible to vote 'no', but equally it depends why you vote 'no' … As a Catholic you can vote 'yes' or you can vote 'no'. I personally will vote 'no' but for quite particular reasons. But I'm not going to stand here and say: you vote 'no'; and you vote 'yes', and you're a Catholic, you'll go to hell. It's not like that.[21]

No matter how we voted, we all now need to accept that the civil law of marriage will permit the exclusive, committed relationship of any two persons to be legally recognised, granting the couple endorsement and respect for their relationship and for their family. There is room in our Church and there is room in our public square for Catholics of goodwill to express varying views about these contested moral and political issues, seeking justice for all and solidarity with all in the mess and complexity of life.

Implications of *Amoris Laetitia*

Let me take you back to Myanmar briefly. When Pope Francis was in Yangon, he met with the Jesuits there. One of these Jesuits is an Islamic scholar from Indonesia. He asked Pope Francis about the problem of religious fundamentalism. Francis replied:

> Look, there are fundamentalisms everywhere. And we Catholics have 'the honour' of having fundamentalists among the baptised. Fundamentalism is an attitude of the

---

[21] Archbishop Mark Coleridge, 28 September 2017. Interview with David Speers, *Sky News*.

soul that stands as a judge of others and of those who share their religion. It is a going to the essential – a claim to be going to the essential – of religion, but to such an extent as to forget what is existential. It forgets the consequences. Fundamentalist attitudes take different forms, but they have the common background of underlining the essential so much that they deny the existential. The fundamentalist denies history, denies the person. And Christian fundamentalism denies the Incarnation.[22]

Within the Catholic Church there is presently strong tension between those who focus too much on the essential and those who overlook the essential in the name of pastoral inclusiveness. In the Catholic tradition, we do state ideals, but we also consider that the application of those ideals to the particular situation is not to be done simply as a matter of logical analysis. There is a need for us to discern God's action and God's call in the midst of the mess and complexity of people's lives and of our world. We need to take account of the existential situation of the person and the consequences which flow from any 'mathematical' application of the principles to the particular.

This tension has been playing out at the highest levels in our Church ever since Pope Francis convened the two synods on the family and then published his post-synodal apostolic exhortation *Amoris Laetitia* in which, as noted earlier, he asserts:

> [C]onscience can do more than recognize that a given situation does not correspond objectively to the overall demands of the Gospel. It can also recognize with sincerity and honesty what for now is the most generous response which can be given to God and come to see with a certain moral security that it is what God himself is asking amid the concrete complexity of one's limits, while yet not

---

[22] Pope Francis, 14 December 2017, quoted in "At the Crossroads of History: Conversations with the Jesuits in Myanmar and Bangladesh", *La Civilta Cattolica*, 10.

fully the objective ideal. In any event, let us recall that this discernment is dynamic; it must remain ever open to new stages of growth and to new decisions which can enable the ideal to be more fully realized.[23]

Gone are the days of seeing the Church as the perfect society, as the hierarchical institution able to set down the rules for good living as if these rules were simply to be applied like a chemical formula. Francis assures us that he is sincere in his belief that Jesus wants a Church attentive to the goodness which the Holy Spirit sows in the midst of human weakness, a Mother who, while clearly expressing her objective teaching, "always does what good she can, even if in the process, her shoes get soiled by the mud of the street". According to Francis, Jesus "expects us to stop looking for those personal or communal niches which shelter us from the maelstrom of human misfortune, and instead to enter into the reality of other people's lives and to know the power of tenderness. Whenever we do so, our lives become wonderfully complicated".[24]

There has to be a holistic connection between our knowledge and our practice. Our ideas and our experience have to inform each other. In February 2018, Cardinal Blasé Cupich who was Francis' 'captain's pick' as the new Cardinal Archbishop of Chicago travelled to Cambridge University to address the Von Hugel Institute for Critical Catholic Inquiry. Cupich was clearly wanting to send a message to the English-speaking world of the Catholic Church. He did it by quoting Pope Francis and Cardinal Parolin at some length to establish that we are now living not just in an era of change in the Church, but in a change of era. Cupich told his British audience that when Cardinal Parolin, the Holy See's Secretary of State, had been asked about the difficulties some seem to have in understanding the post-synodal apostolic exhortation *Amoris Laetitia*, Parolin had responded:

---

[23] Pope Francis, 2016, op. cit., n. 303.
[24] Ibid., n. 308.

[T]he Holy Father is offering a new paradigm in this document, one that calls us to embrace a new spirit, a change of direction in the way the Church carries out its ministry, especially ministry to families. At the heart of this shift is a fully incarnational approach, which the Cardinal explains, is a two-way street. On the one hand the Church embraces the family with the Gospel message. Yet, since the family is already itself a Gospel, the Gospel of the family, there is a reciprocity to this incarnational approach that recognises the contribution that families make to the Church's understanding and proclamation of the Gospel".[25]

Cupich went on to say:

I believe a paradigm shift takes place in *Amoris*. The Pope does this … on a number of levels through a set of interrelated interpretive principles. This allows him to offer a new and holistic response for family ministry. Following up on his appeal for a revolution of mercy, launched with the Jubilee Year, Pope Francis is both inviting and equipping the Church through this new hermeneutic to take up this mission in a new, imaginative, and, yes, holistic way, especially as it relates to her ministry to couples and families.[26]

He was adamant that Pope Francis has introduced a new paradigm, a new hermeneutic, a revolution in thinking for the Church as social actor and moral guide. Francis' oft-repeated call for discernment and accompaniment requires that we be more attentive to the voices and experiences of the laity. Cupich said:

It goes without saying that this will also mean rejecting an

[25] Cardinal Blasé Cupich, 9 February 2018. 'Pope Francis' Revolution of Mercy: *Amoris Laetitia* as a New Paradigm of Catholicity', Speech given at the Von Hügel Institute, St Edmund College, Cambridge, accessed at www.lastampa.it/2018/02/09/vaticaninsider/eng/documents/pope-francis-revolution-of-mercy-amoris-laetitia-as-a-new-paradigm-of-catholicity-skMox0lKtoX5szfKH6QgrL/pagina.html.
[26] Ibid.

authoritarian or paternalistic way of dealing with people that lays down the law, that pretends to have all the answers, or easy answers to complex problems, that suggests that general rules will seamlessly bring immediate clarity or that the teachings of our tradition can preemptively be applied to the particular challenges confronting couples and families. In its place a new direction will be required, one that envisions ministry as accompaniment, an accompaniment, which we will see, is marked by a deep respect for the conscience of the faithful.

Rather than limiting the function of conscience to knowing moral truth about actions in the past and objective truth in the present, conscience also discerns the future, asking: What is God asking of me now?[27]

This has all been a step too far for some bishops, like Archbishop Charles Chaput from Philadelphia, who spoke at Villanova University in March 2018 telling his audience:

[A]nything that enfeebles the believing community from within is so hurtful, not just for the Church, but also for a culture of true freedom. There are no new paradigms; no new hermeneutical principles; no revolutions in thought; and no possible concordats with the world and its alibis, that can erase the radicalism and liberating beauty of Christian anthropology. Key to that anthropology is the nature of our sexuality, expressed in the complementarity of male and female, and ordered to new life and mutual support. Human sexuality and relationships have a God-given purpose. That purpose is a source of true freedom and joy. It can't be changed, or reinterpreted, or medically reimagined away.[28]

---

[27] Ibid.

[28] Archbishop Charles Chaput, 22 February 2018. 'Things to Come: Faith, State and Society in a New World', Address at Villanova University, Philadelphia, accessed at archphila. org/archbishop-chaputs-address-at-villanova-university-things-to-come-faith-state-and-society-in-a-new-world/.

Cupich and Chaput cannot both be absolutely right. But each may have a point. They have set off the dialectic which helps to inform modern life. We so desperately need the respectful dialogue within the Church between those of differing views. For too long, difference and dissent were silenced in our Church with the result that the righteous remnant took charge and many who saw the world and their lives as more complex thought they had no option but to leave. Archbishop Chaput has obviously decided that it is time to lay down the gauntlet with Cardinals Parolin and Cupich. We all need to watch this spot! But we can thank God that we no longer live in a Church where Archbishop Chaput might be despatched by the Holy Father to investigate and put an end to the pastoral ministry of a committed pastoral bishop like our beloved William Morris.[29] Even in our Church, and not just in the public square, we must expect robust differences of view and thus we need to follow Francis's three Cairo principles inside and outside the Church, respecting the identity of all players, courageously accepting our differences, and acting with sincere intentions.

Conclusion

With these reflections on human rights, the Pope's recent visit to Myanmar, the Australian same sex marriage debate, and the episcopal differences over *Amoris Laetitia*, I hope I have helped you in the assessment of our current reality. Discerning our response, we need to take the words justice and solidarity out of our dictionary, working with them so that they become a reality. Together we accept the invitation to build the platform here and now so that the kingdom of justice and peace might break through even in the hardest hearts and on the most sterile ground of the public square.

---

[29] Frank Brennan, 23 June 2014. "Why Bishop Morris Was Sacked", *Eureka Street*, accessed at www.eurekastreet.com.au/article.aspx?aeid=41603.

4

2018 Mary MacKillop Oration

Living through the Holy Saturday of the Church's Life in Australia

Geraldine Doogue AO

Introduction

For some years, Catholic Social Services Victoria, with the support of the Sisters of St Joseph of the Sacred Heart, has sponsored a biennial address, the Mary MacKillop Oration, to honour Australia's first saint, and to reflect the spirit of St Mary MacKillop. When introducing Geraldine Doogue, the 2018 Oration speaker, Gabrielle McMullen noted that the ministries of Australian Catholic social services have much in common with many of the initiatives taken by St Mary MacKillop, who is an inspiration for the sector. The following Mary MacKillop anecdote seems to relate well to the works of Catholic Social Services – it was recounted by Sr Marie Therese Foale rsj in an interview with Doogue on a *Compass* program at the time of Mary MacKillop's canonisation:

> One wonderful story that I love is that about three months after Mary had started in Adelaide she noticed through walking along the streets that there were a lot of kids who weren't coming to school. And when she asked them why, they said "We can't come because we haven't got good clothes". So what did she do? She put an ad in the paper. If anybody's got any clothes that they don't use any more please bring them along to the school at the cathedral and I'll get some of my helpers to make them up into suitable things for children. Then the Sisters went out and presented

the kids with the clothes and of course they came to school. Within six months that school had trebled its enrolment from 60 to over 200.[1]

Some years ago, Pope Francis said: "Following Jesus demands a good dose of courage, a readiness to trade in the sofa for a pair of walking shoes and to set out on new and uncharted paths. To blaze trails that open up new horizons capable of spreading joy, the joy that is born of God's love and wells up in your hearts with every act of mercy".[2] McMullen suggested he might have been talking about the life of Mary MacKillop.

Geraldine Doogue was in Rome in 2010 at the time of Mary Mac-Killop's canonisation. On that occasion Doogue noted in an interview that her experience had been that "big stories get thinner the closer you get to them, and in fact it is the reverse with Mary MacKillop's".[3] Doogue's stirring, thoughtful Mary MacKillop Oration, which is presented below, spoke strongly to the conference theme of *Hearing, Healing, Hope.*

Living through the Holy Saturday of the Church's Life in Australia

Have things ever seemed worse for the Catholic Church in Australia? If it were a boxer, it would look tangled in the ropes, sliding towards the canvas and spitting blood. The past four years have been horrendous. Endless, horrifying accounts of historical child abuse. A royal commission[4]

---

[1] Sr Marie Therese Foale rsj, 10 October 2010. Compass interview with Geraldine Doogue, accessed at www.abc.net.au/compass/s2968600.htm.

[2] Pope Francis, 2016. Address at World Youth Day in Krakow, accessed at www.schoenstatt.org/en/francis/message/2016/08/jesus-is-the-lord-of-risk-the-lord-of-always-more/.

[3] Geraldine Doogue, 16 October 2010. Report from Rome in the lead-up to the canonisation of Mary MacKillop, accessed at www.abc.net.au/radionational/programs/saturdayextra/mary-mackillop/2970738.

[4] The Royal Commission into Institutional Responses to Child Sexual Abuse.

relentlessly critiquing failures of bishops and processes. The media baying for yet more blood. Cardinal George Pell charged with abuse offences … he has the full presumption of innocence, but the communal trauma is palpable. And now a report from the commission eviscerating the Catholic sacrament of confession. How much worse can this get?

These words were written by Professor Greg Craven, the Vice-Chancellor of the Australian Catholic University, in *The Weekend Australian* in 2017.[5] They seemed to me to conclude with a classic Holy Saturday question. It is posed, legitimately, by a struggling, shocked, ashamed people trying to discern our next direction. I would like, however, to read you something of a counter view to those sentiments:

> When you climb out a black well, you are not the same
>
> You come to in the blue air, with a long sore scar circling your chest like the shoreline of a deep new sea
>
> Your hands are webbed, inviting you to trust yourself … in water stranger and wilder than you've ever known
>
> Your heart has a kick, your eyes have a different bite. You have emerged from some dark wonder you can't explain
>
> You are not the same

That is the memorable work of the late, great Australian poet Dorothy Porter in a poem called *Not the Same*, and I would like to suggest that this offers us some psychological, even spiritual road-map: to trust that we can, indeed, emerge.

Maybe we do have to just wait: just pause and reflect on where we are, as people who may have devoted a lot of time to this institution, in some way or the other. And our thoughts may not be particularly coherent. I have always liked one of St Teresa of Avila's lovely statements. At the outset of her classic work *The Way of Perfection*, she

[5] Greg Craven, 19 August 2017. "Besieged Catholic Church is wounded, but will not fall", *The Weekend Australian*, accessed at www.acu.edu.au.

confesses: "Since I don't know what I am to say, I cannot say it in an orderly way!"

Yes, I am struggling mightily with what to say, to feel, to think. And while I am not trying to be trivial, I presume people who have devoted their lives to an institution such as the Commonwealth Bank might have feelings along a similar spectrum right now. That they have given themselves honestly and vigilantly to their big-beast-institution only to discover a range of egregious things were happening around them, in core areas of their institution. Did they not notice? Should they have?

Was the December editorial in *The Tablet* post release of the Royal Commission's report correct, that "the entire Australian Catholic community" had been shown to have failed? Was that a fair verdict? Now of course you might say that the Church's dark-night-of-the-soul is of a different order to say a bank, and of course I would agree with you. But I am making the point that we are not the only institution in this predicament. Many of us knew this institution as something that was precious, unique in its draw on us, offering a glimpse of the Divine, though maybe taken for granted a bit despite all that. Someone was running it, weren't they? It would keep operating, somehow, wouldn't it? We (the laity) would turn up, offer something, confident that it would be there in some form.

As Greg Craven went on to say in that *Weekend Australian* piece, "There is a tremendous tension between these fundamental imperatives. The first is to acknowledge and atone for the atrocious crimes committed under its roof … The second core obligation of the Church is to assess the directions and recommendations of the royal commission on their merits".[6]

In other words, we have to bring our conscious mind to bear. It means reflecting very deeply on that sense of something having

---

[6] Ibid.

possibly died, a confident sense of an institution whose flaws were obvious to us but which we knew were outweighed by its faith, hope and charity. And it was like our personal circulation system, in my view.

Plus, we knew that our Church truly represented far more than the awful stories dominating the headlines: we knew that and could point to evidence. Some 700,000 school children in the Catholic sector, served by 82,000 staff; 66 hospitals including 19 public hospitals run by Church-related entities, surely massive hubs of compassion. The St Vincent de Paul Society is the most extensive volunteer welfare network in the country and the Church is the largest welfare provider outside government. As I have written elsewhere, some of those particularly vulnerable people who have populated the Royal Commission will surely need some of these services during their lives, along with multiple thousands of other needy Australians: "preferential option for the poor" is no theory in these settings, as I am sure many of you seated before me today know better than I!

So where does my Holy-Saturday thinking take me? I have really struggled, I acknowledge, with pitting all the goodness that I know exists, brokered by the Church, against these awful stories, where the Church as Good Shepherd so obviously abandoned its flock. I have felt myself hoist on a particularly acute petard, trying to sort my way through it. It has bedeviled me, and I confess I am not entirely satisfied yet with my answers.

It is as if a virus had entered the organism that I know, this special organism I know, yet I could not really believe it would overtake the body. Was I in denial? Certainly, the wider world seemed to believe this virus was irredeemably metastatic, and sometimes this conviction could seem pretty self-serving. Yet I also knew it was critical that I did face up, as a Catholic, to the level of dysfunction, the lack of kindness above all.

Would these revelations repel people of goodwill and interfere seriously with people's strivings towards something beyond the everyday? Would it simply circumvent people's search for the ineffable, a quest brokered by the Church in unique ways? If so, what a tragedy for searching individuals, and the community, for that matter.

Would it rob us of joy? Another tragedy. Would it limit our abilities to re-imagine a modern faith community here in Australia?

I had quite a powerful, if poignant, experience at Mass in my local church recently, listening to a young Australian-Vietnamese priest who obviously was recently ordained: transparently devout and super-conscientious. His emphasis in his homily quite surprised me, I must say, because he very much saw himself as leading (his word) as the clear guide, the good shepherd I suppose, us, the people in the pews, through the thickets of life, towards greater faith. And then came this moment, which actually brought tears to my eyes, given his sincerity: "I pray every day, dear people, that I will be up to the task, that I will resist all temptations and fulfil my mission". (Or similar words, as if some of those priests in the headlines had not started out the same way, I reflected!)

I could see his total commitment and of course was impressed. But I wanted him to say something like: "I will be there to accompany you, I will learn from you, I will walk alongside you and hope never to deviate as we all attempt, together, to discern God's path for us and our Church in this world"… or something like that.

It helped me focus my thoughts. The only way forward for a thriving Catholic Church in Australia, as I see it, is an institution with much, much more collaboration, power- and influence-sharing and mutual respect between clergy and laity: between the official and non-ordained people.

It is a very different model of both priesthood and Church. The young priest's quite definite emphasis helped me distil my own thoughts, probably quite changed by this crisis, but of course undoubtedly brewed originally in the documents of Vatican II and the whole notion of a Pilgrim Church.

This means a new laity; I fully acknowledge that. I expect real stepping-up by lay people in a way I am just not sure we have been prepared to do. I expect reflection of a big order in terms of what is required, just like I am asked to do on a weekly basis at the ABC, for example. Yes, I expect leadership training, innovative thinking, planning, as well as kindness and generosity of spirit. And to match that, I would hope for humble readiness-to-adapt by clergy: *those who lead are fundamentally called to serve*, which the Jesuits highlighted a decade ago at a conference that I attended.

In trying to sort my way through these last demanding years, I have sought out surprising areas, some sources of hope and energy. I have realised that it requires both humility and perseverance (my word of the year) to be useful, combined with a propensity to plan, as opposed to just ponder. Not passivity, in other words, not surrender, something more deeply bold in fact.

I would like to quote a German writer, the deputy editor-in-chief of the German magazine *Der Spiegel*, Dirk Kurbjeweit, who was in Australia last year and appeared on my programme, speaking about the modern German mood post their 20th century cataclysms, because I have found myself intrigued by how they put themselves back together again.

"Germans once believed they had found a saviour", he has written, "but then *he* tried to destroy the world, and now their belief in salvation has vanished. Sociologist Helmut Schelsky found that there was a 'sceptical generation' of Germans who took part in the war when they were very young and who then went on to build up the Federal Republic of Germany. They rejected all grand ideas, their state religion became Karl Popper's 'piecemeal social engineering', the politics of small measure; turn a screw here, carefully open a valve there, make sure not to create too much hope. That is Angela Merkel's fundamental approach".

Of course, I realise that she has a few problems of her own right now, still being worked out, as you know! But in other words, people at the bottom of the barrel, can become very resourceful and build back, to become the centre of Europe. And after all, they could not exactly abandon their nationality, certainly not easily.

So how might that apply to us, now? Well, I do wonder whether the Church ought to suspend all non-essential activities and listen to what society seeks of it, needs from it, for maybe 12 months, and visibly do so for all the messages that it sends, explicitly and implicitly.

I have also turned to another group that might surprise you: the world of Judaism and the Jewish people, to see whether their experience offered us real guidance in this dark-night time. After all, they truly had to re-create their whole belief and culture twice: when the Babylonians enslaved them and then not long after the time of Jesus, after the Romans destroyed their Second Temple and their whole hierarchy, their kings, their prophets, their priests, their freedom. It was simply impossible to continue as it was. And of course in our own times, the Holocaust is one of the terrible scars of the 20th century, where the Jewish people were again tested to their core.

One of the guiding principles of that community's strength, here and overseas, is summarised by a wonderful phrase offered by the former United Kingdom Chief Rabbi, Jonathan Sacks: the invitation to belong before believing. Personally, I find that so inviting for us right now. I do not believe, of course, that we can simply transpose another belief tradition's whole purpose onto ours.

But as *The Tablet* editorialised again last year – and this time I think it is absolutely right – there is a fundamental continuity between Jewish hope and Christian hope. The Hebrew Bible and the New

Testament as "conjoined narratives of hope ... each looks towards the same ending to the human story, when God will take his own to himself. 'Thy Kingdom Come' is both a Jewish and a Christian prayer of hope, not a passive hope, because the kingdom (however you read that) has to be built: it has to be just and at peace, the lion must lie down with the lamb. The Sermon on the Mount is the template, but the faithful are its builders".

I have several very good Jewish friends, very active in their community, and I have sought them out, to learn more about the way their community is structured. I asked them: "Where does the life lie?"

They are, by choice, a much tighter cultural group. Whereas the Catholic Church is the original multi-national entity, wondrous in its breadth, I have always thought, but not so easy when you are experiencing the type of crisis afflicting the Australian arm. Because to some extent, we are on our own here, discerning a rescue that makes sense to our Australian sensibility, to ensure our children and grandchildren do not consign the Church's wisdom to being a museum piece. (My Jewish friend Stephen says that actually he worries that Jews handle crises well, but he does wonder about their ability to handle what appear to be settled times, without overt repression!)

Rabbi Sacks writes beautifully, and he distilled a particular approach to adapting a belief tradition succinctly when he received the lucrative Templeton Prize for Religion in 2016.[7] Again, I found it very helpful:

> What emerged in Judaism and post Reformation Christianity was the rarest of character-types: the inner-directed personality. Most societies, for most of history, have been either tradition-directed or other-directed. People do what they do either because that's how they've always been done or because that is what other people do. Inner-directed types

---

[7] Rabbi Lord Jonathon Sacks, 2016. 'The Danger of Outsourcing Morality', acceptance speech, 2016 Templeton Prize, accessed at www.rabbisacks.org.

are different. They become the pioneers, the innovators and the survivors. They have an internalised satellite navigation system so they are not fazed by uncharted territory. They have a strong sense of duty to others. They try to have secure marriages. They hand on their values to their children. They belong to strong communities. They take daring but carefully calculated risks. When they fall, they have rapid recovery times. They play it long. They are more interested in sustainability than quick profits. Cultures like that stay young. They defeat the entropy, the loss of energy, that has spelled the decline and fall of every other empire and super-power in history.

Suggesting the West was letting go of some of this, he went on:

> There is an alternative: to become inner-directed again, which means recovering the moral dimension that links our welfare to the welfare of others … helping us tell the difference between the value of things and their price.

Now, you may think: ah yes, he is their Chief Rabbi so obviously he is massively embedded in their recoveries. But no, as I understand it (not in all the different traditions of Judaism of course but in significant ones in Australia), while rabbis and shule are still essentially the symbolic core and known to be, the real locus of energy and commitment is in secular Jewry: benefitting the individuals concerned, and the health of their community.

It is true that they do not explicitly (except in some distinct areas) aim to penetrate the wider community, the way Catholics would. And I want to acknowledge that it is one of our great strengths.

But as my friends say, and it makes such sense: Jews had to enable their own group to survive because they knew no-one else would do it. So, they simply had to work out what was required. They suggested to me that the maintenance of doctrine as such was less emphasised or worried about.

What pre-occupied them was engagement, straddling various age groups, an explicit aim. In fact, rabbis, for example, associated with Jewish schools are said to be responsible for 'Jewish life', a title encompassing a subtly broader concept compared with the brief for our chaplains, and definitely living out that dictum of "belonging before believing".

They set up groups like the Jewish Committee of Australia or Council of Jewish Women (let alone their better-known groups like the Jewish Board of Deputies or B'nai Brith) which are well-funded (an important issue) but which aim to support activities that embody the values of Judaism, more than stated beliefs. Now, of course, we do that too. But I do wonder whether we could articulate this better, especially to younger members, to display a confidence in the values base and its roots, more than we do, to be conspicuously involved. I am told that a big driver of these Jewish groups is:

- engagement before fund-raising, and

- persuading people that Jewish community vibrancy is in their individual and family interest, and

- that the projects chosen were understandable, not abstract, based rather more on action than explicit and stated beliefs, well run and sustainable, to encourage younger talented people to take part.

I also think the Jewish tradition of eating together on Friday night for a Shabbat meal is just so clever. But I admit I cannot see how that can easily be applied, though I would love you to all dwell upon just that because I think it is very affirming in a collective sense. It is personal, it is anti-loneliness (the great need), it exposes people to their spiritual base; it has the potential to be fun! (But, of course, there are also plenty of Shabbat refugees having dinner in Double Bay away from their families as they remind me).

Pope Francis' *Evangelii Gaudium* is quite helpful here. That phrase:

"There are Christians whose lives seem like Lent without Easter"[8] was the most startling challenge issued to me personally in *Evangelii Gaudium*. I liked the way the Pope warned against defeatism, that we could not leave it to the 'professionals'.

What that said to me was that to navigate the way forward, we had to forge more unity with our communities, re-articulate our own values with some confidence, re-examine the structures with a view to borrowing from our secular world.

To me, whether Pope Francis would put it quite like that – or even fully agree with me – I think the Pope is saying to us: do not delay examining the Church's role in your modern life. Do not fall back on the excuse of what you consider non-negotiable foes, like being too busy, or being put off by the clergy, or because you find a "sterile pessimism", and you do not feel capable of breaking through "the grey pragmatism" that develops around daily life. I think it is incredibly important that, in quite colloquial language, Pope Francis is trying to name the beasts that rob us of any chance of a rejoicing faith, partly drawn from people's feeling about an overbearing need to protect their "personal framework", I think he says. I say, "Spot on".

Truthfully, I do not think he does demonstrate that he fully understands why people – including priests and parish workers – feel so powerfully about this need to protect their personal realm, to protect their free time. Many of us feel, I sense, that we have to snatch at securing a quiet life, to preserve a precious core of identity. And snatching is never a thoroughly desirable motive!

But then I think my Jewish friends would say: "Just do it! Show it can be done, and the words will then come". Young people, they say, want it obviously and they will draw the conclusions. Tricky!

---

[8] Pope Francis, 2013. Apostolic Exhortation: *Evangelii Gaudium*. Vatican City: Vatican, n. 6., accessed at w2.vatican.va.

I will finish with words often attributed to Oscar Romero:

We cannot do everything
And there is a sense of liberation in realising that.
This enables us to do something,
And to do it very well.
It may be incomplete, but it is a beginning, a step along the way,
An opportunity for God's grace to enter and do the rest.
We may never see the end results
But that is the difference between the Master-Builder and the worker.

A perfect Holy Saturday prayer!

5

Responding to Abuse, Ensuring Safety and Dedication to Service

Maria Harries AM

The opportunity to engage reflectively with two presentations at a forum called 'Responding to Abuse, Ensuring Safety and Dedication to Service' was greeted with interest and thoughtfulness mingled with a touch of hesitation by those gathered at the 2018 Catholic Social Services conference. No surprises there. Gathered were people of various faith traditions and those of no particular faith, yet all dedicated to service in a variety of Church ministries. While distressed and concerned by the five years of hearings of the Royal Commission into Institutional Responses to Child Sexual Abuse (The Royal Commission)[1] those present were also the people who have worked at the margins and borne witness to the harm of all forms of violence, have accompanied the wounded and know the powers of healing. Some were members of the clergy and religious orders who have fought for justice and for the most disadvantaged. Most have worked with bishops and other clergy and religious for whom they have respect and regard. All were distressed by the horror of the victim accounts that had emerged over five years of hearings. Palpable in the conference and evident in the questions and conversations beforehand, during and afterwards, was an eagerness to confront the truth, understand more, and face the emotional and operational challenges therein.

---

[1] The Royal Commission into Institutional Responses to Child Sexual Abuse presented its findings and recommendations in December 2017. Its report can be accessed at www.childabuseroyalcommission.gov.au/.

At the start of the forum, participants were apprised of the fact that the Australian Catholic Bishops Conference (ACBC) and Catholic Religious Australia (CRA) had instigated the Truth Justice and Healing Council (TJHC) after the announcement of the Royal Commission to enable the Church to "address the past openly and honestly, the good with the bad".[2] Made up of eleven members, predominantly lay but with two senior members of the clergy, the TJHC was set up to allow the Church to speak with one voice before the Royal Commission and to represent the numerous organisations that make up the hugely complex organisational puzzle that represents the Church. As torturous and controversial as it proved to be at times, the way of honesty and openness was set firmly from the start. Francis Sullivan, the CEO of the TJHC, was assiduous in facilitating open dialogue with the Royal Commission, with the public and with organisations represented by those present at the conference.

The questions on participants' minds were implicit in the title of the conference, *Hearing, Healing, Hope* and of the forum, 'Responding to Abuse, Ensuring Safety and Dedication to Service'. Why had this happened? Why have the apparent responses of Church authorities been so inadequate? What can be done now? How to help survivors and victims? How to ensure a safe future for children and vulnerable people?

The two key presenters held promise for providing some answers to these questions as well as enriching the collective understanding of the tragic accounts that continued to challenge all present. These two presenters assisted participants with 'meaning-making' beyond the media turmoil and publicity of the just released Royal Commission's 17-volume report. Robert Fitzgerald AM, a Commissioner with the now finalised Royal Commission, was already known to most of the

---

[2] For information on the Truth Justice and Healing Council, see www.tjhcouncil.org. au/.

audience. A forthright speaker, all were aware that his honesty and personal commitments to those who had been harmed would ensure truth telling and the educationally beneficial discomfort of all attentive listeners. Sheree Limbrick was also known to many of us as a passionate advocate within our service network for those on the margins. Now the CEO of the newly established Catholic Professional Standards Ltd (CPSL),[3] a body recommended by the TJHC and accepted by the ACBC and CRA, she knew well the implications of the findings of the Royal Commission. In her presentation it was evident that CPSL was resolved to tighten the standards in all Catholic organisations but particularly in the myriad Catholic organisations that provide services for children and vulnerable adults.

Alongside the desire of conference participants to understand more and find answers was the potential for despair and loss of hope. The potent, persistent and evocative Commission reporting shocked everyone. Despite being grateful for the final and complete 'outing' of the sinister and endemic nature of sexual abuse and its implications for victims, for all present the risk of a sense of helplessness was palpable. In anticipating such risk, the audience was reminded of the words of Aboriginal leader, Miriam-Rose Ungunmerr-Baumann, at the presentation of the previous day. She talked of the significance of the Aboriginal and Torres Strait Islander spiritual heritage that can assist us all to engage with hope in times of despair. In particular, she said, "We must all remember there is a deep spring that lives in each of us that enables us to hold on to hope". Those present already had intimate knowledge of the inspirational capacity of people to survive struggles and hold on to hope. Most present had borne witness to stories of incredible survival after horrific trauma. The audience was reminded that the inspiration from the pain-filled, truthful honesty of survivors of sexual abuse provides a vital foundation for building a new future.

---

[3] For information on the Catholic Professional Standards Ltd, see www.cpsltd.org.au/.

Confronting the Reality

In acknowledging his ongoing commitment to the shared journey of painful listening of those present, Robert Fitzgerald noted his own unenviable and significant roles in being both a Commissioner and a Catholic. Nevertheless, this had given him a unique insight into both understanding what had happened and how we can move forward. He was unequivocal about rejecting the oft-mentioned opinion that the Royal Commission was anti-religion or anti-Catholic. In presenting first the tensions in the role he had accepted, he enabled many to connect with the tensions for themselves and the need to move beyond the binaries of holding on to a faith or accepting the painful truth of Church failure. He observed sanguinely that he was pleased to be present as "one of them" (a previous Commissioner as well as a Catholic). This was a powerful invitation to be open to the opportunities of hearing the intolerable and imaging the possible rather than resorting to the gloom and hopelessness present in the understandable outrage amongst all present and in the wider community. He was clear that the Church can now forge a new authentic path by accepting the evidence of what has been exposed, listening to the voices of survivors, reflecting carefully upon the recommendations made, and using the talents and gifts of those already engaged with these issues throughout the Church.

Fitzgerald acknowledged his personal sadness at bearing witness to the daily accounts of abuse and the national tragedy of child sexual abuse itself. He opened by asserting that sexual abuse within the Church has been a "scourge for generations" and had impacted upon the lives of thousands of children, now adults. He noted that the awareness of such abuse had been present in the Catholic Church within monasteries and religious orders "throughout the Church's history". Historic documents show abuse within the early Catholic Church in Australia as far back as the late 1800s. The myth in the Church (and undoubtedly elsewhere) is that abuse was a recent phenomenon and short-lived. Such a view minimises the extent of the abuse and the underlying contributory factors present within the Church's culture, structures and practices. Connecting with the emotional disturbance felt by all present, he noted the horror at the emergent reality of the extent of the problem in more recent Church history and at present in our Church and community. Whilst the level of child sexual abuse in institutions appears to have declined, it is still present.

He acknowledged that many in the Church have been aware of this crisis and have been at the forefront of trying to expose and respond to it. The development of *Towards Healing*[4] and professional standards in recent years are examples of the work of those open to the truth of what had happened and could still happen. He confirmed we may not have needed a Royal Commission to know of the endemic nature of sexual abuse of children (for much was already known by the Church authorities), but for this audience he did not mince his words: "For the Church itself, it is a great tragedy. It's a tragedy of epic proportions". About sixty per cent of survivors identified that their abuse occurred in faith-based organisations and of that group just over 60 per cent were in Catholic institutions. Nearly 37 per cent of private session participants identified their abuse as having occurred in a Catholic institution compared to 32 per cent in all government services across Australia. Whilst there may not be historical prevalence studies, these figures alone tell a story.

Forty per cent of complaints related to out-of-home care; that is concerned children who were already vulnerable and in the care of the state, much occurring in "historical boys and girls homes". The

---

[4] *Towards Healing* has been the primary document of the Australian Catholic Church in relation to sexual, emotional and physical abuse. It articulates principles and procedures in responding to complaints of abuse against personnel of the Catholic Church in Australia; see www.catholic.org.au/professional-standards/towards-healing. The Archdiocese of Melbourne has operated an alternative process titled the Melbourne Response; see www.cam.org.au/Professional-Standards/Melbourne-Response.

fact that the majority of such institutional care was provided by faith-based, non-government entities offers no relief from the reality of the evidence. It makes it more perplexing that those of faith conducted such agencies where so much abuse occurred:

> Those who believed that this (the level of abuse in Church) would be something small, just a beat up by media or exaggerated by critics of the Church, have been proven to be wrong.

Fitzgerald noted that the personal and institutional pain of the last five years, which had accompanied the 'lancing of the boil', was necessary and ultimately provides an extraordinary opportunity for institutional reform. The profound appreciation of the "Betrayal of Trust", associated with admitting the sexual abuse that took place within the Church, was acknowledged as early as 2008 by Pope Benedict XVI on International Youth Day in Sydney. It is a term that has continued to resonate painfully and truthfully and was used as the title for the 2013 report of the Victorian parliamentary inquiry into sexual abuse.[5] Fitzgerald noted:

> At the end of the day, it is at the very heart of what we've seen – a betrayal of trust. A betrayal of trust by individuals, by institutions and ultimately by our society as a whole. Child sexual abuse isn't just about an individual's action, it is in fact about the way in which institutions either allowed that to occur or failed to respond. It was not just a few rotten apples but rather there were systemic and cultural issues that enabled abuse and promoted the poor responses that were provided especially before the mid-1990s.

The epidemic nature of sexual abuse in families and communities worldwide is now acknowledged for its terrible long-term effects. The

---

[5] Family and Community Development Committee, 2013. *Betrayal of Trust: Inquiry into the Handling of Child Abuse by Religious and Other Non-Government Organisations*. Melbourne: Parliament of Victoria.

evidence is unequivocal that such abuse has far-reaching consequences personally, psychologically, societally and throughout life. However, the betrayal of trust is experienced by victims and survivors as being particularly brutal and profound when that abuse is perpetrated by those associated with faith-based organisations. This is where they should have been safe.

Fitzgerald challenged participants to provide the evidence that their organisations are child-safe. Even if you answer "Yes, we are a child-safe organisation", you will not be believed without objective evidence, charged Fitzgerald. He noted that past leaders of institutions would have confirmed the safety of children in their charge. They would also, he suggested, have maintained they would have acted immediately and responded appropriately to any evidence of abuse. Such assertions have been proven to be tragically wrong. The absence of evidence-based child safe procedures and practices has, in part, led to endemic abuse and the pervasive lack of trust in Church and other institutions. Fitzgerald also readily acknowledged that many Catholic and other agencies are doing much to rebuild that trust and creating genuinely safe environments for children. But such actions are patchy and not uniform across the Church and community.

How do we deal with the confronting reality of Church abuse? In summary Fitzgerald identified four key points.

First, in order to understand, we must listen carefully and actively, not just hearing the individual voices but listening to their real meaning:

> Listening is an engaged process where you actively try to discern and understand the words and meaning of what is said. And it requires your response, emotionally and practically.

Second, it is essential to understand and accept, as far as it is possible, the enormity of such depravity and the long-term impacts of the refusal to believe victims when they finally come forward. It is important not just for each of us to listen to the individual and collective impact of abuse, but for the Church and its institutions, including its governing bodies, to listen with humility and honesty, to acknowledge the pain and wrong doings. And then to act.

Third is the need to accept the unquestionable evidence as it stands, and acknowledge the need for changes in practice, situate them, implement them and monitor them assiduously. Such evidence is based on the lived reality of victims and survivors in over 50 public hearings, of which 15 related to the Catholic Church, 8,000 private sessions and over 100 pieces of commissioned research:

> The evidence is that the Church has been found wanting especially before the mid-1990s. It has been found wanting in many areas, both in terms of community services and in our parishes and dioceses. There needs to be reform of the culture, governance, policies and practices.

It was noted that community services, heavily represented by their members amongst the participants at the conference, "were implicated" especially in historical out-of-home care settings. That said, the members of Catholic social services who appeared before the Royal Commission provided exemplary evidence of the highest standards in the contemporary care for children. Fitzgerald acknowledged this stating:

> Catholic social services are at the leading edge in many of these child safe practices … what became very obvious to all of us and to all of those that watched the Catholic wrap-up hearings was that part of the Church does get it, does understand it, has gone through reflective processes, has put in place appropriate standards, has embraced good governance, is committed to child safety, and is committed to ensure that where wrong does happen, there are consequences.

Notwithstanding worthwhile efforts by many institutions across Australia, the Commission concluded that no longer should the state rely on "good people doing the right thing". Based on the recommendations, all community services working with children should be subject to a 'reportable conduct regime' with oversight by the relevant state or territory government. Institutions should be legally required to provide proof that they have made every reasonable endeavour to provide child safe environments in any civil case claiming a breach of the duty of care. Expanded mandatory reporting requirements and extensive child safe standards regulations should be enacted in all jurisdictions. Such measures would apply to religious institutions in "all their forms" – parishes, dioceses, health and community services, sporting groups and others working with children and potentially vulnerable adults.

Having accepted the evidence of the extent of abuse, the fourth requirement is to "understand the confluence of other factors in the Catholic Church that have contributed" to this tragedy and be prepared for open dialogue both from within and external to the Church. These conversations and this dialogue must involve all of us. Fitzgerald named clericalism as a significant contributory factor identified by the Commission and recognised by many in the Church, saying it is "a disease that has betrayed us as members of Church, our children and the community at large". It has directly contributed to an unhealthy and unsafe Church culture. And it has done great damage to its own clergy, leaving them ill-equipped for a changing world. For both clergy and lay Catholics, such factors are not comfortable to name, let alone address:

> Contributory factors include mandatory celibacy especially within the diocesan priesthood, the poor selection of candidates for priesthood and religious life, the inadequate teaching of sexual and human development in formation, the failure to require professional development and professional

supervision, inadequate standards to guide people involved in the child-related activities of the Church, the failure to consult effectively when leaders are appointed including Bishops, the lack of the feminine voice within the Church especially in governance, and the lack of understanding of what governance is as distinct from what management is.

Catholic community services have been developed and supported by dioceses and religious congregations and have generally seen themselves as representing the church of the Gospel rather than the hierarchical church of the Roman Empire. While Catholic Social Teaching sits at the heart of their work, these services are run by people of any or no faith for all who need them, regardless of beliefs or values. Good governance is not an alien concept to such services and we now need to share our appreciation and knowledge of good governance as we accept Fitzgerald's challenge. In his words, as an individual Catholic we need to "reject the trappings of a Church that governs *for* us and *for* others and engage instead with a Church that governs *with* us and *with* others". This includes those who have been victims, the clergy, fellow religious leaders and members, people in parishes and those engaged in our community services – in other words, engaged with the people of God. Perhaps the 2020 Plenary Council[6] is one step in that process.

Fitzgerald finished his presentation with an invitation to all present to use the Royal Commission reports as a "rich resource of understanding" to be discerned as we all work on behalf of the children, with those in our Church and outside the Church, with those who hurt, those who do not understand, and those who struggle with some of the Commission's interpretations and recommendations. In asserting that the Church has within it the answers and solutions it needs (if only it were truly open to them and the possibilities they

---

[6] Planning is underway for a Plenary Council in 2020-2021 about the future of the Catholic Church in Australia; see plenarycouncil.catholic.org.au/.

provide), he reminded all of the compelling words of Micah that we should hold close as we work with children and vulnerable people and with victims and survivors: "To act with justice, to love with tenderness, to walk humbly with your God" (*Micah*, 6:8).

Establishing a Standards Body for the Church

Recognising very early in the findings of the Royal Commission that the Church along with so many other organisations had failed to pay heed to Micah's exhortation, or even to listen to, respect, value and provide consistent quality standards of care for children, one of the earliest recommendations of the TJHC was to propose to the ACBC and CRA the establishing of a standards body for the Church. It was very apparent to the TJHC that the "Church leadership had not previously been held to account" in relation to the safeguarding of children and vulnerable people engaged with the Church in Australia. As a second step, after acknowledging the implications of past abuses, it was essential that Church leaders accept the need to be accountable and to be seen to be accountable for the activities under their jurisdiction.

Despite misgivings on the part of a number of agencies which, for various reasons, saw this as 'just more regulation', 'more red tape', 'duplication' etc., this recommendation to establish Catholic Professional Standards Ltd (CPSL) was accepted following a national consultation process with service providers, congregational leaders and clergy. The new body was established as a company limited by guarantee in November 2016 and its inaugural CEO, Sheree Limbrick, was appointed in 2017. The full complement of board members of "formidable and independent thinkers" from a range of disciplines was finalised in 2018.[7]

One of Many Important Solutions

Limbrick introduced participants to CPSL, noting its functional independence from the Church and that it has "national coverage of

---

[7] Catholic Professional Standards Ltd, op. cit.

all activities of the Catholic Church – our initial focus is on ACBC and CRA entities, whilst continuing dialogue with trustees from [ministerial] public juridic persons,[8] the St Vincent de Paul Society, the Catholic tertiary education sector, and establishing links with others such as Associations of Christ's Faithful".

She identified its mission: "To promote the dignity and welfare of all persons who come into contact with the Church and its works, especially the young and vulnerable". In pursuing its mission, the purpose of CPSL is:

> To endeavour to ensure that all persons within and those who engage with the Church, in liturgical, ministerial, social or pastoral spheres, will be treated respectfully, professionally and in accordance with Gospel values.

CPSL's real and perceived independence was always likely to cause concern, if not distrust and disbelief, on the part of many inside and outside the Church. The Royal Commission found most organisations, including the churches, had improperly governed and monitored themselves, which in turn led to dire consequences. Hence, the Commission asserted the need for external auditing and monitoring. In response, the ACBC and CRA set up CPSL, which Limbrick described "as functionally rather than structurally independent of the Church".

She clarified that "a company established, owned and paid for by the Church is not structurally independent – we wouldn't exist if the institutional Church (the bishops and religious) had not established the company and committed to funding it". To validate this position, Limbrick employed the words of The Hon. Neville Owen, Chair of the Truth Justice and Healing Council and a member of Pope Francis' Pontifical Commission for the

---

[8] Public juridic persons (PJPs) are Church entities established under both civil and canon law. These are the Church's canonical equivalent of a corporation established to deliver a variety of services.

Protection of Minors, who had noted in his evidence to the Royal Commission:

> ... I've always taken a view that you must distinguish between structural independence and functional independence ... by functional independence I mean the capacity to bring an objective, dispassionate and informed mind to the decision-making process ... A situation where those who are operating the company, managing the company and making the decisions at that level will be functionally independent.[9]

The analogy used by Limbrick is one familiar to those in governance in our community and health services, that of the use of 'external auditors' for financial oversight: "The organisation hiring them pays the bill, but the audit firm operates independently and makes assessments and decisions based on their professional knowledge, skill, clear policies and capacity".

An express purpose of the bishops and religious in setting up CSPL was that compliance and reporting against the standards would promote accountability, transparency and trust in the life of the Church. However, the additional and more progressive roles of CPSL go beyond implementing standards and retrospective accountability to ones familiar to the Church. These were described as follows by Archbishop Mark Coleridge of Brisbane at a Royal Commission hearing:[10]

- AWARENESS – increasing awareness across everyone in the Church as to what child safeguarding (and, latterly, safeguarding of other vulnerable groups) entails and how to go about it.
- ACCOUNTABILITY – this applies to the Church as a whole and to individuals within the Church – 'there has

---

[9] Royal Commission, 2017, op. cit.; see Case Study 50, 20 February 2017.
[10] Ibid.

been a tendency … for bishops and the Church to have a sense of themselves as a law unto themselves. Now that has to change'.

- CONSISTENCY – to have consistency across states is not easy, to have it within the Church is difficulty multiplied; but achieving 'genuine consistency of approach' to critical matters and issues will 'represent genuine cultural change'.

- COMPASSION – 'to address all of these issues in their complexity and their intense practicality, their urgency, but to address them with the sense that the child or the vulnerable person must take priority and that all of these issues must be seen through their eyes. That's what I mean by compassion.'

As noted earlier, Fitzgerald indicated that the Royal Commission had identified the failure of governance within the Church as one of the many serious factors responsible for the levels of abuse. Of necessity, CPSL will both introduce and be able to monitor changes in governance and reporting within Church entities such as dioceses and congregations. Examples of work to be undertaken at these early stages in the development of the role of CPSL are:

- safeguarding resources/policies/reporting being centralised across a diocese rather than separated between parishes, education and social services,

- clearer lines of accountability and reporting being established between incorporated ministries and their congregational/diocesan 'owners',

- combined efforts in a location between dioceses, congregations, public juridic persons, the St Vincent de Paul Society and other Church entities.

Limbrick emphasised that, whilst the governance changes are focused on Church entities, a key effort is to promote the core philosophical position that the care of children and vulnerable people in the Church is everyone's business. The aim, she said, is:

> To increase the broader Catholic community's knowledge and understanding of crimes such as grooming and physical and sexual abuse, the devastating impact of abuse on individuals and the ripple effects into families and communities, and to strengthen the Church's awareness, prevention and protection focus.

The first and foundational activity for CPSL is the development of standards for safeguarding children and young people. In doing so, it will adopt the ten Child Safe Standards recommended by the Royal Commission and "contextualise them for application across the Church":

- Child safety is embedded in institutional leadership, governance and culture.
- Children participate in decisions affecting them and are taken seriously.
- Families and communities are informed and involved.
- Equity is upheld, and diverse needs are taken into account.
- People working with children are suitable and supported.
- Processes to respond to complaints of child sexual abuse are child focused.
- Staff are equipped with the knowledge, skills and awareness to keep children safe through continual education and training.
- Physical and online environments minimise the opportunity for abuse to occur.
- Implementation of the Child Safe Standards is continuously reviewed and improved.
- Policies and procedures document how the institution is child safe.[11]

---

[11] Royal Commission, 2017, op. cit., Vol. 6.

Having listened to input, CPSL will be integrating the range of concerns from within and outside the Church with the ten standards and the wisdom and expertise present already in community services and make recommendations specific for the large range of institutions across the Church.

Alongside the articulation of the standards, CPSL's second activity will be constructing a comprehensive quality assurance and audit framework across vastly different Church entities. CPSL will employ a "responsive and risk-based approach" to monitor compliance with the standards.[12] In acknowledging the concerns, if not confusion, within Catholic services about the intent and utility of CPSL's mandate, Limbrick also acknowledged the quality assurance, compliance and audit expertise within the sector. For example, she noted the role that it could play in assisting other parts of the Church in developing competence, and adopting best governance practices. She reassured the participants that CPSL would be "releasing its draft work and seeking wide-ranging feedback". She encouraged everyone to provide individual and/or collective feedback.

Limbrick advised participants that CPSL was keen to avoid duplicating the substantial audit compliance to which agencies are already subject. She assured participants that they would not have to engage in 'yet another audit' as, in the first instance, CPSL would be implementing "a self-attestation model for services/agencies which already have in place some form of external accreditation or assurance". All that agencies would need to do at this stage would be to provide details of current accreditation and assurance mechanisms and safeguarding work. Additionally, Limbrick confirmed that CPSL would continue to be consultative and involve engagement with a wide range of stakeholders in workshops in each state and territory. Such consultation, she said, would include experts and groups in the social services sector and, importantly,

---

[12] Ibid., Recommendation 6.10.

children, young people and victims and survivors of Church sexual abuse. The intent of this process is to map and understand better the range of "regulatory and accreditation requirements already in place as well as how the sectors are integrating child safeguarding into existing systems/processes".

In conclusion, Limbrick observed, "There is no doubt in my mind people in the Church know what needs to be done, we just have to get on and do it … which is where we come in". In supporting this observation, she identified the ten issues that had emerged from national consultations to date and noted they were consistent with those raised by the Royal Commission:

- Code of Conduct – review of *Integrity in Ministry* and *Integrity in Service of the Church*,[13]
- complaint management – review of *Towards Healing*[14] and The Melbourne Response,[15]
- credentialing and management of movement for clergy and religious – review of the Australian Catholic Ministry Register,
- specific guidance for recruitment, screening and support for overseas clergy/religious,
- ongoing development of healing and support services for survivors and families,
- management and support for respondents and offenders and those on ministry restrictions,
- records management,

---

[13] *Integrity in Ministry* (2004) is a document of Principles and Standards for Catholic Clergy and Religious in Australia and *Integrity in the Service of the Church* (2011) a comparable resource document of Principles and Standards for Lay Workers in the Catholic Church in Australia. They were developed by the National Committee for Professional Standards, a committee of the Australian Catholic Bishops Conference and Catholic Religious Australia; see www.catholic.org.au/documents/.

[14] *Towards Healing*, op. cit.

[15] Ibid.

- information sharing between and across Church entities on a range of issues,
- clinical supervision and ongoing formation for clergy and religious,
- development of appropriate safeguarding modules/curriculum for use in seminaries and religious formation.

In summary, CPSL is charged with the responsibility for:

- articulating and setting standards,
- training, support and advice to support all Church entities to meet the standards and improve practice,
- overseeing the audits of compliance using out-sourced, independent skilled auditors,
- publishing the findings of audits.

The Journey Ahead

We have witnessed the inexorable suffering and dire consequences for the many who have come forward to tell of their experiences of abuse, often for the first time, during the five-year course of the Royal Commission. Thousands of lives have been damaged, some lost. This has been a period of profound disturbance for our Australian community, our institutions, our churches, our families and for many in our ministries whose work has been to relieve suffering. Along with other implicated institutions, we share in the loss of legitimacy and credibility of the Catholic institution for which we work. Feelings of shame, impotence, horror, hopelessness and anger have accompanied the findings and the processes of the Royal Commission. Undoubtedly, there have been many conversations tainted with secondary guilt at being associated with Church agencies connected with these terrible acts of abuse. Many identify with the victims and survivors and voice feelings of helplessness. Many are victims and survivors and often deep hurt and rage accompany feelings of confusion and uncertainty.

Reflecting on the conversations following the presentations of Fitzgerald and Limbrick, what was apparent was a mixture of ongoing disturbance, pain, anger and, yes, just a hint of denial amongst some. There remain a few for whom scepticism is the chosen stance. And there is some justification for some scepticism relating, for example, to the Royal Commission's methodology in calculating percentages of clergy responsible for abuse[16] and the conflation of the terms sexual abuse and paedophilia. However, most importantly, what was most prominent among conference participants was compassion, a commitment to social justice, a clear-eyed acceptance of the 'evils' uncovered by the Royal Commission and a resolve to accept the findings, embrace the need for change, and move beyond the pain to resolution. The invitation of conference organisers for people to come to a conference titled *Hearing, Healing, Hope*, with a forum titled 'Responding to Abuse, Ensuring Safety and Dedication to Service', was an invitation to listen deeply, dialogue thoughtfully, and find individual and collective ways to respond to the invaluable if confronting outcomes of the Royal Commission.

The people who manage and work in Church ministries have a myriad of skills and the resilience that comes, in some part, from being with and learning from those on the margins whom they accompany on their generally tough and tender journeys. They are active witnesses and respondents to those who suffer. It was identified during the Royal Commission, and confirmed in the presentation by Fitzgerald, that considerable governance sophistication and expertise are evident in the service arenas within the Church. It is axiomatic then that the Church needs community service leaders to share their knowledge about governance and healing and participate in the necessary renewal. Our Church faces significant challenges to its governance

---

[16] Virginia Ingram, 2017. 'Child Sexual Abuse and the Catholic Church in Australia: What the Royal Commission Tells Us', ABC Religion and Ethics; see www.abc.net.au/religion/articles/2017/12/22/4784037.htm.

structures that have been identified for a long time – and accentuated now – namely as being too hierarchical, patriarchal and masculine. We did not need the Royal Commission to tell us about the problems of clericalism and the significance of the absence of women in decision-making positions in the Church. In all of our services we have become painfully aware of the international scourge of abuses of power and associated socio-cultural structures in patriarchal systems that have led to sexual violation and violence. The dominance of patriarchal values has influenced the abuse of women and children generally and is named by the Royal Commission as a contributing factor in the abuse, and deficiency of response to this, of the scourge of sexual abuse in our Church. The reminder of the implications of the denial of the feminine is a poignant and salutary one.

It is vital that lay leaders, in partnership with clergy, grasp the importance of challenging the traditional power differentials that have accommodated abuse in all its forms. Human service ministries have struggled with softening their hierarchical structures to engage more humbly with cultural, religious and gender diversity and are, consequently, well-placed to support the changes required. Not only have community service leaders successfully confronted multiple governance challenges and worked to build accountability and compliance, they are at the coal face with the people on the periphery, including now the many thousands of survivors and victims.

Despite the heroic work that has been achieved in the name of the Church, this institution for which we work has been shown to have failed in a profound and public way. It is now time to help repair and rebuild it in ways that ensure a safe place for all. Whatever our secular, spiritual or faith journeys, our work is grounded in the call of Catholic Social Teaching that contests poverty and social injustice. We work for and with dedicated religious people, the majority of whom have given their lives selflessly to the Church. It is a Church that, along with others, has made and continues to make valuable contributions to our community and world and on which many thousands of Australians rely for much needed services.

The women and men at the conference involved in lay and clerical leadership are amongst those who now have a major role in helping to reshape our Church. The bishops have work to do and so do we. In observing the risks of the resistance to change by the Church hierarchy, Archbishop Coleridge observed, "A long and arduous task lies before us" as Vatican II efforts at reform and renewal are reinvigorated post the Royal Commission.[17] In saying this, he challenges us to work separately and together. The 2020 Plenary Council is a time when the faithful, the clerical Church and others come together, not to finalise the outcome of our individual and collective work, but to look closely at what needs to change, acknowledge what has changed, and discern a different Gospel-inspired future.

Conclusion

In summarising, what the forum and the conference enabled all to see is that we are in a transformative time for our Church. The world feels weary. There are ever increasing numbers of people ostracised, dispossessed and suffering. At the same time, the institutions in which they placed their trust and hope have been found severely wanting. Now is the time to hold on to hope as we work together to build our services for the increasing number of people on the periphery of life's opportunities and to challenge the structures that create such injustices. Pope Francis comes to us serendipitously at this time. As a champion of the work done by community services, he notes that God is not a God of doctrinal orthodoxy represented by an all-controlling magisterium but rather a pastoral God who asks us to accompany with compassion and love each other and all who suffer.

We need to pursue a post-institutional Church in which the laity

---

[17] Mark Coleridge, 23/30 December 2017. "'A long and arduous task lies before us': Will the Church resist the Royal Commission's recommendations?", *The Tablet*, 5.

no longer see themselves simply as subject to the authority of a Church hierarchy. In doing so, we must, of course, first refine and monitor well the work of making sure the services to all children and vulnerable people enable them to be and feel safe. However, as someone said recently, 'Legitimacy is not renewed by regulation". It is what we do now to acknowledge and help the healing of victims and survivors, and how we do it, that will help lead the Church back to a Gospel focus and facilitate the progress of our vitally important ministries. Alongside the already mighty struggle in which we engage on behalf of the countless numbers of people who have not only been marginalised but also been ostracised for their marginalisation, we need to contribute our wisdom and knowledge to the struggle ahead. As Sr Joan Chittister OSB says so eloquently: "It is not the struggle that defeats us, it is our failure to really engage with the struggle that depletes the human spirit".[18]

---

[18] Joan D. Chittister, 2003. *Scarred by Struggle, Transformed by Hope.* Grand Rapids, MI: William B. Eerdmans Publishing Co.

Healing – Communities
with which we Work

6

Effective Advocacy of Public Policy

Patrice Scales

The workshop on 'Effective Advocacy of Public Policy' at the Catholic Social Services *Hearing, Healing Hope* conference brought together three voices from organisations that have decades of experience in providing services to the most disadvantaged groups in our community. A key 'take-away' from this workshop, and perhaps the starting point for any effective advocacy of public policy, is the message that "it's not okay" for disadvantage and injustice to go unchallenged as organisations pursue their mission to make a difference to individuals' lives and to our community.

Sally Parnell, Executive Director of Programs at Jesuit Social Services, Phil Glendenning, Director of the Edmund Rice Centre and President of the Refugee Council of Australia, and Karen Lococo, Manager of the Journey to Social Inclusion Program at Sacred Heart Mission, shared specific case studies of how their organisations have put advocacy into action to improve the lives and circumstances of those in their care. Bernie Geary, former Victorian Commissioner for Children and Young People, and a great advocate himself for disadvantaged young people, chaired the session, and led discussion on what are the key elements of effective public policy advocacy today.

Advocacy has many definitions but for the purposes of this workshop, the presenters aimed to show how their organisations were using their experience in working with the most disadvantaged: to have the voices of those people heard in the wider community, to speak up with and for them, to influence policy makers and decisions, and to improve the life opportunities for those in their care. The workshop aimed to provide some insights into how organisations like these turn action into influence to improve both the community's understanding of the issues and their own services to their client groups.

Each of the presenters spoke about particular programs on which their organisations have worked, giving context to the problems, issues and raison d'être for those programs, how they gave a voice to the people whose lives were affected, and how their organisations have aimed to make an ongoing difference through combining action with advocacy.

Justice for Young People in an Unjust System

In providing some context to her work, Sally Parnell explained that Jesuit Social Services calls itself a 'social change' organisation. She expressed it as: "We do, and we influence". While its work is focused on service delivery, it also has a strong focus on advocacy, and in seeking to produce some change within government or other decision makers around improving the lot of the most disadvantaged people in our community.

In her presentation, Parnell reflected particularly on issues around the youth justice system, and the learnings from a 2017 Jesuit Social Services' study tour to Europe and the United States to look at places that were improving outcomes for young people caught up in the justice system.

Jesuit Social Services has worked in the justice 'space' for over 40 years. It began as a very small organisation that has now grown to over 300 staff and 250 volunteers, with expansion of its work to areas as far away as the Northern Territory. Parnell reflected on current media attention on youth crime which gives the impression that there is a major crisis in youth justice in Victoria, that crime rates are increasing, and that our community is a lot less safe than it used to be. In fact, the reality is the opposite – data show that youth crime is going down while high-profile crime activity is gaining media visibility.

From an advocacy point of view, Jesuit Social Services is concerned about the 'knee-jerk' reaction happening on both sides of parliament, which leads to a lack of focus on sound evidence and good policy. As Parnell remarked: "When you have a Minister for Children and Families in Victoria saying that young people in the prison system are thugs, they're the worst of the worst, some don't deserve to be in a youth facility but should be in adult prisons … I think we know we've got a problem".

In Victoria, the youth justice system has been transferred to the department that also runs adult prisons. This means, in effect, that a system that once was managed within a child welfare framework will now operate alongside an adult system where the mindset is on control, compliance and a 'no last chances given' approach. This is quite the opposite of the Northern Territory's approach where, after a Royal Commission into the Protection and Detention of Children in the Northern Territory,[1] it has gone the other way and taken youth justice out of the adult system and put it under the child welfare system.

In this environment Jesuit Social Services recognised that it needed to have more understanding about best practice in youth justice to be able to influence decision makers. Thus, two Jesuit Social Services staff, Parnell and Chief Executive Officer Julie Edwards, took a study tour to Norway, Germany and Spain to study their models of best practice that were showing success. In parallel, the Jesuit Social Services Director of Advocacy and Strategic Communications and the Chair of the Board went to the United States to look at some

---

[1] For information on the 2017 Royal Commission into the Protection and Detention of Children in the Northern Territory, see childdetentionnt.royalcommission.gov.au/Pages/Report.aspx.

successful models of youth justice. Some of their observations included:

- In Germany, Norway and Spain, the age of criminal responsibility is 14 or 15 years. In Victoria, the age of criminal responsibility is 10 years meaning that a child as young as 10 can be jailed for offences.

- There was much less politicisation of juvenile crime in European countries than in Victoria. In fact, Parnell and Edwards noted that there was no 'front page' news around juvenile crime; it was not an issue and the system was stable. Parnell felt that this approach might reflect a different cultural and political mindset around human rights and citizenship because of the many war experiences those countries had experienced.

- What the Jesuit Social Services team saw overseas as best practice was around normalising of behaviour, with education at the centre and highly qualified staff. There was a perception in some communities that a job working in a prison was a career pathway. Parnell was impressed with a training academy for prison officers in Norway where a logo on a t-shirt read: "If nothing changes, nothing changes". For Parnell, this was a very powerful message.

- There was also a different attitude towards crime that did not mean the end to any other rights or benefits. If, for example, someone had committed a crime, and their punishment was being detained, then that person was still able to access other services such as education and health services. Many people were detained at night but were still able to work in the community during the day. In contrast to this, in Victoria a 224-bed facility is being built, which the Government has referred to as a 'supermax prison' for young people. To Jesuit Social Services, this seems a negative use of resources with money going into the wrong end of the system, instead of keeping young people out of prison.

- In the United States, despite the fact that more people are incarcerated per head of population than in other countries, there are many states that are running progressive justice systems. In Missouri, for example, the State is closing youth prisons and moving towards much smaller facilities, outside walls rather than within walls, with a strong focus on education. While some secure facilities will need to operate for challenging youth, systems like the Missouri model show that contemporary policy sees effectiveness in different approaches.

- This overseas experience has given Jesuit Social Services a renewed sense of what their organisation should be doing around advocacy. The current debate around juvenile crime is focused on dehumanising and demonising young people. While Jesuit Social Services will continue to liaise with government using evidence, writing submissions, etc., it also plans to put more energy into changing the message about the way young people are being treated. It is a fact that the younger a person goes into the prison system, the higher is the likelihood that they will stay in there and have a life in prison. As a community, we need to change the mindset that the community has become unsafe, and we need to change the way we treat young people in the justice system.

Breaking the Cycle of Chronic Homelessness

Sacred Heart Mission is a grassroots-based organisation which began in 1982 when St Kilda West Parish Priest Fr Ernie Smith opened his door and shared a meal with a man who was hungry and experiencing homelessness. Within a year, this first act of generosity and compassion had grown to a meals service provided by parishioners to more than 70 people. Today, Sacred Heart Mission provides a daily meals program to around 400 people, together with a range of innovative and individualised support services for people who experience homelessness, including crisis accommodation, aged care services, women's services, counselling and health services.

It was the ongoing issue of chronic homelessness and its resultant problems that led to the trial of the program called Journey to Social Inclusion (J2SI) in 2009.[2] Karen Lococo is manager of the J2SI Phase 2 program. She reminded the workshop participants that a quarter of a million people in Australia access government-funded homeless services annually, with around 116,000 people homeless. Some 22,000 of those people are deemed to be chronically homeless.

J2SI is an intervention program geared towards people who are chronically homeless. The first incarnation of the program ran from 2009-2012 with 40 participants recruited mainly from the St Kilda area with a caseload ratio of one case manager to four participants. Its purpose was to trial whether working intensively with chronically homeless people for a period of up to three years, rather than the usual 90-day or four-month support period, would change the outcomes for participants.

The program looked not only at accommodation needs, but also addressed employment, addiction, physical and mental health, trauma and social inclusion or connection to community. It was thoroughly

---

[2] For reports of the J2SI Pilot at Sacred Heart Mission, see www.sacredheartmission. org/about/publications-research.

evaluated from a financial, social and economic perspective, both quantitatively and qualitatively, to ensure that the outcomes could be used as evidence to secure future funding to continue the program.

A study undertaken a year after the three-year pilot came to an end showed 75 per cent of participants remained in stable housing after four years, 80 per cent had seen a decline in the need for health services, and the pilot generated savings to government of up to $32,080 per participant. The Australian Government acknowledged the pilot with a National Homelessness Services Award for excellence and innovation in 2013, and it also received a Council to Homeless Persons award for excellence in ending homelessness for adults.

Overall, the evaluation of the first phase of J2SI found that the lives of people who have complex needs and have been homeless for long periods of time, with the right interventions, could change dramatically. And while the program is an expensive service model, ultimately the cost to government is less than having a person chronically homeless.

As Manager of the second iteration of J2SI, Lococo explained that J2SI continues to work on a three-year, trauma-based model. In the first year, the primary case manager develops the primary strong relationship with the client. In the second year, once housing is stable and trust is built, more people on the team are introduced into the relationship. In the third year, the team embeds the services and supports within the broader community. They help the client find a job, if possible, or an interest they like, and help connect them with family and their immediate community.

Getting people back to work is the most challenging aspect because it can take time to understand what motivates people to believe they have the capability to do a job. Lococo reported that, in February 2018, 13 people out of 58 on the program were in paid employment. While these numbers may seem low, in actual fact, it is a huge step for people who may not have been employed for years, to be in paid employment.

Sacred Heart Mission has effectively used the results of the J2SI evidence-based model to advocate to government for a different approach to investing in the lives of people who are homeless. In August 2018, the J2SI program will be funded for a third phase; 60 more people who have been long-term homeless will enter the program, with 60 more the year later, and a further 60 a year after that. So, in total over a five-year period, Sacred Heart Mission will be working with 180 people to improve not only their accommodation needs, but to change their life opportunities and connectedness with community. Significantly, armed with the results and evidence of the first and second phases of J2SI, Sacred Heart Mission was able to say to government, "These are the results we have had", and convince government that longer-term investment in chronic homelessness has real benefits. As Lococo said: "It's really, really exciting".

Justice for 'The First Peoples' and the 'Last Peoples to Arrive'

Phil Glendenning spoke about Edmund Rice Centre's (ERC) advocacy work in relation to Indigenous rights, in particular the Sea of Hands campaign, and policy in relation to asylum seekers deported back to their countries. From the outset, Glendenning made the pertinent point that the most effective advocacy is when people with lived experience get to lead the advocacy process, whether they are Indigenous people, refugees or asylum seekers.

Australians for Native Title and Reconciliation (ANTaR) began in 1997 in response to a swell of public anger towards Federal Government moves to wind back Indigenous native title rights. In Victoria, more than 30,000 people became involved, forming groups in most of the 37 Federal electorates in the State.

The idea of a 'sea of hands' came from a delegation, of which

Glendenning was part, to study the Northern Ireland peace process. To break the nexus of Northern Ireland Protestants talking to Northern Ireland Catholics with few outcomes, the process brought together people from other reconciliation situations, particularly young people. Walking out at the end of one of the workshops, Glendenning and his colleagues were confronted by the impact of the powerful symbol of crucifixes representing each person who had been killed in the Irish 'troubles'. So, emerged the impetus for the Sea of Hands campaign.[3]

The Sea of Hands campaign started with an Eminent Citizens Statement from people as diverse as film stars, authors, football players and Olympic athletes. They signed off on the statement and this was followed by support from a further 150,000 signatories, with the involvement of around 200 national organisations, a coalition of people and organisations that shared the same values and were willing to take action.

On 12 October 1997, the Sea of Hands paved its way into Australian history books when 70,000 members of culturally diverse communities in Australia protested outside Parliament House in Canberra. Today, the Sea of Hands is a prominent Australian symbol of Indigenous rights to land, the ongoing process of Reconciliation, and the desire for greater mutual understanding and respect between Indigenous and non-Indigenous communities. Almost 300,000 Australians have put their signatures on a hand in the Sea of Hands. Each one of the hands symbolises the Australian peoples' rights-based movement towards Reconciliation.

Glendenning also spoke about ERC's work in relation to "the last people to arrive", asylum seekers and refugees. In 2005, ERC became aware of stories that some of the people whom Australia had deported back to countries like Afghanistan, Iran, Iraq, Colombia and

---

[3] For information on the 1997 Australians for Native Title and Reconciliation (ANTaR) Sea of Hands campaign, see www.antar.org.au/sea-hands.

Rwanda had been killed. ERC was vitally interested in this but needed to know more. Glendenning related a story about how they came to have the capacity and capability to research and advocate on this issue:

> Word got around [about us wanting to research this issue]. I got a knock on the door the next day from a magnificent Dominican sister, Carmel Leavey, who is a great researcher and writer. She was then about 78 years of age. She said, 'I hear you need some research done. I want a job. I can write, I can research, and I don't want any money'. I said, 'Man, you must have been born in a stable. Come on, then, let's go'.

Sister Carmel recruited the resources of another Dominican Sister, Mary Britt, and together with the Australian Catholic University the research began. While ERC raised resources, Sisters Carmel and Mary tracked down 183 people in 22 different countries, with full details of addresses, telephone numbers, etc. Their work found that 31 people had been killed in Afghanistan, four in Iraq, four in Colombia, two in Bogota, nine in Sri Lanka. All of these people had told the Australian Government that if they were sent back, they would be killed. Sadly, they were proven to be correct.

Rather than taking the first phase of the research to the public, ERC went to the United Nations and here Glendenning made the point again that evidence is crucially important. "You've got to get the evidence of the evidence of the evidence. Take the polemics out of it, and just get your information absolutely dead, rock-solid straight, and then get ready for the incoming mortar rounds".

The ERC research paper titled 'Deported to Danger: Investigation into the Fate of Deported People'[4] has led to the publication of several reports, submissions and testimony given to Federal parliamentary enquiries, public meetings, investigations by Federal

---

[4] For information on the methodology, various reports and submissions concerning the Edmund Rice Centre's *Deported to Danger: Investigation into the Fate of Deported People*, 2003, see www.erc.org.au/deported_to_danger_publications.

Police into allegations of illegal actions by immigration officials, extensive media coverage, and in 2008 production of a documentary film, *A Well-Founded Fear*.[5]

Glendenning made the point that what goes on publicly in advocacy is not necessarily what is happening behind the scenes in order to deliver the result. On the one hand, the Australian Government was virtually berating the research findings, with the Minister for Foreign Affairs stating that ERC was publishing lies and innuendo, masquerading as facts, while at the same time ending the deportation of people back to Afghanistan and congratulating ERC on a job "well done".

In concluding, Glendenning made observations about the broad principles learnt from these advocacy case studies: "Accurately analyse the situation, get your information right, and gather the evidence of the evidence of the evidence. Then develop a campaign for education and for the media, ensuring that the media is 'on tap', not 'on top'. Even though access to the media might be denied from time to time, [this] does not deny the importance of what you are doing. And, sometimes, the best thing you can do is shut up!"

Advocacy Learnings from the Case Studies

Following the presentation of the workshop case studies, a number of participants contributed to the discussion and commentary around advocacy, including possibilities and opportunities for organisations wishing to improve their advocacy work. The following points have been summarised from the workshop input and may provide some guidance on developing effective campaigns and advocacy.

Evidence is a core requirement of a sound advocacy strategy. As Phil Glendenning put it, "evidence of evidence of evidence" will make the argument 'rock solid'. Karen Lococo noted that the second phase of J2SI is already showing improvements on the

[5] The documentary film, *A Well-Founded Fear*, 2008, is accessible at www.imdb.com/title/tt1272048/?ref_=nv_sr_2.

first J2SI pilot. By the time Sacred Heart Mission has a further 180 people through the program in Phase 3, the evidence is expected to be irrefutable.

Relationships with government and decision makers are also a critical component of effective advocacy, even if at times the message seems to fall on silent ears. But relationships with decision makers must be accompanied by relationships with others who have influence, such as high-profile groups and individuals who have a passion to make a difference in the community.

People with the 'lived experience' must be front and centre of the advocacy efforts, rather than sitting to the side while others do the talking for them. This was the case with the Sea of Hands campaign, the purpose of which was to get a group of non-Indigenous Australians to support the Indigenous voice, and that approach made a significant impact in the community.

Be prepared to fearlessly put your case to anyone in order to help a broader audience in understanding the issues, including opponents of the cause. Having a conversation only with people who understand the issues does not bring about change. Conservative media outlets, radio and newspapers etc., generally feed on contrarian arguments. If you can be 'that argument' and persuasively put your case, your advocacy is more likely to change attitudes or misperceptions than speaking with those who agree with you.

Work collaboratively with other agencies, bodies and individuals as a way of strengthening the advocacy effort. If more than one agency or organisation is working with the same social problems and issues, the credibility of the argument will be substantially enhanced, making it difficult for policy makers to ignore the problem.

Be prepared to change the campaign strategy if governments and decision makers are complacent and not prepared to hear and act. As well as standard advocacy steps, such as writing submissions and speaking to politicians and decision makers, be prepared to use a 'grass roots' approach to influence community perceptions and attitudes and spread the conversation more broadly.

Catholic parishes and schools should be considered as a way of continuing the conversation on social issues, such as asylum seekers and disadvantaged young people. Schools, in particular, often foster an understanding of social justice issues and young people are very open to hearing about the lived experience of those their own age, for example, the life of a young person in prison or young people who are living in poverty.

Use other formal and informal community gatherings to spread a message about the need for change. Groups such as 'spirituality in the pub' and 'politics in the pub' offer a venue for discussing issues and advocating for change, not only in metropolitan areas but also in regional and country areas. Be prepared to bring up issues, challenge perceptions and offer a different view wherever groups of people informally together, the golf club, a group of friends, a book group.

Never give up, even if no gains have been made, or only partial gains have been made. Where injustice, unfairness or disadvantage is concerned, every issue is worth fighting for, no matter how long it takes. Go back to the basics: build the evidence, build the relationships, and challenge the *status quo*. Where there is still more to be achieved, look to the mission of your organisation, renew the advocacy campaign and forge on.

The Motivation for Advocacy: "It's Not Okay"

Karen Lococo summed up cogently the motivation for her work: "It's not okay that people are sleeping on the street. It's not okay that they don't have enough to eat. It's not okay that there are 4,000 kids homeless, or even rough sleeping, in Australia. That's not okay".

As Catholic organisations pursue their mission to make a difference

119

to individuals' lives and to our community, the 'take-away' of this workshop, and perhaps the starting point for any effective advocacy of public policy, is the message that "it's not okay".

7

Support for Asylum Seekers: Sharing Information and Insights from around the Country

Adrian Foley

Introduction

At the *Hearing, Healing, Hope* Catholic Social Services national conference I hosted the workshop entitled 'Support for Asylum Seekers and Recently Arrived Communities: Sharing Information and Insights from around the Country' presented by Sr Brigid Arthur csb from the Brigidine Asylum Seeker Project and Tracey Cabrié, who is Centre Manager of the Cabrini Asylum Seeker and Refugee Health Hub. This chapter captures insights from that workshop. The chapter also considers the current refugee context, the needs of asylum seekers and new migrants, and some areas in which the Church might improve its support.

How asylum seekers are treated in Australia can be considered as:

- *A political issue* – Politicians have used the issue as a very effective tool over the past twenty years or so to polarise, shape and harden public attitudes and thereby achieve political success.

- *A social issue* – As the official treatment of asylum seekers has become progressively harsher, many Australians have asked what has happened to the 'fair go' on which as a nation we used to pride ourselves. Meanwhile, many compassionate and generous people have been doing their best to welcome asylum seekers and refugees and ensure they get the best support possible in the current environment.

- *A moral issue* – The treatment accorded to asylum seekers and refugees has often been unfair, unjust, morally wrong, even in the face of rationalisations for its implementation – for example, "preventing deaths at sea", "protecting our borders" and so on.

If we are to support asylum seekers and refugees, we need to do so at each of these levels.

For 'new migrants', I limit my comments to refugees sponsored by the Australian Government under the United Nations Humanitarian Resettlement Program. These new migrants, who face a different set of issues than asylum seekers, also need our help settling into Australian life.

The Current Australian Context

In early 2018 there were around 19,000 people who had arrived in Australia by sea, so-called "illegal maritime arrivals" (IMAs), living in the Australian community on bridging visas pending the resolution of their asylum claims, 334 IMAs in detention in Australia including on Christmas Island, and 336 in detention in Nauru.[1] In addition, there were around 870 people who had sought asylum in Australia but are now living on Manus Island, and 650 living in the Nauru community.[2]

In addition to those who arrive by boat without a visa, many people arrive by air each year and subsequently apply for protection. The Government does not appear to publish statistics currently on this category of asylum seekers. However, in 2014 the Department of Immigration and Border Protection reported that 9,646 people

---

[1] Immigration Detention and Community Statistics Summary, 31 January 2018, Department of Home Affairs, 4, accessed at www.homeaffairs.gov.au/.

[2] Refugee Action Coalition Sydney data, accessed at www.refugeeaction.org.au/.

had arrived in this way in 2013-2014, an increase of 13.8 per cent over the previous year.[3] Many people in this group have limited means, relying on friends, generous people and social service agencies for support.

Currently the Australian Government is reviewing applications for protection from those IMAs living in the community under its "legacy caseload" legislation,[4] while some of those on Manus Island and in Nauru may be resettled in the United States. What will happen to those who are not successful?

At one level, it is reasonable to expect that those who do not satisfy refugee eligibility requirements should return home. However, many of those whose claims for asylum have been rejected have endured detention for years, resisting financial inducements from the Australian Government to return home, hoping they might be resettled in a safer country. Many suffer from severe and permanent mental illness. Should we return them to their countries, possibly to danger? Should we not extend mercy, compassion and the benefit of the doubt to welcome these poor souls into our country?

Clearly, Australia should have a controlled immigration program, including an agreed process for its intake of refugees. Our participation in the UN Humanitarian Resettlement Program[5] goes some way towards responding to Australia's moral obligation to resettle displaced people, and towards achieving an orderly intake of refugees.

There seems to be a sense that once the Government has resolved the current "legacy caseload", Australia's obligation to the refugees of

---

[3] *Asylum Statistics—Australia: Quarterly Tables—June Quarter 2014*, Department of Immigration and Border Protection, accessed at www.homeaffairs.gov.au.

[4] Migration and Maritime Powers Legislation Amendment (Resolving the Asylum Legacy Caseload) Act 2014; see www.legislation.gov.au/Details/C2014A00135.

[5] Australia will welcome approximately 18,000 refugees in 2017-2108 under the United Nations Humanitarian Resettlement Program, about 10 per cent of its permanent intake; see *Discussion Paper Australia's Humanitarian Programme 2017-18*, Department of Immigration and Border Protection, accessed at www.homeaffairs.gov.au/.

the world will be fully expressed in its participation in the resettlement program and foreign aid grants. Will the future be that ordered and contained?

The Chaotic Long-term World Refugee Situation

In 2016 there were 65.6 million displaced persons around the world, 22.5 million refugees, 40.3 million internally displaced people, and 2.8 million people seeking protection.[6] Refugee numbers are growing rapidly each year. With ongoing wars in Afghanistan, Syria and Sudan, and war threatening to break out in various places, it seems likely that large numbers of people will continue to be displaced by wars well into this century.

Further, climate change is expected to increase displacement of people in years to come, creating "climate refugees". Permanent displacement due to climate change is not currently a basis for recognition as a refugee under the United Nations Convention on Refugees, highlighting the need for a new definition of what it means to be a refugee.

In the South-East Asian region, Australia's international neighbourhood, there were 520,000 refugees and asylum seekers in 2014, with the great majority of these from Myanmar.[7] The numbers have grown since then, with large scale expulsions from Myanmar over the past year.

Will Australia be able to insulate itself from unforeseen population

---

[6] United Nations High Commissioner for Refugees (UNCHR), 2016. *Global Trends: Forced Displacement in 2016*. Geneva: UNCHR, accessed at www.unhcr.org/. 'Refugees' are persons forced to leave their homes for reasons including conflict and violence. An 'asylum seeker' is a person who has sought protection as a refugee, but whose claim for refugee status has not yet been assessed. 'Internally displaced persons' are people who are forced to flee their home, but remaining within their national borders. Internally displaced persons are not refugees under the Refugee Convention.

[7] UNHCR Regional Office for South East Asia Fact Sheet, September 2014, accessed at www.unhcr.org/.

flows in years to come? Surely it is more likely that desperate people will continue to present themselves to us seeking admission, and that Australia will be called upon to take additional refugees to help respond to catastrophes, such as occurred after the Second World War and the Vietnamese displacement in the 1970s.

What is the Typical Situation of Asylum Seekers and Refugees?

We have already touched on some of problems facing asylum seekers in Australia, on Manus Island and in Nauru. Let us look a little more closely.

Many asylum seekers in Australia and offshore, including some who arrived by air, have been waiting four or more years to have their asylum claims assessed, while their lives have been placed on hold. They are unable to make plans for the future or be reunited with their families. In many cases they have little English and little income, and experience difficulty obtaining work, accommodation, access to education and health services. They suffer isolation from family, friends, culture and country of birth, and often have difficulty locating identity papers to substantiate their claims for protection. Many have been traumatised before they came to Australia, and many have then been traumatised further, particularly those transferred to offshore detention. Even if they are accepted as refugees under current policy, they are only granted temporary visas (Temporary Protection Visas or Safe Haven Enterprise Visas), and are still unable to sponsor their families to join them. They live in fear and uncertainty, not knowing if they may be returned to their countries, not able to move on with their lives.

Resettling New Migrants under the United Nations Humanitarian Program

The Australian Government has a range of programs to help settle refugees under its humanitarian entry scheme, including assistance with initial accommodation, income support and English language training. Apart from ongoing income support where required, official support tends to be limited to the first year.

Successful resettlement requires much more than this. Refugees and migrants, particularly if coming from countries culturally, linguistically, religiously and technologically different from ours, often feel deep loss and loneliness living in suburbia, separated from family and friends, where neighbours may not speak to them or acknowledge them, where they struggle to speak the language and find dignified work, where their children may not be welcomed at school, where their social mores concerning family relationships and discipline are very different from those they encounter in Australia. They struggle to understand us, while we wonder why they cannot integrate, as previous waves of migrants have done before them.

While governments can go some way to addressing these needs, the remainder comes down to the new migrants themselves, and to us. We can do this as Pope Francis said, by "welcoming, protecting, promoting and integrating".[8]

The Role of the Church

There are many organisations, non-faith-aligned as well as faith groups, helping those in need. Would it not be better for Christians to support non-faith-aligned organisations, rather than setting up their own support arrangements? Would fewer, larger organisations not make for more efficient use of resources and be more effective in lobbying for better policies?

While we should support all organisations doing valuable work assisting people in need, I think Christians must be involved, *as Christians*, because we have been given a responsibility to represent Christ in a world that needs him. St Paul told us that we are

---

[8] Pope Francis, 2018. Message for the Celebration of the 51st World Day of Peace, accessed at w2.vatican.va/.

"ambassadors for Christ" (2 *Corinthians* 5:20), representing Christ our physically absent Sovereign to those who need him.

In a book published in 2010 with authorship as Joseph Ratzinger, Pope Benedict XVI said: "The Church must accept her responsibility for society in various ways ... she must help society to find its moral identity".[9] We thus have a two-fold responsibility: to come to the aid of the asylum seeker and new migrant as Christians (though we do not wear a label), and to the rescue of a society that often seems to be losing its conscience.

Pope Francis

Pope Francis has shown us by word and example that the Church needs to be involved at every level in supporting refugees, and all in need of help. We wish him grace and strength as he leads the Church and the world in standing up for the rights of the oppressed and showing us how to welcome and serve those in need of our help.

Australian Bishops

The Australian Catholic Bishops Conference and the bishops individually lead the Catholic community in supporting refugees and others in need through advocacy, periodic social justice statements, and day-to-day leadership. We trust that they will continue to provide vital leadership and encouragement at national and diocesan levels, advocacy for justice and fair play. Active diocesan leadership is essential to encourage and resource parishes and agencies to reach out to those needing assistance, including asylum seekers and new migrants.

Parishes

Parish priests and parish leaders encourage and energise parishioners – for example, through Prayers of the Faithful, homilies, financial

[9] Joseph Ratzinger (Pope Benedict XVI), 2010. *A Turning Point for Europe? The Church in the Modern World: Assessment and Forecast.* San Francisco: Ignatius Press, 179.

and other support, to reach out to support asylum seekers and the organisations that support them. Pope Francis says of the parish:

> The parish is the presence of the Church in a given territory, an environment for hearing God's word, for growth in the Christian life, for dialogue, proclamation, charitable outreach, worship and celebration. In all its activities the parish encourages and trains its members to be evangelisers. It is a community of communities, a sanctuary where the thirsty come to drink in the midst of their journey, and a centre of constant missionary outreach We must admit, though, that the call to review and renew our parishes has not yet sufficed to bring them nearer to people, to make them environments of living communion and participation, and to make them completely mission-oriented.[10]

Many parishes have social justice and other groups working on behalf of their parishes to bring the "joy of the Gospel", as proclaimed by Pope Francis, to asylum seekers and others in need. They may work with other organisations, Catholic or otherwise, to provide that support. Many committed parishioners volunteer their time and resources to help. Some provide accommodation in their own homes, rental assistance, or material aid. The possibilities for providing help are numerous.

The capacity of parishes to offer services to their own members and others varies greatly. While some parishes have abundant human and financial resources, many others need assistance from outside if they are to reach out to those in need. Many appear to be barely surviving.

I would like to see parishes become less 'parochial', and those parishes and parishioners that can, reaching out to other parishes and parishioners to encourage, seed and create more vital, missionary

---

[10] Pope Francis, 2013. Apostolic Exhortation: *Evangelii Gaudium*. Vatican City: Vatican, n. 27-28.

parishes across the whole Church. While there are still many parishes capable of initiating outreach, I fear their numbers may be diminishing as Catholics stop attending church for lack of engagement. The research project by the Pastoral Projects Office (now Pastoral Research Office) *Catholics who Have Stopped Attending Mass* and other publications on parish vitality from this Office are relevant here.[11]

Catholic Service Agencies

Agencies including the St Vincent de Paul Society, Brigidine Asylum Seekers Project, CatholicCare, Mercy Connect, Good Shepherd Australia New Zealand, CAPSA (Catholic Alliance for People Seeking Asylum), Catholic Social Services and many others work closely with parishes, providing essential services to the poor, asylum seekers, the homeless and others, and advocating on their behalf.

As Tony Nicholson noted at the 2016 Catholic Social Services conference, many charitable organisations often grew out of community and parish initiatives and continue to rely upon them in part for their ongoing vitality.[12]

I would like to see Catholic agencies working more with parishes to build parish capacity and outreach. This interaction is vital for the continuing 'health' and growth of the Church, parishes, the organisations themselves and for those in need of our support.

Schools

Many Catholic schools, as well as others, take in migrant and asylum seeker students at significant financial cost, providing outstanding programs of encouragement, engagement and support. They

---

[11] Robert Dixon, Sharon Bond, Kath Engebretson, Richard Rymarz, Bryan Cussen and Katherine Wright, 2007. *Research Project on Catholics who Have Stopped Attending Mass.* Melbourne: Pastoral Projects Office, accessed at pro.catholic.org.au/pdf/DCReport.pdf.
[12] Tony Nicholson, 2016. "The Mission or the Money or Both" in Gabrielle McMullen, Patrice Scales and Denis Fitzgerald (eds), *Review, Reimagine, Renew: Mission Making a Difference in a Changing World.* Redland Bay, Queensland: Connor Court, 115-124.

nurture an awareness of social justice in all their students and often encourage and support them to provide direct support to groups in need. These schools deserve our recognition, gratitude and our encouragement. Although schools are very busy places, I would like to see more schools working with parishes and service agencies to provide support to those in need, and to be further enculturated in the social justice ethic.

What Needs to be Done to Help Asylum Seekers and New Migrants?

Our volunteers, parishes, agencies and schools must continue the great work that they are already doing. Many vulnerable people depend upon them for participation in society and for material and social support.

We need to be alert to changing circumstances which asylum seekers face, and be ready to respond wherever we can. At the Catholic Social Services conference workshop, Sr Brigid noted that the Government has been withdrawing income support payments from many asylum seekers. If this trend continues it will leave many families destitute and support agencies stretched in their capacity to respond.

We need to call out abusive and cruel treatment of vulnerable people wherever we see it. We need to resist measures to punish unfortunate people who are doing no more than exercising their international rights.

We should focus more on educating and informing the Australian public, not least youth and students, on the experiences of asylum seekers, the personal hardship caused by current policies, and ways we can help.

I would like to see Catholic leaders, Catholic agencies and parishes collaborating more closely with faith-based and other organisations, including the Australian Christian Refugee Taskforce,[13] social networks and media, working to influence public attitudes for good, while becoming a powerful national voice for change.

Catholic organisations employ some 220,000 people.[14] I would like to see them examine areas where they might employ refugees and new migrants in their organisations and introduce affirmative employment practices to ensure this happens. As employers, they have a wonderful opportunity to inform their employees of refugee and asylum seeker issues, and to support them in participating in relevant activities and networks.

We need to continue to visit politicians and write letters opposing harsh treatment of people in distress. Feedback from politicians tells us this is a very effective means of keeping the issues before decision makers.

Regarding new migrants, I would like to see the Church and the general community doing more to help new communities, particularly those from war-torn parts of Africa and the Middle East, to settle into our way of life. To be effective, we need to learn first about their cultures, values and experiences, as we have as much to learn about them as they do about us.

Conclusion

Barring a decision by one of the major political parties to break the current policy deadlock and opt for a more humane approach to refugees, it seems likely the Government response will continue indefinitely. Consequently, we should expect that the struggle to achieve more humane treatment for asylum seekers will be a long one, and we need to be thinking and working within that context.

---

[13] For information on the Australian Churches Refugee Taskforce (ACRT), see www. acrt.com.au.

[14] Robert Dixon, Jane McMahon, Stephen Reid, George Keryk and Annemarie Atapattu, 2017. *Our Work Matters: Catholic Church Employers and Employees in Australia*. Canberra: Australian Catholic Bishops Conference.

I recently saw an interview between Jenny Hutcheon and Ai Weiwei on ABC's *One Plus One* program. Asked why he supported the refugee cause, Ai Weiwei said the refugee issue is:

> … about understanding our humanity today. It's a crisis not just about refugees, but about us. If we give up these most important values, there is no future for us and no future for our children.[15]

---

[15] Jenny Hutcheon and Ai Weiwei, 2018. Interview on ABC's *One Plus One* program, accessed at iview.abc.net.au/programs/one-plus-one/NC1813H008S00.

8

Church Leadership in Preventing and Responding to Family Violence: Sharing Resources and Insights from around the Country

Fiona Basile

Family violence is a crisis in Australia – each week a woman dies at the hands of her partner or ex-partner. It is estimated that one in four children experience the fear and distress of witnessing their mother being abused. Family violence in all its forms offends against a vision of family as a place of love and safety, where children learn to respect and live with others. Our goal must be a society where all people are safe in their homes, families and close relationships; where violence and abuse are not acceptable; and where all relationships respect the equality and dignity of each person. This is part of the Gospel vision of love and respect.

This chapter explores the challenges and opportunities within Catholic social services and the broader Church:

- to prevent family violence,
- to respond to the needs of victims and survivors, and
- to discuss and determine how our Catholic social service organisations, parishes and Church leaders can best resource a pro-active approach in responding to the needs of those impacted by family violence.

In discussing the above, speakers at the 2018 national Catholic

Social Services conference, *Hearing Healing Hope*, shared their experiences and ideas relating to extending awareness of the nature of family violence – its incidence and causes – and how to best provide support for victims and survivors. The speakers included Di Swan, Director of Family and Relationship Services, Centacare Brisbane; Jocelyn Bignold, Chief Executive Officer of McAuley Community Services for Women in Melbourne; and Charlie King OAM, an ABC broadcaster based in Darwin, who has long been involved in the fight to end family violence. In writing this chapter, the author has drawn upon the information and wisdom shared by the workshop speakers.

What is Family Violence?

The Victorian *Family Violence Protection Act 2008* defines family violence as harmful behaviour that occurs when somebody threatens or controls a family member through fear. It can include physical harm, sexual assault, and emotional and economic abuse, and includes control over social contact. Physical and sexual assault are also criminal offences.

The key element of family violence is coercive control and fear. Fear is the most powerful way a perpetrator controls his victim. Fear can be included by giving a certain look across a room, making a gesture, possessing weapons (even if the perpetrator does not use them), destroying property, cruelty to pets and any behaviour that renders the victim powerless. As noted by Di Swan in her presentation, "We're seeing an increase in women accessing our services as well as an increase in the types of violence – more non-lethal strangulation, choking, pet abuse, and threats to kill".

There is a difference in the way violence is perpetrated towards men and towards women. Men face a higher risk of physical assault, usually by another man who is a stranger, and usually in public as a one-off event. Family violence, on the other hand, is predominantly perpetrated by men against women, and it is usually by men known to the women, in their own home. Women are more likely to experience multiple forms of violence that include physical, sexual and psychological abuse. When women experience violence, it is more likely to be part of a pattern of behaviour that happens over time, and women are more likely to be in fear of their lives. Research also indicates that when a woman makes an effort to leave a situation of abuse, the abusive male is more likely to tighten control.

One of the main drivers of family violence is inequality, for instance, men's control over decision-making and limiting women's ability to be independent in public and private life. The following cultural factors also contribute to higher rates of violence against women: the adherence to stereotypical roles that men are strong and women are weak; men are the breadwinners, women stay at home; men are better suited to positions of power, women are too emotional.

In the last decade a number of major state-based and national reviews have been undertaken addressing family violence, for example:

- National Plan to Reduce Family Violence against Women and Children 2010-2022,[1]

- Federal Parliamentary Enquiry into the Family Law System 2017,[2]

- Queensland Child Protection Commission of Inquiry,[3]

- Queensland's *Not Now, Not Ever* report,[4]

- Victoria's Royal Commission into Family Violence.[5]

---

[1] Details of the plan can be accessed at www.dss.gov.au/women/programs-services/reducing-violence.

[2] The report of the enquiry is available at www.aph.gov.au/fvlawreform.

[3] The final reports of the commission are at www.childprotectioninquiry.qld.gov.au/.

[4] For the *Not Now, Not Ever* report, see www.communities.qld.gov.au/gateway/end-domestic-family-violence/about.

[5] The report and recommendations of the Royal Commission are available at www.rcfv.com.au/Report-Recommendations.

In most instances, it is too early to evaluate the impact of their wide-ranging recommendations.

Roles of the Church in Preventing and Responding to Family Violence

The Catholic Church is working in various ways toward the elimination of family violence. For example, following the 2016 national Catholic Social Services conference and the Royal Commission into Family Violence, the Victorian Bishops released a public statement condemning family violence and provided each parish with a resource kit in order to help it respond better to family violence. The kit contents are also available online.[6] In Queensland, the Archdiocese of Brisbane has implemented a Domestic and Family Violence Taskforce, which includes members from the Archdiocese and other key stakeholders from the Catholic social services sector.

Centacare Brisbane's Family and Relationship Services[7] cover 77,000 square kilometres in the south-east of Queensland and the White Bay-Burnett regions. In terms of domestic violence services, in the 2017 calendar year, Di Swan reported that its services provided 32,000 output hours, supported 4,000 clients across nine domestic violence and family services. Staff undertook just over 3,000 risk assessments, each of which can take up to 1.5 hours, and just over 700 child protection and 282 suicide risk assessments. According to Swan, "Risk fluctuates so any time a client re-engages with the service another risk assessment is undertaken to ensure that our support intervention is matching what is happening for the client and family at that time". Staff work closely with Queensland Police, magistrates, child safety authorities, other non-government organisations (NGOs) and the Department of Corrections.

---

[6] To access the Parish Resource Kit, see www.css.org.au/Domestic-Violence.

[7] For information on Centacare Brisbane's Family and Relationship Services, see centacarebrisbane.net.au/family-relationship-services/overview/#.

McAuley Community Services for Women[8] responds daily to women and children who are experiencing family violence. It provides crisis accommodation, basic necessities, emotional support and access to legal services. Recognising it is not enough to simply respond, McAuley also has a women's education, training and employment program. Another of its programs, Engage to Change,[9] raises awareness of family violence and helps people to develop the confidence to respond appropriately. In her workshop presentation, Jocelyn Bignold said, "If employers understand what family violence is and put the policies in place, then we have an opportunity to keep employees safely employed and reduce the incidence of violence and the risk of slipping into homelessness. This is the same message we'd like to give faith-based communities: if you understand what's going on, you can address it. We're not asking you to solve it, and you don't have to intervene. Just know what it is, understand the implications and refer appropriately to specialist services".

Challenges

Swan advised that, in Queensland, while there is significant reform work underway in both the domestic violence and child safety spaces, this still requires coordination across all key government and non-government stakeholders. Further, there are enhanced opportunities for improved services with the domestic violence reforms in Queensland, but the pace and intensity of the reforms is impacting the effectiveness of the sector. Swan noted that, along with funding reform, there remains a gap in fully resourcing NGOs to deliver specialist DFV (domestic and family violence) services. Further, the number of women and families coming forward has increased, so under-resourcing remains a serious issue.

---

[8] McAuley Community Services for Women takes care of women and their children who are escaping family violence, and women who are homeless. For details of the services, see www.mcauleycsw.org.au/.

[9] For details of this program, see www.mcauleycsw.org.au/our-services/engage-to-change.

Challenges addressed by Bignold include the fact that family violence is difficult to identify, and it is dangerous if mistakes are made. In addition, alcohol, drugs, mental illness and financial stress mask family violence, and can be used to minimise what is happening. "People become afraid to intervene. They say it's not our business, they don't want to get involved and don't want to make things worse", she said. "Our message is that you don't need to intervene. We're asking you to listen, to believe what people are saying, to respect their decisions and to help them find specialist support". Compassion, mercy and sympathy are important elements.

Prevention of Family Violence

Family violence is prevalent to a high degree in Indigenous communities. According to the third workshop speaker, Charlie King, Indigenous women are 35 times more likely to be hospitalised from an act of family violence than non-Indigenous women. In his presentation, King outlined a number of preventative initiatives taking place in the Northern Territory and having a positive impact.

Founder of the 'No More' campaign[10] in the Northern Territory, King, who has worked for 25 years in the media, believes sport has an important role to play in preventing family violence. "If we could get the sporting community of Australia to take a stronger stand against family violence that would make a big difference", he said. In one Northern Territory community, family violence has been reduced by about 60 per cent just by getting women involved in running the football competition.

Another community in the Northern Territory experienced violence on grand final day annually for ten years. An incident would happen on the ground, which would inevitably spill out onto the streets and into homes. A decision was made to cease playing

---

[10] For information on the 'No More' campaign, see www.nomore.org.au/.

grand finals and this was the case for a number of years. Eventually, when the decision to resume playing a grand final took place, Bishop Eugene Hurley of Darwin went onto the ground and blessed the game. Bishop Hurley and King talked to the players about respecting the game and playing with respect for each other. "We explained that two teams play. One team wins and one doesn't and it would be nice if, at the end of the game, you went over to the team that didn't win and said to them 'Try again next year; don't get bitter, get better'; and it worked", said King. Two years ago, a grand final was played, with the final goal at the last minute deciding the winner. When the siren went, there was no violence. There had been no violence during the game. Further, after the game and even one month later, the police confirmed that there had still been no violence. "We have to challenge the way we play sport", said King. "If we can change the attitude in sport on the field, that spills over into the community and it makes a difference".

Today the 'No More' campaign has links with more than five sporting codes and nearly 100 teams. It is still growing. Sporting clubs are assisted in making Domestic Violence Action Plans,[11] which outline their approach to reducing family violence. The voice of children is being heard by way of creative music endeavours and communities are taking a stand in public marches. Strong, male community leaders are teaming up with women and children, to lead an integrated plan of action to prevent family violence.

In the Northern Territory, however, there is one particular challenge in the fight against family violence, namely distance. It is difficult to provide services to women and children affected by family violence because they are so far away from vital facilities. In one community where there are high levels of family violence, it takes six hours to travel out to the community, and another six hours to get

---

[11] Ibid.

back. This is where strong partnerships are so important. King explained, "The Northern Territory Police give us free flights whenever they're going out to visit communities and whenever the magistrates fly out, they do the same. When Correctional Services go out to court and have a free seat on their charter, they'll also offer us a free flight, which is really good of them".

Public awareness of the 'No More' campaign continues to grow through its increased engagement with the sporting community and increasing media coverage. As the campaign grows, its aim stays the same: to reduce family violence by engaging men in the sporting community both at the grassroots and national level to join the battle to create a future free from family violence.

Some Recommendations

According to the workshop speakers, a number of recommendations and future actions could usefully be implemented by the Catholic social services sector and the wider Church moving forward.

Catholic Social Services Sector

While there are pockets of work taking place among Catholic social service agencies to combat family violence, Swan noted that the approach is not systemic and coordinated. It is recommended that more effective and focused advocacy from the Australian Catholic social services sector take place, both at state and Federal government levels. Social change is more likely to take place when there is collective, structured input. Agencies need to organise a 'Collective Impact forum' to focus solely on this issue, to share ideas and strategies, and to put forward key recommendations and actions. The dent that Catholic social service agencies could make in combating DFV through a Collective Impact initiative cannot be overstated. It is further recommended that a national Catholic social services statement be released to speak powerfully out against family violence.

Cultural Change in the Community and within Catholic Parishes

Culturally, changes need to be made within the community, and more specifically within parish communities. The *Not Now, Not Ever* report[12] recommended that leaders of all faiths and religions take a leadership role in fostering and encouraging respectful relationships. Faith communities need to be educated to understand that coercive control and violence are never acceptable. Parishes and community groups need to know where to direct someone who needs assistance. Any time a victim comes into a parish or a community seeking help, it is so important to assist him or her to get to the right service and to ensure that the appropriate risk assessment can be made – this can be a matter of life or death. It is not at all appropriate to advise someone seeking help to "go back and work it out with your spouse", or to "seek couples counselling". Safety must be the priority, as is the removal of any stigma and shame. It is imperative that parish personnel are provided with adequate resources and referral information.[13]

Collaboration between Catholic Social Services and the Wider Catholic Church

Gender inequality is one of the main driving factors of family violence. Given the Catholic Church is a patriarchal system, it needs to address any gender imbalances or potential blind spots. The Victorian Bishops are to be applauded for their official statement condemning family violence following the Royal Commission into Family Violence and the provision of resources for parishes, however concerted efforts must continue. This is particularly important given the recent conclusion of the Royal Commission into Institutional Responses to Child Sexual Abuse and its wide-ranging recommendations, which may take resources and attention away from the fight against family violence. The Catholic community, including bishops, priests, parishioners and Catholic social services must continue to take a collective and

---

[12] *Not Now, Not Ever report*, op. cit.
[13] Parish Resource Kit, op. cit.

collaborative stand against violence in any form. It is recommended that the Australian bishops release a statement reinforcing their commitment to end family violence, and that they continue to work in collaboration with the Catholic social services sector on this goal. It is also recommended that faith communities refer to 'Safer',[14] an online resource aimed to help Australian churches to understand, identify and respond to family violence.

Conclusion

The 'Safer' resource uses the term 'brokenness' to describe the suffering of men who are perpetrators of family violence. It talks about a profound woundedness. Rigid stereotypical roles and expectations trap men into outdated ways of being, just as they trap women. Power, control, competition and having to live up to these stereotypes are disempowering and damaging.

We must replace these outdated models with Christ's model of peace, respect, trust and 'caretaking' of each other. Women, men and children will then have a chance of better, happier and safer lives. Now is the time to challenge the culture that enables family violence to take place. We do not want to be saying in another thirty years that we knew about this and did nothing. The framework to address family violence exists and these atrocities are preventable. We all have a role to play in helping end family violence. We need many voices from all walks of life to communicate a message that violence has to stop. This chapter contributes one voice to this urgent agenda.

---

[14] For access to the 'Safer' resources, see www.saferresource.org.au/.

9

It's Time – Working for Wellness and Empowerment for Our Aboriginal and Torres Strait Islander Brothers and Sisters

Darlene Dreise

If we are very lucky, there may be an occasion or two in our lives when we are privileged to witness for ourselves a story of great transformation … These episodes may have an indelible effect on our spirit, far beyond that of mere happenstance. Jade's story is powerful in that it speaks of promise and potential and, while it is composed as a personal memoir, it reflects the author's present recollections of experiences over time. Names and characteristics have been changed to protect the privacy of individuals and institutions, and the personas of several Aboriginal and Torres Strait Islander people have been woven together to create 'Jade' who could be a daughter, sister, grandchild or Aunty from any Indigenous community today. The author has also exercised creative imagining in the composition of story events, however Jade's journey highlights for us themes of challenge, growth and resilience, which are universal and timeless.

First, let us meet Jade …

For all of us, there comes a time when personal happiness and professional credibility align, perhaps with the realisation that "My work is rewarding, I'm good at what I do and feel as though I am truly making a difference!" And then … the challenge comes … the call for help that tilts the axis of your world and drags you out of your comfort zone.

In this story, the central character is 'Jade' who we learned about via 'cold calls' from one of the teachers at a local Catholic secondary college in our city. This teacher had spent several hours contacting Catholic agencies in town trying to secure an employment opportunity for one of the college's Year 12 graduates. More than a little intrigued, I invited the teacher to tell me more.

A picture was painted of a young Aboriginal woman who had completed 12 years of education but was yet to attain employment. Jade had moved into town with her family several years ago. During the course of the conversation it was revealed that no-one in Jade's family was employed and, while they were keen to support her in seeking employment, they did not have the necessary lived experience to assist her.

The teacher's only motivation for relaying this story was his desire for this young woman to fulfil her potential – "I'm just contacting all the Catholic agencies to see if between us, one of us – any one of us – can help this kid. We call ourselves Catholic, and the Church is one of the biggest employers in this region, so now's the time to live up to our identity!"

That did not go down too well, let me tell you! First, he starts with a cold call, and then plays the 'Catholic' card to find employment for a young woman who might be able to find it herself if only she tried harder … contacted more people … knocked on more doors … don't people realise that hospitals are busy places? That we have employment policies and processes? That we can't go around creating jobs for people even if their stories do tug at the heartstrings?

My response? "Sure, I'll take your number and 'get back to you' if I become aware of any opportunities". (Note to self – file in the 'too hard basket' ASAP!)

But that's not how the Spirit works, is it? Sometimes things 'stick' … and agitate … and take you into uncomfortable places …

Long story short: Nobody likes being called out by having their comfort zone and Catholic identity prodded … but this was a time when the Spirit truly agitated.

Senior hospital staff were consulted as to 'the possibilities'. Opposition was respectfully noted.

We prayed.

This challenge kept rearing its head – and hope was expressed that perhaps another Catholic agency would offer an opportunity to this young woman.

We reflected.

We thought we should at least make contact with this young woman and invited her in to meet with us.

We discerned.

And we employed Jade.

Yes, there was some resistance, but as staff got to know her over the course of two years, they took her under their wing, offering assistance with transport, donations of household items when she moved into her first unit and supported her during her dark times when social and cultural pressures threatened to be all-consuming.

Jade was successfully employed with us for two years and then left when her life got 'too hard'.

Two years later, Jade re-established contact with us. Her former manager was happy for her to re-apply for employment, and Jade has since re-commenced working with us. She consistently demonstrates professionalism and is a powerful role model for her younger siblings and she was recently an active and engaging participant at St Vincent's Health Australia's national Aboriginal and Torres Strait Islander staff forum, connecting with cultural peers from across Australia. She is part of our St Vincent's family.

Introduction

Our Indigenous people have always acknowledged the power of story in the role of the characters or tale tellers.[1] Dance, art, oral re-telling and song … these skills have served well to preserve heritage and illustrate lessons for living. Jade's story can be viewed as a parable for today as it is a touchstone for those involved in Catholic

---

[1] Bruce Pascoe with the Australian Institute of Aboriginal and Torres Strait Islander Studies (AIATSIS), 2010. *The Little Red, Yellow, Black Book – An Introduction to Indigenous Australia*. Canberra: Aboriginal Studies Press.

support service ministries, tying together the threads of what might otherwise be regarded as disparate phenomena – that is, wellness and empowerment for our Aboriginal and Torres Strait Islander people. The reality is that wellness for these groups is rarely thought of in terms of physical functioning alone, but as the result of the impact of historical trauma (including enforced removal from traditional lands and stolen children), and the social determinants of health (education, employment, housing and so on) which, in turn, influence the spirit of individuals, families and communities alike. When one link in this chain is weakened, the domino effect on every other aspect of living can be devastating. Consequently, the psychological defence mechanism of compartmentalising may not be effective or understood easily by these groups.

As professionals within ministries serving society's most vulnerable individuals, we understand that the wellbeing status of populations is identified according to criteria including employment, housing, education and health outcomes. Against such criteria, our First Nations people and communities continue to score at rates considerably lower than other cultural and population groups nationally and internationally. So, while we have a sense and understanding of the complexity of challenges affecting our Indigenous peoples today, yesterday and, inevitably as it would seem, tomorrow, we are also challenged to recognise the deep impact and interconnectedness of holistic wellness for these groups. Joe Roe, an elder of the Karajarri and Yawuru peoples captured this sentiment beautifully:

> When people's emotional, spiritual, physical and social needs are met, then their Inner Spirit feels strong because they are in a good state of health. When one or more of these needs are not met, people's health deteriorates. This will affect your Inner Spirit and make you feel weak or no good.[2]

---

[2] Joseph Roe in Kate Smith and Lianne Gilchrist, 2017. "Well-being of Older Aboriginal Australians: The Importance of 'Keeping Spirit Strong'", *Australasian Journal on Ageing*, 36(2), 112.

This interconnectedness of health, wellness and spirituality has been interpreted by this Torres Strait Islander author as follows:

> Our health is not just a physical reality, but impactful on our minds and spirits. Our health is strong when we are able to care for our families and communities ... when we have homes and beds for our children and food on the table ... when our children attend school and appreciate the value of education ... when we are fit and strong and don't have to rely on handouts. When we feel good going to work and have a stable income ... when we can care for our elders and continue to learn from their wisdom and stories ... when we have true friends who laugh and cry with us ... when all of Australia knows the story of our land and appreciates our place as the descendants of the first peoples. In this way, our dignity is strong, and I feel that I am someone of worth. Know us ... beyond the faces that you see in the everyday maelstrom of life ... know our struggles and pain, our joys and achievements and work with us to enable positive change for our families and communities.[3]

Jade's story is but one in a landscape of complex historical and contemporary narratives, but it is important as it speaks of hope and possibility in an arena of seemingly insurmountable barriers. Media stories and government reports often contribute to a view of Indigenous cultures as being disenfranchised – broken beyond the point of healing. As a result, a 'numbing' or desensitising effect, or sense of being overwhelmed at an apparent inability to change or even impact on our current state of affairs, may impact both our Indigenous and non-Indigenous people.

The roles of those in Catholic ministry who work and minister in this space are significant, privileged and challenging as they offer social support defined by Christian values while operating in a secular

---

[3] Darlene Dreise, reflection.

society, serving clients who live in worlds of multiple realities. In times of both spiritual fragility and of joy our Catholic ministries are called to stand with Aboriginal and Torres Strait Islander individuals, families and communities, our ultimate goal being their empowerment and flourishing. In this way, we move towards the vision of Pope St John Paul II in his address to Aborigines and Torres Strait Islanders in Alice Springs on 29 November 1986:

> Your Christian faith calls you to become the best kind of Aboriginal people you can be. This is possible only if reconciliation and forgiveness are part of your lives. Only then will you find happiness. Only then will you make your best contribution to all your brothers and sisters in this great nation. You are part of Australia and Australia is part of you. And the Church herself in Australia will not be fully the Church that Jesus wants her to be until you have made your contribution to her life and until that contribution has been joyfully received by others.[4]

These words continue to provide inspiration for our work within the health and social support services arenas with the realisation that the ultimate fullness of our Church in this nation has yet to be revealed and can only occur through the welcoming and acceptance of the contributions of Aboriginal and Torres Strait Islander peoples. Each of us is therefore called to work towards the unknown possibilities to be revealed through the true flourishing of the original peoples of this land.

One Organisation's Approach to Working with and for Our Aboriginal and Torres Strait Islander Peoples

When the first five Religious Sisters of Charity set foot on this continent in 1838, they came with the knowledge that this land was occupied prior to the arrival of Europeans. It is said that their congregational leader,

---

[4] Pope St John Paul II, 29 November 1986. Address to the Aborigines and Torres Strait Islanders in Alice Springs, accessed at w2.vatican.va/.

Mother Mary Aikenhead, included a black crucifix amongst the Sisters' belongings as a symbol of their respect for the Aboriginal people.

These pioneering religious women and their Australian Congregation have as one of their legacies today St Vincent's Health Australia (SVHA), in whose hospitals, aged care facilities, research entities and outreach programs, staff, through words and actions, proclaim the organisational mission: "We bring God's love to those in need through the healing ministry of Jesus".[5]

These powerful words guide SVHA's ongoing commitment to working with and for Australia's Aboriginal and Torres Strait Islander peoples. Foundational to this work was the development of a national Reconciliation Action Plan (RAP) recognising the value of formal and informal relationships and partnerships with Indigenous people and communities and which focuses on positive developments in the areas of Relationships, Respect, Opportunities and Reporting Accountabilities.[6] Initiatives within this plan range from very simple ones to those that could possibly effect inter-generational change. For example, each of the SVHA hospitals, aged care facilities and administrative centres adheres to an Acknowledgement of Traditional Owners protocol, displays the Aboriginal and Torres Strait Islander flags and extends inclusive hospitality to Elders and local community members for significant events.

A Cultural Awareness Training package has also been developed for all staff across the organisation. This resource has become part of a suite of tools to be utilised in the clinical and non-clinical dimensions of care of, and communication with, Aboriginal and Torres Strait Islander people and organisations.

---

[5] St Vincent's Health Australia is now part of Mary Aikenhead Ministries. In 2009 the Religious Sisters of Charity of Australia transferred their hospitals and other ministries to this new ministerial public juridic person, established by the Holy See at the congregation's instigation. For more information on SVHA, see svha.org.au/home.

[6] The SVHA Reconciliation Action Plan (RAP) can be accessed at svha.org.au/home/about-us/reconciliation.

SVHA also hopes to enable positive inter-generational change through its strategic approach to targeted employment and its ambitious target to increase its Aboriginal and Torres Strait Islander workforce to 500 employees by 2020 as part of its commitment to the Commonwealth Government's Employment Parity Initiative. The success of this initiative has the potential to improve the wellness of many Indigenous families and communities, and this level of workforce representation will also enable Indigenous perspectives to be considered with an enhanced profile both within the organisation and in the wider political landscape.

In recognition of the critical nature of peer support as a tool supporting the retention of employees, SVHA also supports all Aboriginal and Torres Strait Islander staff and representative senior staff to gather once a year at a staff forum. The forum provides a valuable opportunity for formal and informal engagement with Aboriginal and Torres Strait Islander staff allowing for the sharing of challenges and success stories alike through yarning, formal presentations and the presence and shared wisdom of Elders.

The SVHA Reconciliation Action Plan Collaborative Art Project, 'Reconciliation: Towards Excellent Health, Happiness and Equality 2016' powerfully acts as both sign and symbol of what reconciliation means to the people of SVHA.[7] This artwork, completed by both Indigenous and non-Indigenous staff, including senior managers, is a triptych combining works from Queensland, New South Wales and Victoria, representing the breadth of the artists' vision for Aboriginal and Torres Strait Islander people in SVHA facilities. The final artwork is a reflection of reconciliation on an individual, state and national level. A copy of the triptych is on display at each facility of St Vincent's Health Australia. It is a vibrant symbol of our RAP commitment, our own reflections, and our collective experience of the reconciliation journey we are all on.

---

[7] Ibid.

Figure 1: The 2016 triptych arising from the St Vincent's Health Australia Reconciliation Action Plan Collaborative Art Project and entitled 'Reconciliation: Towards Excellent Health, Happiness and Equality'[8]

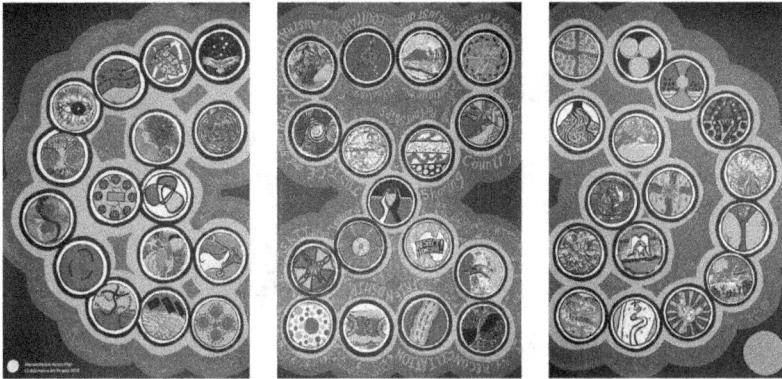

Looking Forward, Looking Back

Many of us have been called to work in ministries of care with our Aboriginal and Torres Strait Islander brothers and sisters, whether in education, social services, health or aged care. As capable and competent professionals, let us not be deceived by the commentary of social analysts and nay-sayers who by word, action or the deliberate omission or positioning of historical truths attempt to sway our collective consciousness to apathy and indifference for the descendants of the original peoples of this land. As we learn about the unceasing challenges facing the wellbeing of these groups, we can also acknowledge their capability for resilience and their prioritisation of familial connections – invaluable tools in the slow work of liberation for families and communities.

Let our hearts not be heavy, for these people have not succumbed, but demonstrated a capacity for resilience, influence and, yes, great humour in the face of intergenerational trials. The wisdom and

---

[8] Ibid., reproduced with the kind permission of St Vincent's Health Australia.

intellectual acuity of these people to survive in this environment – the longest endurance of any culture – speak volumes of the unleashed potential and 'of what could be'.

Know too that these people were called to care for and nurture their wellness long before the good news of the Gospels came to these shores. Sherry Balcombe, Co-ordinator of Aboriginal Catholic Ministry Victoria, paints a poignant picture with her understanding that "Aboriginal people were living rich and full lives and caring for Mother Earth for many thousands of years before the birth of Father Abraham".[9]

Further north, the Meriam people of the Torres Strait continue to honour Malo Ra Gelar or Malo's Law – a collection of rules and behaviours for harmonious and moral living.[10] The people of this community have abided by these laws for millennia, and other similar understandings have guided life in island communities since 'the time before time'. It would therefore appear that the pursuit of peaceful and productive lifestyles has always been prioritised by our traditional peoples, certainly long before the coming of European settlement. Their struggles, triumphs and realities of living are thus interwoven with the fabric of this land and our surrounding seas, yet our Aboriginal and Torres Strait Islander people too must listen to the heart call of their ancestors and children and rise to the challenge of flourishing in communities to be all that they can be. And we must believe and trust in the capability and competence of non-Indigenous Australians who work with us as we heal, for then we will truly be empowered to have a voice in our national dialogue.

---

[9] Sherry Balcombe, personal conversation; for information on Aboriginal Catholic Ministry Victoria, see www.cam.org.au/acmv/.

[10] For information on Malo's Law, see Nonie Sharp, 1993. "No Ordinary Case: Reflections Upon Mabo (No. 2)", *Sydney Law Review*, 15(2), 143-158, accessed at www.austlii.edu.au/.

Epilogue

Picture this:

Five years on from our first meeting with Jade, our setting is a twilight welcoming event being held for new Year 7 high school students at a local Catholic secondary college. Amongst the assembled crowd of nervous students and parents stands a young Aboriginal woman – Jade – who became known to us as a result of requests for employment assistance by a former teacher of this college.

Jade was at this event with her younger brother who was starting at the college and her mum and very much taking a protective and proactive role with them. It was lovely to have a yarn with her and find out that she was still working in healthcare and loving it, and the pride her mum had in her achievements was obvious. It was gratifying to see Jade in attendance with her mum, supporting her little brother and acting as a great role model for him and her other younger siblings.

Jade's future may have taken a very different direction if it were not for the combined efforts of local Catholic ministries acting with fidelity to their respective mission and values. In times of seemingly insurmountable challenges, may we let Jade's story act as a compass guiding us to our true north – a state of sustainable, celebrated wellness and energised empowerment for the descendants of the original peoples of this land.

10

The National Disability Insurance Scheme: Opportunities and Challenges for Mission-based Agencies

Ingrid Hatfield

The National Disability Insurance Scheme (NDIS) is one of Australia's most significant social reforms, fundamentally changing the way disability services are funded and delivered. The scheme is transforming the disability support sector to a competitive market model, where 'consumers' have control over an individualised package of funding, and choice in the support services they receive. Transition to the NDIS presents very significant challenges and opportunities for service providers, and Catholic agencies must discern how to navigate the fundamental changes in service delivery and discern how to express their organisational mission and values in a new environment. The 2018 Catholic Social Services conference presented the opportunity for Catholic social service providers to engage with these issues across two workshops.

In the first workshop, facilitated by Camilla Rowland, Chief Executive Officer of Marymead, expert panellists explored areas of convergence and tension between NDIS policies and practices and the mission values of Catholic agencies. Panel members were the Hon Kevin Andrews MP, Chair of the Australian Parliament's Joint Standing Committee on the NDIS; Dr Ken Baker AM, Chief Executive of National Disability Services; and Christine Macqueen, Manager Disability Futures at CatholicCare Diocese of Broken Bay.

The second workshop, facilitated by Kate Venables, Director

of CatholicCare Social Services in Toowoomba, provided an opportunity for agencies to connect with the collective expertise of Catholic agencies delivering services in the NDIS. The workshop included presentations from Tony Hollamby, Chief Executive Officer of St John of God Accord; Peter Selwood, Executive Director of Centacare Brisbane; and Anne-Marie Mioche, Chief Executive Officer of CentaCare Wilcannia-Forbes. Attendees at the workshops represented the wide diversity and strong commitment of Catholic agencies delivering disability support services across Australia.

An Ambitious Reform

The NDIS is a national insurance model designed to reform the previously underfunded, unfair and inefficient disability support system. The scheme was developed through an in-depth inquiry into the disability support sector, and established following a strong support campaign from people with disability, their families and carers, and service providers. The aim of the NDIS is to ensure access to reasonable and necessary supports for every person with disability, with appropriate funding based on individual need, and genuine choice and control for participants regarding the disability support services they receive.[1]

The NDIS was established in trial site areas in 2013, with a progressive national rollout according to age groups and geographical areas beginning in July 2016. The scheme is expected to reach full operation by 2020, supporting an estimated 475,000 people and costing $22 billion in the first year of full operation. The disability care workforce will need to double to meet this demand for services.[2]

The NDIS is a remarkable social policy initiative with strong

---

[1] Productivity Commission, August 2011. *Disability Care and Support - Inquiry Report*, accessed at www.pc.gov.au/inquiries/completed/disability-support/report.

[2] Productivity Commission, October 2017. *National Disability Insurance Scheme Costs – Study Report*, accessed at www.pc.gov.au/inquiries/completed/ndis-costs/report.

political and community support. However, as each of the workshop panellists acknowledged, there have been significant difficulties and frustrations with the implementation of the scheme so far. Many people with disability have benefitted from the NDIS, but as expressed by Andrews, the current experience of too many participants and providers is one of inconsistency and inadequacy.

The Productivity Commission has found that the participant intake rate for the scheme is falling behind schedule, and the rollout is unlikely to meet the ambitious target time frame. Further, the Commission reports there has been too great an emphasis on reaching target numbers of participants at the expense of the quality of the implementation of the scheme, to the detriment of participants and providers' experience.[3] In acknowledging these difficulties, workshop panellists emphasised that we must not lose sight of the empowering vision of the NDIS, and the strong political and community support to see it implemented well and to improve the lives of people living with disability.

Convergence and Tension: Mission Values and the NDIS

The underlying mission, vision and values of Catholic agencies are founded in on a belief in the inherent dignity of the human person. Catholic Social Teaching emphasises that a "just society can become a reality only when it is based on the respect of the transcendent dignity of the human person".[4] This respect for the dignity and worth of every human being is fundamental to the work of Catholic social service agencies. It inspires the commitment of agencies to working with all people regardless of their background and, in particular, to support those who are most vulnerable and disadvantaged.

---

[3] Ibid., 96, Finding 2.1.
[4] Pontifical Council for Justice and Peace, 2004. *Compendium of the Social Doctrine of the Church*. Vatican: Libreria Editrice Vaticana, par. 132.

Further, there is an underlying understanding in the Catholic social tradition that people are inherently interconnected with and interdependent on one another. As Andrews articulated, human beings are not "atomised" individuals, but situated in the context of family and community. This is consistent with the values and approach of the community sector, which recognises the importance of family and community and seeks to support people in a holistic way.

The fundamental aims of the NDIS are in line with these strong mission values. As stated by the National Disability Insurance Agency (NDIA), "The NDIS aims to give people with disability better access to personalised, high quality and innovative supports and services. A specific focus is to enhance the independence, social and economic participation of people with disability and their carers".[5] As emphasised during the workshops, there is strong alignment between the underlying vision of the scheme and the mission values of Catholic social service providers. The NDIS offers a national, inclusive scheme which promotes the dignity and participation of people with a disability, and the provision of high-quality, person-centred support services.

However, as each of the workshop speakers also acknowledged, there is considerable tension between this ideal and the reality. While there is strong convergence between the values of Catholic social service providers and the aims of the NDIS, there are considerable differences in the way the scheme is being implemented. For example, as Rowland argued, the scheme still sits within a tightly controlled bureaucratic structure which lacks true flexibility to meet the individual needs of people with disabilities and their carers. For many people entering the NDIS, the aims of the scheme remain largely aspirational.

A strong theme of the workshop discussions was the tension within the NDIS of the focus on the individual, and the need to

---

[5] National Disability Insurance Agency Service Charter: www.ndis.gov.au/about-us/our-service-charter.

better balance this with regard for the importance of the role of family, carers and support staff. The NDIS is predicated on the ability of individuals with disability to self-direct the services that they want. While this is strongly aligned with an understanding of the inherent dignity of every person, it has become imbalanced without a corresponding acknowledgement of the importance of family and carers and the varying capacity of people with disability to articulate their needs and goals and navigate a complex market system.

As workshop presenters outlined, while there is strong support for the founding principles of the NDIS, the emphasis on the individual and their self-determination has driven some disregard for contextual factors and those surrounding and supporting the individual. For example, in the planning conversation with participants, the NDIA has been reluctant to involve others beyond the individual participant in developing their personal plan and funding package. There are some legitimate concerns regarding protection against conflicts of interest and respect for self-determination. However, excluding staff with extensive knowledge and experience in supporting an individual from being present in their planning interview (where this is desired by the participant), means that plans are less likely to reflect the genuine needs and aspirations of participants, to the detriment of the participants and the scheme overall.

This is particularly critical for people with complex or high support needs, who rely on the support of family, carers or service providers. Workshop speakers and attendees expressed concern that the NDIS system is becoming biased towards those with high capacity and ability to articulate their own needs and aspirations. The emphasis on individual self-determination has meant that those without such capacity, or the support of family and carers, are falling behind.

This tension between an emphasis on the individual and acknowledgement of the role of family, carers and service providers is yet to be properly addressed in implementation of the scheme.

Capacity for self-determination is a continuum, and the scheme overall needs to find a better balance in supporting people across the full length of this spectrum.

Rowland further outlined the tension between the approach and implementation of the NDIS and the values and practice of mission-driven service providers, in regard to five particular areas:

- Providers work with people and their families in contexts of complexity. Within a family there may be multiple people with a diagnosis. Providers work with carers as much as we they work with people with disabilities – however, the individual focus of the NDIS leaves little room for acknowledgement of family context and there is little in the scheme to support carers' needs.

- Providers work towards long-term transformation. While the NDIS is predicated on an early-intervention model to support the best outcomes for participants over their life-time, in reality the scheme has meant short-term plans and ever shrinking funds with each subsequent plan. This does not allow for any short-term crises or episodes which might arise, and the support of people towards long-term goals.

- Providers work flexibly with people, noting that many conditions have both episodes and some vulnerabilities which are permanent. As evidenced by reductions in support coordination over time, and expectations that most participants will move towards self-management, the NDIA appears to assume, incorrectly, that everyone is on a straight trajectory towards complete recovery with ever-decreasing need.

- Providers believe that planning needs to be very flexible, with inclusion of opportunity for changes by the participant, rather than finalised with the judgement of the NDIA planner.

- Providers work to build community capacity and work collaboratively with other agencies. However, the NDIS, along with other new government funding structures, focuses on individual transactional services rather than consideration of long-term community building, and forces agencies into competition with one another.

These significant differences reveal a tension between the values of the community sector and the approach of the Government and NDIA in implementing the NDIS. The challenge remains to navigate these differences in continuing to promote the establishment of an accessible and equitable scheme, which respects both the dignity and self-determination of people with disability and enables the supportive role of family, carers and service providers.

Case Study: A Crisis in Short-Term Accommodation

The disparity between the aims and reality of the NDIS is clearly illustrated in a case study provided by Rowland during the first workshop. This case study, regarding short-term accommodation, which essentially replaces previously funded respite services, demonstrates some of the significant challenges of the implementation of the NDIS both for participants and carers and for service providers.

In April 2016 following some months of discussion, all the service providers of short-term accommodation in the Australian Capital Territory (ACT) trial site developed a joint letter to the then CEO of the NDIA outlining major concerns regarding the service price for short-term accommodation under the NDIS. Both the criteria which underpinned the service price, and the actual price itself, differed substantially from the reality of service provision cost, especially for clients with complex needs.

Essentially, the criteria modelled the services as always being delivered by one staff member to three clients, though this was far from the reality. Across all the agencies in the ACT, the average requests and needs of clients required a minimum of 1:2 staffing. In Marymead's case, more than two-thirds of clients required either 1:1 or 1:2 staff to client ratios. No matter how the costing analysis was modelled, agencies could not come up with the price rate that had been set by the NDIA actuaries. In fact, the NDIS rate was almost half that required to operate a service with skilled staff and meet basic employment and disability service standards.

In talking with CEOs across other areas, Rowland found that many other providers, including large organisations, had also done the modelling and decided they were either going to 'cherry pick' clients or stop providing short-term accommodation altogether. As providers were now in a competitive market situation, Rowland found few agencies were doing any advocacy to their state governments or the NDIA. As such, most Government representatives were unaware of the looming market crisis.

Marymead chose to remain committed to their clients and advocate for service rates to meet the provision of services to all NDIS participants, including those with high or complex needs. Marymead invested significant time and resources in organising independent costing modelling by accountants, developing case studies for every single affected client, and attending meetings with the NDIA and local government representatives to discuss the looming crisis.

Unfortunately, it came to a crisis point where some carers were facing relinquishment of care of their children with high support needs. Together with the clear evidence and advocacy from providers and the sector peak body, this crisis finally triggered change and the NDIA reconsidered the criteria and rates for short-term accommodation. The NDIA set in place new rates for short-term accommodation from November 2017, which allowed greater variability in staff ratios for clients with complex needs.

As Rowland emphasised during the workshop, it should not take a crisis to instigate the necessary changes to meet the needs of the most vulnerable clients and their families. It required a significant investment of resources from providers and the sector peak body before flaws in NDIA policy were resolved, and the NDIS system could support provision of services to participants with the greatest needs. This advocacy required the collaborative effort of providers, advocacy agencies and peak bodies, who together held the NDIA to account to deliver a scheme which reflects the original vision and values of the NDIS reform.

Challenges in Implementation

As outlined by the case study above, while the aims of the NDIS are strongly supported, there are serious challenges for service providers and participants in ensuring the implementation of a sustainable and accessible scheme. The workshop presentations and discussions focused on a number of areas of particular challenge and concern, as summarised below.

Pricing

As indicated in Rowland's case study regarding short-term accommodation, there is a lack of transparency in the way the price for support services is determined by the NDIA. Workshop panellists expressed concern that the pricing framework appears to be based on unrealistic assumptions divorced from the reality of service provision. This includes minimal provision for staff training and development, inappropriate assumptions of the number of hours staff can spend in direct support with clients, and a lack of recognition of staff to client ratios required for safe provision of services for people with complex needs.

Workshop attendees reported that the inadequacy of NDIS prices, particularly for personal supports and community participation, is severely impacting the viability of these services and constraining the ability of providers to invest in developing a quality workforce. Some providers are heavily subsidising provision of NDIS services, while others are withdrawing from provision altogether. As Baker said, these concerns are reflected in an annual survey from National Disability Services, which found that inadequacies in NDIS pricing are dampening business confidence across the sector.[6]

It was acknowledged that the NDIA had commissioned an independent price review, due to be released in March 2018, which panellists hoped would go some way to address these immediate concerns. In the medium- to long-term, there was support for shifting the role of price-setting from the NDIA to an independent agency, such as the Quality and Safeguards Commission, and eventually progressing towards price de-regulation.

Market Failure

Related to the inadequacies of prices for key supports, workshop attendees raised significant concerns regarding the current and real risks of market failure for disability services in their communities. One representative said there had been a systemic reduction of services in their area, as many providers lacked the required infrastructure or reserves to continue in service provision under the NDIS.

Andrews agreed this was an area of very real concern into which the Joint Standing Committee on the NDIS has been inquiring. Thin markets and market failure are issues facing major cities as well as rural areas where there has traditionally been a lack of service providers. Workshop presenters predicted that market failure would not occur uniformly, but rather according to particular types of services and locations. As Andrews emphasised, it is particularly concerning that the way in which the NDIS market is constructed may lead to greater

---

[6] National Disability Services, 2017. *State of the Disability Sector Report 2017*, accessed at www.nds.org.au/news/state-of-the-disability-sector-report-2017-reflects-sector-under-pressure.

reduction in services, with providers withdrawing in areas where there have not previously been problems.

Panellists argued that there needs to be a much better system of data collection and analysis to provide early warning signs of market failure and to support timely intervention. It is not an option for the Government to wait for the market to fail and then react – peoples' lives are at stake.

Rural and Regional Provision

The challenges of ensuring the availability of services in rural and regional areas were well articulated by Mioche, drawing on the experience of CentaCare in the Diocese of Wilcannia-Forbes. This Diocese covers 52 per cent of New South Wales, but of the 7.5 million people who live in the state, only 143,000 of them reside in this western half. The largest population centre in the Diocese is Broken Hill, which has around 20,000 residents and is an 8-9 hours drive from the other most significant population centres.

Along with these extreme distances and low population density, the area has high levels of disadvantage across almost all social and health indicators. There are relatively high levels of disability, including psychosocial disability, and an already poor service system. As Mioche emphasised, it is very hard to see how a market model can be expected to be successful in such areas.

People face multiple barriers to accessing the NDIS in rural areas, from a lack of the health professionals necessary to provide diagnosis for qualification for the scheme, to an inability to see an NDIA planner and lack of service providers delivering in the area. As acknowledged during the workshops, it is extremely concerning that some NDIS prices are unrealistic even in areas of high-population density, let alone when applied to rural and regional areas.

While there is some rural and remote loading in the NDIS price guide, this is not proportionate to the extremely high travel and service delivery costs in such areas. As Mioche argued, given these clear issues, there needs to be much greater consultation with communities and service providers in rural areas to identify sustainable models of service before the scheme is fully rolled out. This could include a mixture of block-funding and a market approach, or identifying a lead agency with responsibility to ensure availability of services across a region.

Workforce

As discussed in the second workshop, one of the most significant challenges facing providers is the recruitment and development of a disability care workforce sufficient to meet demand for services. This is consistent with the Productivity Commission's finding that the workforce is unlikely to be sufficient to meet demand for NDIS services by 2020.[7]

It was agreed across the workshops that governments must do more in stewarding the NDIS market to support the necessary increase in the workforce. Providers argued that the salary price point severely constrains their ability to invest in developing a quality workforce. As such, part of the solution to these challenges must be adjusting the price framework to allow for appropriate staff training, development and career progression.

Safety Net

Where State and Territory Government agencies previously provided assurance of services as the provider of last resort, no such arrangements yet exist under the NDIS. The lack of safety net provisions or clear guidelines to ensure appropriate services in crisis situations and cases of break-down of family care is extremely concerning. As argued by Macqueen, this is a severe implication of the imbalanced shift to a focus on the individual, without due regard for the necessary underlying social support systems.

---

[7] Productivity Commission, 2017, op. cit., 336, Finding 9.1.

As Andrews reported, the Joint Standing Committee on the NDIS has found a number of situations in which, because there is no provider of last resort, a person with disability has been in jail for no reason other than they do not have an NDIS support plan. This unjustifiable situation is indicative of a systemic failure, consistent with the experience of Catholic Social Services Australia (CSSA) members, of the extreme lack of clarity and support for people with disability in such crisis situations. Appropriate safety net arrangements must be implemented as a matter of urgency.

Carers

There were significant concerns raised during the workshops that the individualistic focus of the NDIS has meant there is lack of support for carers. The necessity to support carers was well articulated by Baker: "However much the NDIS expands provision of formal services, and it will considerably, most care and support will still rely on family carers ... if they are not supported to do that, through respite services and other help, then the pressure on the scheme will just increase".

Workshop attendees strongly advocated for the extension of funding for the Commonwealth Respite and Carelink Centres (CRCC), to ensure carers are enabled to continue in their crucial support roles while the long-term policies of care support under the NDIS are devised. Providers at the workshop attested to how crucial the support of the CRCCs have been in preventing the relinquishment of children and tearing apart of family units. There is significant concern that, in the transition to the NDIS, policy progress in recognising the crucial role of carers will be lost.

Issues with Planning Process

Providers have witnessed extensive variability in the suitability of participants' support plans, with vast discrepancies between funding allocations for individuals with similar needs and with some participants much worse off than under the previous funding model. The current planning system does not allow flexibility to cater for changing client needs or episodes within the life of a plan. Participants should have the ability to use their resources flexibly for different needs as they arise.

As Macqueen argued, these inconsistencies and difficulties in the planning process reflect a disconnect between the founding purpose and current processes of the NDIS. It was acknowledged that the NDIA has undertaken a review of the planning process and is implementing changes to improve the participant and provider experience.

Vulnerable Clients

There is an inherent assumption in the way NDIS plans are designed and funded that after a certain period of time, most participants will be able to navigate the system largely independently. However, this is not realistic for many of the participants that CSSA members serve, who require far more support to navigate the NDIS system than is currently billable. Such participants may have high or complex needs, no family or informal carer support, significant psychosocial disability or a history of trauma. The complex and ongoing nature of such vulnerabilities mean that many participants do not have the capacity to engage with a market system independently and will continue to require extensive support to access services they require.

A concern was raised by a service provider during the workshops, namely support for very vulnerable and isolated people with significant psychosocial disability. This provider advocates on behalf of people in such situations, to assist them in the very complex process of proving eligibility and registering for the NDIS. This is time-consuming and unfunded work, but is incredibly valuable in enabling vulnerable people to access the supports they need. Without this support, many of these clients would move prematurely into the much more expensive aged care system. There must be further recognition of the support needs of vulnerable clients, with funding for ongoing support coordination and enabling of agencies to continue this vital advocacy and support.

Intersection with Other Services

Finally, as Rowland raised, there are significant challenges for service providers aiming to work with communities in a holistic and long-term way, as there is a wide funding gap for people who require information, support and care but do not yet qualify for the NDIS. Under the NDIS, there is a relatively small Information, Linkages and Capacity Building fund which provides short-term block grants, to cover such supports. However, this funding is not at all adequate for what is required to support people who are not yet approved under the NDIS and are awaiting diagnosis or who have fluctuating need. There remains significant confusion regarding what is included in the NDIS and what is not, with much greater clarity required around the boundaries and interface between the NDIS and mainstream services.

Opportunities

Despite these significant challenges, there is strong commitment to the vision of the NDIS and the opportunities it provides for people with disability and their families and for the disability support sector.

For many people with disability, their lives have already been remarkably changed through engagement with the NDIS, as the scheme has finally given many people access to resources and supports appropriate to their needs. As outlined by Rowland, so far the NDIS has been particularly beneficial for people with a clear diagnosis and prognosis, and those who are motivated and articulate, and have supportive family or social networks. The NDIS provides significant opportunity for clients with clear goals.

The NDIS also presents significant opportunities for providers. Hollamby emphasised how St John of God Accord has engaged very positively with the NDIS, viewing the reform as a tremendous opportunity to enrich the lives of people they support. Though the NDIS has been a complete "disruption" to the previous way of doing things, it has opened up possibilities for the organisation that would never have been available before, including significant organisational growth.

St John of God Accord approached the transition to the NDIS through work in four key strategic areas:

- becoming a leader in disability services,

- reviewing finance, IT and infrastructure,

- ensuring responsiveness to the NDIS environment, and

- promoting partnering and capital optimisation.

Engaging with the new system helped the organisation sharpen its thinking regarding how it supports clients, with the articulation of a positive behavioural support model, innovations in service delivery and customer care, development of new IT platforms and new organisational partnerships.

The move away from block funding has promoted greater efficiency and maximisation of funding available. In moving from a centralised block-funding model to a de-centralised approach, the NDIS offers opportunities for flexibility, responsiveness and innovation in development of services. The participant, or customer, rather than the government, becomes the core negotiator of funding and service expectation.

As such, Hollamby argued, customer experience is the focus of everything. For St John of God Accord, this meant putting a lot of time and energy into thinking through the end-to-end customer experience, as well as providing significant pre-planning preparation and support for clients, and ongoing communication with clients and families. For the first time, the organisation developed a strong brand

and marketing position, building on the clear mission and values of the organisation to make a difference in the lives of the people it supports.

The NDIS presents a particular opportunity for faith-based organisations. As demonstrated in the second workshop, Catholic organisations are strongly positioned with a clear mission and values, extensive experience in providing support to those in need, and a strong people-centred culture. As Peter Selwood put it, the mission of Catholic agencies means that they are committed to the provision of disability support services, and have an opportunity to set the bar for provision of quality services, enforcing a high standard of care for clients and staff in a new market setting.

Moving Forward

Significant hurdles remain in ensuring transition to a sustainable, equitable and accessible NDIS. While the challenges are immense, the workshop panel expressed a shared optimism that the approach of the NDIA is changing and it has heard the need for improvement. Panellists were encouraged that, under relatively new leadership, the NDIA has a greater energy and openness to engage with providers and participants, hear the concerns of the sector and address the problems. The NDIA is mindful of the difficulties and large task ahead, and, as acknowledged by the panel, is undertaking system reviews and improvements.

A key theme of the workshop discussions was the changing nature of and need for advocacy in the transition to the NDIS. Baker encouraged attendees to realise that change is achievable, and the lesson from the success of the campaign for the NDIS is that the unity of voices across the sector is incredibly powerful. The message now is that the "NDIS is the right destination, it's just that the road getting there is difficult". We need to continue to advocate in a united way to ensure the destination we reach with the NDIS is the one for which the sector fought so hard.

A key element in ensuring this, as the panel agreed, will be a much greater emphasis on market stewardship. There has tended to be a narrow focus from the Government on the overall budget and time frames of the scheme. However, in Baker's words, the core focus should be ensuring that "people with disability get the supports they need, when and where they require them, at a level of quality that both protects them from harm and enables them to realise their goals". True market stewardship will ensure a "sustainable and enduring market" for both providers and participants. This requires a balance between the innovation and flexibility of open competition, and assurance of essential services through regulation.

Appropriate market stewardship of the NDIS moving forward will require:

- clarification around the respective roles of government agencies, as the NDIA, Department of Social Services, the newly established Quality and Safeguards Commission and State and Territory Governments all have responsibility, but so far lack clarity about their distinctive roles in ensuring market sustainability,

- appropriate collection of data and timely dissemination to demonstrate market trends, so that government agencies planning market intervention are well-informed, service providers are able to invest in places where there is known demand for services, and participants have greater informed choice,

- adequate pricing to allow efficient organisations to deliver quality services and generate enough surplus to stimulate expansion.

As Baker emphasised, if the prices for core support services continue to limit expansion, there will be an increasing shortfall between the demand for and supply of services, with direct consequences for participants. Beyond the independent price review, CSSA has strongly supported the Productivity Commission's recommendation that the role of price setting be moved from the NDIA to an independent body, to remove the conflict of interest with the NDIA managing both the overall budget of the scheme and pricing of supports. Shifting this role to the Quality and Safeguards Commission, as recommended by the Productivity Commission,[8] would promote a direct connection between pricing and service quality, while long-term progression is made towards deregulation of prices.

The workshop panel also emphasised the need for a better balance between a focus on the individual participant and acknowledgement of the essential role of family, carers and service providers. Though the NDIS will considerably expand the provision of formal services, the vast majority of care will still be provided by family members. If they are not supported to continue in this work, through respite services and links to other support, then the pressure on the scheme will inevitably increase. As outlined by Macqueen, part of the solution to the policy issues faced by the NDIA must be coming back to the principles of co-design, allowing those with the lived experience of disability, and the experience of providers who support them, to be part of the process of generating solutions.

As discussed during the workshops, further specific changes that agencies would want to see include:

- appropriate safety net arrangements for crisis situations, developed as a matter of urgency,

- development of alternative approaches in rural areas, drawing on consultation with communities and co-designed with experienced service providers,

- greater flexibility in NDIS plans to account for people with complex and ever-changing needs, and to allow for

---

[8] Productivity commission, 2017, op. cit., Recommendation 8.3.

situations where there are multiple members of a family with a disability,

* development of the Information, Linkages and Capacity Building fund to support people better through their communities as a secondary service layer to the NDIS,

* implementation of the participant and provider pathway review by the NDIA,

* improvement in the experience of the NDIS for participants with psychosocial (mental health-related) disability,

* greater support for vulnerable and isolated individuals engaging with the NDIS.

Overall, the NDIS represents a significant opportunity, in line with the mission of Catholic social service agencies, to transform the lives of people and communities. Throughout the workshops, agencies were reminded of the need to hold true to the founding vision of the NDIS, as together government and providers navigate the task of large-scale sector reform, and the significant challenges, tensions and risks of the implementation of the scheme. As Venables aptly reminded us, the NDIS is a brand-new world which may be like the Promised Land – let us just hope we do not spend 40 years wandering in the desert before we can make it work!

11

Social Housing: Exploring Opportunities for Affordable Housing Initiatives

May Lam

This chapter draws on presentations made during the social housing workshop at the Catholic Social Services conference in February 2018 in Melbourne. The session was chaired by Chris Hall, Chair of the Australian Catholic Housing Alliance and CEO of MercyCare Western Australia. Contributors included Tony Fitzgerald, CEO of Centacare Ballarat; Tim Gourlay, CEO of CatholicCare Tasmania; Andrew Goelst, Property Development and Asset Manager for Centacare Evolve Housing; Claire-Anne Willis, Senior Policy Officer at Catholic Social Services Victoria; and Mark Philips, CEO of CatholicCare Sydney.

Forming a Catholic Housing Alliance and Activating Networks

The Australian Catholic Housing Alliance (ACHA) came together in 2012 as an informal network of Catholic service organisations from across the country to share learnings and find ways more cooperatively to meet the needs of many people left behind as a result of very high real estate prices across the country. The latter is not just a problem for those on low incomes. More and more people on middle incomes are also unable to access suitable and affordable housing for themselves, whether renting or buying. On any given night in Australia, over 116,000 people are homeless.[1] Further, there are around 200,000 people on waiting lists for social housing.[2]

Catholic Social Services Australia and Catholic Health Australia are the auspicing bodies for ACHA, reflecting the importance of affordable housing as a means to support human dignity, avoid family breakdown, and maintain social inclusion and general and mental health. Over the past six years, members of ACHA have been able to deepen their understanding of the diverse ways that Catholic social services and the dioceses might create housing solutions. This can mean buying or leasing land from Catholic or non-Catholic sources, or re-purposing buildings that are no longer needed for their original function.

All kinds of experiences have been shared by the group: raising finance for social and affordable housing, accessing the government funding and rent subsidies that are available, design solutions for large scale property development or small-scale homes in clusters, ways to manage tenancies, and getting the social mix right for multiple-dwelling developments.

The Alliance has also been following the work of regional Catholic networks established in the Archdiocese of Sydney and in Victoria to explore ways to generate more affordable housing. The strength of all these groups coming together is in their diversity, with cross-learning possible between experienced housing developers and service providers, and those just getting started, now enriched by the more recent involvement of the Catholic Development Funds.

This article reports on the work and housing projects of two organisations, Centacare Ballarat and CatholicCare Tasmania, to

---

[1] Australian Bureau of Statistics 2018. No. 2049.0 *Census of Population and Housing: Estimating Homelessness 2016*, accessed at www.abs.gov.au/.

[2] Australian Institute of Health and Welfare, 2017. *Housing Assistance in Australia 2017*, accessed at www.aihw.gov.au/reports-statistics/health-welfare-services/housing-assistance/overview.

illustrate some of the housing solutions they have delivered. This is followed by 'work in progress' reports from the housing action networks in Sydney and Victoria.

Centacare Housing in Ballarat

Centacare Housing is a subsidiary of Centacare Catholic Diocese of Ballarat (Centacare Ballarat) – its outreach encompasses the western region of Victoria. Centacare research has shown that typically in Ballarat there are 75 people sleeping on the street each night and 400 in insecure accommodation, such as couch surfing or living in a caravan.

Centacare Housing and VincentCare are the only two Catholic agencies in Victoria among the 30 community organisations registered as providers of affordable housing. This kind of provider generally manages rental housing, often on behalf of the State Government's Director of Housing, and may own some properties. It often specialises in a particular client group, for example people with disabilities, aged people, or youth. A registered provider of this type can only charge low-income people affordable levels of rent, based on their income. This is normally a defined percentage of their unemployment allowance or pension, whether from government-funded settlement services or Veterans Affairs. Community housing providers must also report against a set of standards for various aspects of housing services. For example, there are tenant surveys about responsiveness to maintenance issues, or evaluation of information provided to prospective tenants when they are considering renting a property.

All of that is challenging, but Centacare Housing currently manages and rents out various properties on behalf of the Director of Housing, which include 10 stand-alone dwellings of two, three or four bedrooms, a 15-unit rooming house, an eight-unit supported crisis accommodation facility, and some crisis accommodation units, and is preparing itself to participate in the transfer of the management of the State Government's social housing units to community housing providers.

Centacare Housing also manages 41 other properties on behalf of Centacare Ballarat. Among these are 29 smaller affordable housing units ranging from small studios up to a three-bedroom unit, acquired from the redevelopment five years ago of a 41-unit motel. The units are set around a half acre of public open space that includes community gardens, a children's playground, a gazebo with barbecue facilities, a 10-kilowatt solar system, a laundromat, and community hub room.

This development was made possible, and is able to be rented at affordable rates, because of top-up Federal Government funding received through the National Rental Affordability Scheme. The priority of those with highest needs is balanced with renting to a cross-section of the community, based on research findings that there are fewer problems where the tenant mix resembles a 'normal' street. Some of the older residents keep an eye on the younger tenants and call Centacare to suggest checking on tenants if issues arise.

A number of other Centacare Ballarat programs support tenants with wrap-around services, such as parenting, or integrated family services. Centacare also refers tenants to other providers in Ballarat for services that it does not deliver, such as treatment of alcohol or drug dependency.

In another development in Ballarat, Centacare Housing has built 13 stand-alone dwellings of two, three or four bedrooms. This too was possible because of funding from the National Rental Affordability Scheme, which unfortunately is no longer available. If it had more funds, Centacare would provide increased housing stock. A couple of parishes have identified blocks of land that could be developed, but the challenge is getting access to capital. Further, there is a definite need for more crisis accommodation in Ballarat. Centacare Housing operates one facility, but could fill five and, in particular, there are many women locally with unmet needs for housing.

CatholicCare Tasmania

Growth in the value of properties in Tasmania has led to higher rents, more people in housing stress and 4,000 people on the housing waiting list in Tasmania. The average income in suburbs where CatholicCare Tasmania has tenants is about $667 a fortnight; the Australian average is $1,200. Eighty-one per cent of people aged over 75 years in Tasmania are fully dependent on Centrelink payments for their main source of income, and the 65-plus aged cohort is set to double in the next 35 years.

CatholicCare became involved in housing and property development after its Board decided over eight years ago to move into housing and children's services and reduce the organisation's dependence on government grants. At around the same time, the Federal Government mandated that the States would have to transfer 35 per cent of their social housing stock to community housing providers.[3] That initiative in Tasmania was called Better Housing Futures, and CatholicCare sought to be prepared for it.

Being only a small player in housing, CatholicCare Tasmania decided to partner with another agency outside Tasmania, resulting in Centacare Evolve Housing (CEH), a registered community housing provider able to operate nationally. Today, CatholicCare has a total portfolio of around 1,500 properties located in some of the areas of greatest social need in Australia. Of those, 450 properties are owned and managed directly by CatholicCare; 1,050 are managed through CEH.

---

[3] Hal Pawson, Vivienne Milligan, Ilan Wiesel and Kath Hulse, October 2013. *Public Housing Transfers: Past, Present and Prospective*, AHURI Final Report No. 215. Melbourne: Housing and Urban Research Institute, accessed at www.ahuri.edu.au/research/final-reports/215.

CatholicCare started by buying properties from Red Cross, namely 50 very small motel-type accommodation units. It then bought another property of 50-plus units on the site of a retirement village that was facing financial difficulties. Having acquired the whole complex, Centacare was able to build more units on the site.

As other Federal Government funding came online, the existing assets were able to be utilised to leverage more finance. It was possible to buy land, or access it, from the Archdiocese of Hobart, either through outright acquisition or long-term lease. Land bought from the diocese has always been priced at market value.

Over time, CatholicCare tried different approaches to make more and better housing available. While maintaining traditional weatherboard housing for the Government, it has added new-build units in the backyard, because many people living in social housing cannot care for their yard, which decreases the amenity of the area. Smaller yard sizes also mean lower maintenance.

In other developments CatholicCare is building housing with an appearance that would not be out of place in any suburb in Australia. This ensures, through using diverse and more contemporary styles of architecture and layout, that it looks just like a traditional subdivision, while staying with smaller housing lots. Elsewhere, it is building specialist disability accommodation to platinum standards. These building projects have been supported by loan finance from the Catholic Development Fund Tasmania, Catholic Development Fund Melbourne and Diocesan Development Fund Paramatta, whose understanding of the needs for finance and shared Catholic mission have been very enabling.

CatholicCare's philosophy is to plan and build communities and futures, not just houses. It has also accessed funding to create a parkland. For example, on land adjacent to an industrial estate, it has planted screens of trees to provide additional residential land, as part of a larger master plan. In another illustration of building communities and futures, in a collaboration with the Museum of Old and New Art (MONA), CatholicCare is working to secure land that will be used to take disengaged youth and inspire them to become talented computer programmers, based on a model from New Orleans in the United States of America.

If Centacare Evolve Housing had adequate finance, its vision would be to eradicate the housing waiting list. While that is a big and audacious goal, it believes that it is achievable.

Housing Initiatives Working Group in Victoria

The Housing Initiatives Working Group has its origins in the 2017-2018 Bishops' Social Justice Statement, 'Everyone's Business',[4] and the growing need to address housing issues. These developments came together with the Victorian Government's 2017 announcement of the 'Homes for Victorians' strategy,[5] which includes various initiatives to increase access to housing and improve its affordability: improved planning and approvals processes, assistance for first home buyers, affordable and social housing funding measures, and improved homelessness services. The Victorian Government had also foreshadowed other initiatives, including a $1 billion Social Housing Growth Fund. This is set to generate $70-80 million in annual dividends to be applied to social and affordable housing.

The Fund will mean that new social and affordable housing developments can be realised in more diverse ways than in the past and can include units of private housing. Government funding can also be used to subsidise rentals for people who need housing

---

[4] Australian Catholic Bishops Conference, 2017. 'Everyone's Business: Developing an Inclusive and Sustainable Economy', Social Justice Statement 2017-2018, accessed at www.socialjustice.catholic.org.au.

[5] Victorian State Government, 2017. *Homes for Victorians: Affordability, Access and Choice*, accessed at www.vic.gov.au/affordablehousing/about.html.

assistance but not necessarily intensive long-term housing. All this opens up new housing services and solutions for housing providers and agencies to consider, and Archbishop Denis Hart of Melbourne asked Catholic Social Services Victoria to consider the potential to take action. A working group formed, chaired by the Episcopal Vicar for Social Services, Fr Joe Caddy, and including representatives of Catholic housing agencies and of the Catholic Development Fund Melbourne as well as the Property Manager for the Archdiocese of Melbourne.

The Housing Initiatives Working Group is exploring options to develop projects utilising Church land or underutilised properties in parishes or religious communities in Victoria to increase the level of social housing for people in need. The working group developed a discussion paper,[6] and then a survey which went out to parishes and also to religious congregations, to find out the extent of social housing currently being provided by the Church and to identify underutilised property that might be used to extend this provision. The survey initially covered the Archdiocese of Melbourne[7] and is being extended to the other Victorian dioceses.

The response has been encouraging, with 42 parishes (approximately 21 per cent of parishes in the Archdiocese) and four religious congregations reporting that they already provide low-cost housing, much of that for elderly people. These residences were largely developed in the 1970s and 1980s when 30- to 50-year leases were made available for this purpose with the Victorian Government providing capital to build the accommodation. There are also other types of accommodation for different groups of people being reported. A common finding is that parishes are asset-rich but income-poor,

---

[6] Catholic Social Services Victoria, 2017. *Discussion Paper: The Catholic Church in Victoria Working to Increase Social Housing,* accessed at www.css.org.au

[7] Catholic Social Services Victoria, 2018. *Victoria Catholic Social Housing: A Report – Melbourne Archdiocese,* accessed at www.css.org.au.

and either lack the means to redevelop their properties or need to utilise their assets as part of their overall financial management. For example, a number of parishes have properties on land that is not really being utilised as well as it could be or have houses that are too dilapidated to use but lack the funds to renovate them.

By taking stock of relevant properties, the working group hopes to link relevant parishes to Catholic housing agencies in order to support more partnerships and collaborations for social housing proposals, including some that can be taken to government. The working group is also engaging with the Church agencies to consider diocesan-wide planning and the management of property portfolios. The aim is to develop a framework or guidelines in relation to building social housing into future property development proposals for the Victorian dioceses.

New South Wales Developments

The Sydney Alliance is an advocacy group with around 45 members, spread across a wide array of unions, churches, community groups and schools. For the past few years, this Alliance has been lobbying the New South Wales Government for 'inclusionary zoning'; that is for new housing developments on private land to ensure that 15 per cent of dwellings built provide affordable housing, increasing to 30 per cent where public land is used. While the current New South Wales Government does not support this policy, the Opposition does.

In particular, the Archdiocese of Sydney has convened a group of Catholic organisations to come together to consider the possibility of achieving some form of transformational change to tackle homelessness. St Vincent's Health Australia, the St Vincent de Paul Society, the Mercy Foundation, Catholic HealthcCare and the Archdiocese itself, represented by CatholicCare Sydney, have been looking at the challenge of eliminating rough sleeping in Sydney. A proposal is to go to Archbishop Anthony Fisher OP of Sydney asking the Church to act as a catalyst to eliminate rough sleeping in Sydney. Other cities around the world, including London, have also taken on this challenge.

Two years ago, the New South Wales Government called for proposals to build social and affordable housing. The St Vincent de Paul Society, through Amelie Housing, won some of that funding, with a proposal for 500 housing lots. In fact, all the winners of the first funding round were faith-based organisations. In 2018 the New South Wales Government is inviting proposals for a second round of funding, for a total of 1,200 housing units. While several partners, including the Archdiocese of Sydney, were interested, it proved hard to get access to land, an important element of any proposal. For example, decision-making in the Church can be challenging; Canon Law can be an impediment; and it is not easy to determine properties that might be available and applied to social housing.

Some properties identified in the dioceses of Sydney and Parramatta could have been put into the mix for a proposal to Government but, disappointingly, these only added up to about 100 housing units. The Government was seeking proposals for minimum tenant numbers of around 400. What emerged from that exercise, however, is the identification of properties that could be used in future.

The Sydney Alliance has also been keen to promote the use of Church property for social services in general, not just affordable housing. This is being called the Community Care Strategy, and is work linked to the Parish 2020 initiative of the Archdiocese of Sydney, which is exploring ways to renew and strengthen parishes.[8]

Conclusion

This chapter, like the corresponding workshop at the Catholic Social Services conference, has addressed issues of relevance to Church

---

[8] For information on 'Parish 2020: Building Vital Faith Communities', see www.sydney-catholic.org/parishes/parish2020/.

agencies seeking to tackle the shortage of social housing and provide affordable options to their clients. It has explored key issues that underpin finding solutions, namely access to finance and to land, imperfect Church decision-making processes, and strategies that lead to successful outcomes. Such strategies include good planning, being prepared for opportunities both to tender for government funding and to utilise available land and property, and a determination to address this challenging social problem.

12

Excellence in Caring for Vulnerable Clients: Going beyond the Rhetoric and Compliance to Explore Excellence in Care

Robyn Miller

This chapter explores the concepts that were presented in the workshop of the same name at the Catholic Social Services conference in February 2018.

In Australia the national Royal Commission into Institutional Responses to Child Sexual Abuse (Royal Commission)[1] has redefined what it means to provide excellence in care and has led to increased awareness of the rigor required to be a child safe organisation. The harmful treatment of vulnerable children in faith-based, community-based and government institutions alike, that was outed during the Royal Commission, has galvanised each state's commitment to reform. Underpinning the reform agenda now afoot in every jurisdiction is the pervasive acknowledgement of the rights of children, families and Aboriginal and Torres Strait Islander communities.

Children Needing Care

Over the past decade, the number of children and young people in care in Australia has grown from 25,454 in 2006 to 46,448 in 2016,[2] an

---

[1] The 5-year Royal Commission into Institutional Responses to Child Sexual Abuse concluded in December 2017; see at www.childabuseroyalcommission.gov.au/.

[2] Australian Institute of Health and Welfare (AIHW), 2007. *Child Protection Australia 2005-*

increase of 82 per cent. In 2015-2016, 36 per cent of these children were from Aboriginal and/or Torres Strait Islander backgrounds[3] when they form only 5.5 per cent of the population. The factors associated with increases in demand over this period are largely driven by changes in community attitudes, increased expectations on professionals to report concerns, and the inclusion of emotional harm, especially relating to family violence, as a reportable form of abuse.

It has never been clearer that what mainstream systems have been doing up until now, in a general sense, is not working, and that innovative, relationally based and long-term solutions to support families and to prevent harm and children coming into care are needed. At MacKillop Family Services we totally support the drive to resource Aboriginal Community Controlled Organisations properly to provide community-based family services and to support the transfer of Aboriginal children and young people to be cared for by Aboriginal families and communities. Our goal is to use our strength as an organisation to support families and to prevent any child being harmed and removed, reducing residential care and improving the quality of care, with greater emphasis on keeping siblings together and to reunify families wherever possible. We know much about the poor outcomes of child removal, the unsustainable costs for governments, and that children are staying longer in care and generally have poorer outcomes than their peers.

The research-based knowledge on the impact of child abuse and neglect has been well articulated in the professional literature. The literature on trauma and the evidence from neuroscience research have stimulated change in the approach to child and family practice. For

-06. Child Welfare Series No. 40. Cat. No. CWS 28. Canberra: AIHW, 51 and AIHW, 2017. *Child Protection Australia 2015-16*. Child Welfare Series No. 66. Cat. No. CWS 60. Canberra: AIHW, 62, respectively.
[3] AIHW, 2017, op. cit., 52.

186

example, Glaser,[4] Perry[5] and Shonkoff and Garner[6] have reported on the neurophysiological processes experienced by maltreated children and young people alongside behavioural, cognitive, emotional and relational impacts. It is clear that the impact of traumatic events at different times in the life cycle will have different consequences.[7] Importantly, the authors also outline evidence that a secure attachment with a primary carer has a buffering effect and promotes healing.

Organisations providing care, like individuals, are living, complex, adaptive systems and being alive, they are vulnerable to stress, particularly chronic and repetitive stress. Our social service organisations are facing significant stressors from a wide range of sources – for example, budget shortfalls, increased workload, staff and foster care decreases and turnover, less experienced staff, increased expectations and community criticism. Organisational trauma when it occurs can be devastating – for example, occupational violence, layoffs, child or staff deaths, and negative media exposure. The National Disability Insurance Scheme (NDIS) has radically changed the policy and practice landscape and there are multiple legislative, policy and regulatory changes, before we even begin to focus on the practice challenges of working with traumatised children and families.

[4] D. Glaser, 2000. "Child Abuse and Neglect and the Brain – A Review", *Journal of Child Psychology and Psychiatry*, 41(1), 97-116.
[5] B. D. Perry, 2002. "Childhood Experience and the Expression of Genetic Potential: What Childhood Neglect Tells Us About Nature and Nurture", *Brain and Mind*, 3(1), 79-100; B. D. Perry, 2006. "Applying Principles of Neurodevelopment to Clinical Work with Maltreated and Traumatized Children: The Neurosequential Model of Therapeutics" in N. B. Webb (ed.), *Working with Traumatized Youth in Child Welfare*. New York: The Guilford Press, 27-52.
[6] J. P. Shonkoff and A. S. Garner, 2012. "The Lifelong Effects of Early Childhood Adversity and Toxic Stress", *Pediatrics*, 129(1), e232-e246.
[7] J. Atkinson, 2002. *Trauma Trails: Recreating Song Lines – The Transgenerational Effects of Trauma in Indigenous Australia*. North Melbourne: Spinifex Press; J. L. Herman, 1992. *Trauma and Recovery: The Aftermath of Violence – From Domestic Abuse to Political Terror*. New York: Basic Books; B. A. van der Kolk, 2006. "Clinical Implications of Neuroscience Research in PTSD", *Annals of the New York Academy of Sciences*, 1071(1), 277-293.

The ubiquitous presence of family violence, drug and alcohol abuse, and the radical impact of social media on our children have created unprecedented challenges for organisations which seek to go beyond the rhetoric and compliance and provide excellent care.

Impact of the Royal Commission – Child Safety

Through the case studies and in private sessions at the Royal Commission, we heard many stories of where institutions had failed to protect children in their care from sexual abuse. What we heard showed that child sexual abuse in institutions continues today and is not just a problem from the past. We learned that institutional cultures and practices, that allowed abuse to occur and inhibited detection and response, continue to exist in contemporary institutions. It has never been clearer that children's safety and best interests must be at the core of an institution's operations and be supported by a well-informed community.

The Royal Commission examined the elements that define a child safe institution, noted the reasons that institutions fail and considered what standards could be applied to make them safer places for children. From this work ten Child Safe Standards were identified that would contribute most effectively to improve the safety of children in institutions: "The standards work together to articulate what makes a child safe institution" and "are of equal importance and are interrelated". The Royal Commission stressed that the Child Safe Standards should be reviewed and seen as dynamic and not static.[8] The chapter in this book by Maria Harries provides a detailed discussion of the Child Safe Standards and how they have been adopted by Catholic Professional Standards Ltd to operationalise the safeguarding of children and young people across Church entities.

---

[8] Royal Commission, 2017, op. cit., *Final Report*, Vol. 6, 13.

Trauma-informed Care: The Sanctuary Model

In 2012 MacKillop Family Services adopted the Sanctuary Model as its approach to care and over a four-year period became an accredited institution in 2016.[9] The Sanctuary Model, developed by Dr Sandra Bloom in the United States of America, is a trauma-informed method for creating or changing an organisational culture.[10] The Sanctuary Model, at its core, promotes safety and recovery from adversity through the active creation of a trauma-informed community. A recognition that adversity is pervasive in the experience of human beings forms the basis for the Sanctuary Model's focus not only on the people who seek services, but equally on the people and systems who provide those services.

Creating a Sanctuary organisation is a deeply rooted organisational change initiative that requires sustained commitment and work over the course of years and is an approach to care based on the principles of trauma theory and an understanding of systems theory.

Sanctuary asks us to change a basic question by recognising the influence of a person's experiences, namely beginning with the premise: "What's happened to you?" rather than "What's wrong with you?" This becomes a cornerstone of engaging with another person while developing a solutions approach. It recognises the inherent resilience in people and the belief that they can heal. We change the language we use to describe behaviour, moving away from words like 'manipulating', 'attention-seeking', which evoke negative feelings about the child, to terms that more accurately describe what the child is doing in relation to their experience.

We change their experience by acting differently to the people who have hurt them, moving away from punitive responses that replicate their past trauma experiences. When we think of trauma,

---

[9] For information on MacKillop Family Services' adoption of the Sanctuary Model, see www.mackillop.org.au/sanctuary-model.

[10] For background on the Sanctuary Model, see www.sanctuaryweb.com/.

we often think of discrete events, like a car crash, accident, assault, but we also know that experiences that are repetitive and emotionally overwhelming and affect development may be as damaging, things like physical or sexual abuse, witnessing family violence or being neglected and helpless. And when these things happen in childhood, they often occur in the context of a household where adults are using illicit substances, may be mentally ill or may only be occasionally present. Research also shows us that poverty, racism and neglect can have a profound effect on a person's development.

In 1990, a landmark study demonstrated that these types of traumatic experiences in childhood have a strong relationship with poor physical, mental and social health in adulthood. The study, undertaken as a collaboration between Kaiser Permanente and the Centre for Disease Control looked at the relationship between adverse childhood experiences (ACEs) and later health outcomes in adults.[11] The study provides powerful evidence of the direct link between adverse experiences, disrupted brain development, the inability to function at a social, emotional and cognitive level, and the adoption of high-risk behaviours, which eventually leads to early death.

In this state of chronic hyperarousal, the brain is not able to attend effectively to the basic tasks of emotional and cognitive development, so we may see problems with judgment, mood and behaviour. Exposure to chronic stress also means exposure to extreme emotional responses, which are often too intense for the brain to tolerate. Traumatised people may seem numb to distressing experiences to which other people react strongly. Instead of showing what they feel, they may act out what they feel, resulting in a wide variety of behavioural disturbances. Exposure to chronic stress or adversity also perpetuates a sense of helplessness created by the inability to stop the trauma or escape from it. This may result in controlling behaviours as a way to mitigate that sense of helplessness.

---

[11] Details of the Centre of Disease Control-Kaiser Permanente Adverse Childhood Experiences Study are available at www.cdc.gov/violenceprevention/acestudy/about.html.

Essential to Sanctuary is forming a safe, non-violent environment for clients and assisting them in forming healthy relationships with staff and their carers, who are role models for caring and safety. Sanctuary teaches young people to cope effectively with stress and trauma and heal their emotional and behavioural health issues. It also teaches residential caring facilities to form communities that are safe and caring and maintain a culture that reflects these qualities at every level within the organisation.

The Sanctuary model is based on seven core commitments that serve as goals for resolving trauma-based issues. Everyone, in every part of the organisation, staff, carers and service users, is expected to practice these commitments in their daily interactions. The commitments are:

- non-violence,
- emotional intelligence,
- inquiry and social learning,
- democracy,
- open communication,
- social responsibility, and
- growth and change.[12]

A Change in Perspective

The Sanctuary Model challenges each individual involved in the life of a child to examine old models of thinking, behaviour management, conflict resolution, and crisis intervention. Below in Table 1 are some examples (adapted from the Bethany Children's Home Sanctuary Reference Handbook) of the differences in beliefs between traditional models and the trauma-informed Sanctuary Model.

---

[12] Sanctuary Model, op. cit.

Table 1: Differences in Beliefs between Traditional Models and the Trauma-informed Sanctuary Model

Traditional	Sanctuary
To ask, "What is wrong with you?"	To ask, "What has happened to you?"
Children are sick or bad	Children are injured but capable of recovery
The most important part of treatment is individual therapy	Everything is therapy and every experience a child has can be important in their recovery
Care plans for service users are made by a select few who are identified as 'the experts'	We do true multidisciplinary team work regularly
Physical safety is paramount – seclusion, restraint and coercion are acceptable	Paying attention to psychological, social and moral safety prevents violence
Violence is accepted as a routine part of the work	Violence is the exception to the rule of non-violence
Children's problems are largely viewed as biological or genetic	Children's problems are viewed as complex and related to trauma and attachment problems
Emotional control is essential for an orderly environment	Learning to manage emotions is more important than controlling them
Institutional responsibility is to protect society from these damaged children	Together with the staff and children the organisational function is to create a "living learning environment"

Work on the Child Sexual Abuse Prevention Project

In Australia and globally, child-to-child sexual abuse and sexual exploitation are problems of significant proportions, particularly in residential out-of-home care (OOHC) settings. Yet there is a paucity of research identifying effective ways to prevent sexual abuse and violence specifically in these settings and an urgent need to develop, trial and evaluate new approaches anchored in best available evidence.

This was a recommendation of the Royal Commission.[13] The Victorian Commission for Children and Young People had earlier, in 2015, inquired into the adequacy of the provision of residential care services for Victorian children and young people who had been subject to sexual abuse or sexual exploitation whilst residing in residential care. The report argued that there is very little consistent education provided to children and young people in residential care about healthy and safe relationships, sexual health and the safe use of the internet and social media. Sexual health and wellbeing education for children in residential care should include information about sexual health, positive relationships, reproduction, issues related to consent, safe use of the internet and social media platforms, and protective behaviours as well as information that counters the influence of pornography.[14]

In November 2016, MacKillop Family Services partnered with the University of Melbourne to co-design harmful sexual behaviour and child sexual exploitation prevention strategies to be trialled and evaluated at four MacKillop residential houses. Through this successful and strongly collaborative partnership, work has been carried out to establish which interventions could effectively prevent sexual abuse.

The project addresses the problem of sexual violence for children and young people living in OOHC, including harmful sexual behaviour (HSB, behaviours carried out by children and young people that are developmentally inappropriate and abusive towards self or others) and child sexual exploitation (CSE, adult-perpetrated sexual abuse that involves a child or young person receiving goods, money, power or attention in exchange for sexual activity), and domestic and family violence (DFV) in dating relationships. Children and young

---

[13] Royal Commission, 2017, op. cit., *Final Report*, Vol. 12, *Contemporary Out-of-home Care.*

[14] Commission for Children and Young People (CCYP), 2015. *"... As a Good Parent Would ...": Inquiry into the Adequacy of the Provision of Residential Care Services to Victorian Children and Young People Who Have Been Subject to Sexual Abuse or Sexual Exploitation Whilst Residing in Residential Care.* Melbourne: CCYP.

people in out-of-home care have a significantly increased risk of experiencing HSB and CSE, both being forms of child sexual abuse.[15] Our focus is directed to the carers and caseworkers in community service organisations and is designed initially to prioritise residential care settings.

In Australia during 2015-2016 there were 55,614 children and young people living in OOHC. Approximately five per cent of those children and young people were living in residential care settings.[16] A disproportionate 33 per cent of child sexual abuse reports to statutory child protection related to those children and young people living in residential care.[17] Further, children and young people from Aboriginal and/or Torres Strait Islander backgrounds and children living with disability were vastly overrepresented in these data.[18]

In the Victorian context, data from the Department of Health and Human Services[19] indicate that almost one in three children in residential care has been identified as at risk of sexual exploitation. This is also borne out by data from MacKillop's critical incident reporting system, which indicate staff are increasingly being called upon to respond to the elevated risk of sexual exploitation by predatory individuals and groups.

Many children and young people are living in care because they have experienced violence in their families of origin.[20] When children and young people live with violence they are more susceptible to

[15] Royal Commission, 2017, op. cit., *Institutional Responses to Child Sexual Abuse in Out-of-home Care*, 2016 consultation paper.

[16] AIHW, 2017, op. cit., 42 and 47.

[17] Royal Commission, 2017, op. cit., *Institutional Responses to Child Sexual Abuse in Out-of-home Care*, 5.

[18] AIHW, 2017, op. cit.

[19] Department of Health and Human Services, 2017, unpublished data.

[20] Royal Commission into Family Violence, 2016. *Report and Recommendations*, Vol. II. Melbourne: Victorian Government Printer, Melbourne.

Table 2: Three Prevention Strategies

	Core Components of Three Prevention Strategies
Prevention strategy 1 – Whole-of-house respectful relationships and sexuality education	• Train workers in whole-of-house approach, including recognising and responding to Harmful Sexual Behaviour (HSB) and Child Sexual Exploitation (CSE), as well as context of Domestic and Family Violence (DFV) • Educate children and young people about respectful relationships and sexual health and safety • Proactively engage in developmentally appropriate sex education • Facilitate Life Story work for children and young people
Prevention strategy 2 – Missing from home strategy	• Establish practice partnerships between each child or young person and residential house workers (involving social media) to counter grooming • Assertively engage children and young people who are missing from placement • Work consistently with Enhanced Response Model and Sexual Exploitation Protocol
Prevention strategy 3 – Sexual safety response	• Implement early identification, safety planning, advocacy and therapeutic treatment for HSB • Proactively support exit strategies for CSE • Join up MacKillop workers with local HSB and CSE professionals

developing abusive behaviours or to being victimised in the future.[21] These abusive behaviours are sometimes sexually harmful and at other times involve intimate partner violence. Further, DFV is the

---

[21] S. Holt, H. Buckley and S. Whelan, 2008. "The Impact of Exposure to Domestic Violence on Children and Young People: A Review of the Literature", *Child Abuse and Neglect*, 32, 797-810.

key risk factor for harmful sexual behaviours carried out by children and young people.[22]

The outcome of the MacKillop-University of Melbourne project to date is the co-design of three interventions that, when implemented and as detailed above in Table 2, will prevent harmful sexual behaviour and child sexual exploitation for children and young people living in out-of-home care. We have trained our staff for implementing these strategies and employed a nurse practitioner as part of the team, and the pilot program is underway.

Conclusion

At MacKillop Family Services, we are committed to providing excellence in care. However, the overall culture of any agency needs to be the supportive and driving force that strives for accountability and professional dedication. As former Royal Commissioner Robert Fitzgerald AM said in his keynote at the MacKillop Family Services conference on 21 March 2018: "If in ten years' time, you have every policy and procedure in place, and you meet every mandatory standard, but you do not have a genuine culture of safety, then you will fail. What we have seen over the decades is that bad culture breeds bad conduct". We must all take responsibility for developing and sustaining healthy cultures where our values are lived and walked each day, and celebrate the people who are champions of excellence.

---

[22] R. Pratt and R. Miller, 2012. *Adolescents with Sexually Abusive Behaviour and Their Families: Best Interest Case Practice Model – Specialist Practice Resource*. Melbourne: Victorian Government Department of Human Services.

Hope – Our Engagement
with the Challenges

13

A Healthy Earth for a Flourishing Society: Implementing *Laudato Si'*

Mark Monahan

Leading into the 2018 Catholic Social Services national conference in Melbourne, on 21 February 2018, the conference sponsors hosted a forum entitled 'A Healthy Earth for a Flourishing Society: Implementing *Laudato Si'*'. It brought together many of the conference attendees and others interested in exploring implementation of Pope Francis' landmark encyclical, *Laudato Si'*.[1] The forum was facilitated by Jacqui Rémond, former National Director of Catholic Earthcare Australia and co-founder of the Global Catholic Climate Movement. The other presenters were Dr Miriam-Rose Ungunmerr-Baumann, an Aboriginal elder from Nauiyu (Daly River); Gavin Dufty, Manager Policy and Research at the St Vincent de Paul Society in Victoria; and Bronwyn Lay, Ecological Justice Policy Officer at Jesuit Social Services. This chapter captures the input at the forum of these four presenters and discussion of the topic by attendees.

Introduction

In preparation for the forum it become apparent that our Catholic Social Services community connects with ecological thinking, reflection and action in very different ways. Some consider that until we 'fix' our human community, we cannot look at the natural environment, while others find much grace in the support and friendship of

---

[1] Pope Francis, 2015. Encyclical Letter, *Laudato Si': On Care for Our Common Home*. Vatican City: Vatican, accessed at w2.vatican.va/.

a forest. The forum therefore aimed to welcome everyone along this continuum and challenge them to consider how they might further their response to the call of ecological conversion in Pope Francis' encyclical.

The language of 'our common home' recognises that our Earth community is not just made up of, nor dominated by, human beings, but rather it is an interconnected ecosystem, which includes all creatures, plants, water and our planet itself. Between these sub-groups exist intimate relationships, dependencies and a fine balance necessary to maintain a healthy ecosystem. Global warming has reached most people's consciousness, but now we are also starting to recognise links between the health of our planet and the health of our human communities.

Thus, the forum aimed to assist participants to connect Earth, culture and human flourishing, to consider how our organisations place themselves within Earth and our services could be more environmentally sustainable, and to increase understanding of how those already vulnerable within our community are impacted upon by environmental and sustainability issues such as rising energy costs. This chapter, like the forum, invites us to reflect on our personal situation, on our ministry's role and, lastly, on how the Catholic Social Services sector can champion this critical topic.

The first peoples of Australia, the Aboriginal and Torres Strait Islander Australians, have a rich wisdom to share as they have lived in relationship with Mother Earth for up to 80,000 years. They recognise that they belong to Earth, and through her keep connected to their tribe and spirit. So, we began the forum connecting ourselves to Earth led by Sheree Balcombe, Coordinator of Aboriginal Catholic Ministry Victoria. She encouraged us to look, feel and think through the prism of Earth, as she offered an Acknowledgement of Country and conducted a smoking ceremony. As she shared with us: "The smoking ceremony cleanses our hearts and minds so that at the beginning of the ceremony all people gather in unity".[2]

The Appeal of Pope Francis

The question at the very heart of *Laudato Si'* is "What kind of world do we want to leave to those who come after us, to children who are now growing up?" (n. 160). Pope Francis says:

> Everything is related, and we human beings are united as brothers and sisters on a wonderful pilgrimage, woven together by the love God has for each of his creatures and which also unites us in fond affection with brother sun, sister moon, brother river and mother earth. (n. 92).

> I urgently appeal, then, for a new dialogue about how we are shaping the future of our planet. We need a conversation which includes everyone, since the environmental challenge we are undergoing, and its human roots, concern and affect us all. (n. 14)[3]

The way that the encyclical is structured is dialogical.[4] The forum also sought to be dialogical to capture an array of knowledge, opinion, wisdom and ideas. So, to underpin a prophetic dialogue, the forum commenced with a brief overview of each chapter of the encyclical presented by Jacqui Rémond.

Chapter 1: What is Happening to Our Common Home?

The first chapter of the encyclical presents the most recent scientific findings on ecology in a way as to evoke the reader to listen to the cry of creation, "to become painfully aware, to dare to turn what is

---

[2] Aboriginal Catholic Ministry Lismore, accessed at acmlismore.org.au/pray/ceremonies/smoke-water-blessing/.

[3] Pope Francis, 2015, op. cit.

[4] Jacqui Rémond, 2018. "In Dialogue with Francis' Eco Manifesto", *Eureka Street*, 28(4), accessed at www.eurekastreet.com.au/.

happening to the world into our own personal suffering and thus to discover what each of us can do about it" (n. 19). We need only take a frank look at the facts to see that our common home is falling into serious disrepair: "If we scan the regions of our planet, we immediately see that humanity has disappointed God's expectations" (n. 61).[5]

Chapter 2: The Gospel of Creation

To address the problem illustrated in the previous chapter, Pope Francis offers a comprehensive view from the Judeo-Christian tradition. He articulates the "tremendous responsibility" (n. 90) of humankind for creation, the intimate connection among all creatures and the fact that "the natural environment is a collective good, the patrimony of all humanity and the responsibility of everyone" (n. 95).[6]

Chapter 3: The Human Roots of the Ecological Crisis

This chapter gives an analysis of the current situation, "so as to consider not only its symptoms but also its deepest causes" (n. 15), in dialogue with philosophy and the human sciences. Pope Francis says: "scientific and technological progress cannot be equated with the progress of humanity and history" (n. 113). Humans have become self-centered and no longer recognise their place in the world. This results in a 'use and throw away' logic that justifies every type of waste, environmental or human.[7]

Chapter 4: Integral Ecology

The heart of the encyclical's proposals is integral ecology as a new paradigm of justice. It "will help to provide an approach to ecology

---

[5] Pope Francis, 2015, op. cit.
[6] Ibid.
[7] Ibid.

which respects our unique place as human beings in this world and our relationship to our surroundings" (n. 15). "Nature cannot be regarded as something separate from ourselves or as a mere setting in which we live ... We are faced not with two separate crises, one environmental and the other social, but rather one complex crisis which is both social and environmental" (n. 139).[8]

Chapter 5: Lines of Approach and Action

This chapter addresses the question of what we can and must do. Analyses are not enough. We need proposals "for dialogue and action which would involve each of us as individuals, and also affect international policy" (n. 15). They will "help us to escape the spiral of self-destruction which currently engulfs us" (n. 163). Pope Francis states: "The Church does not presume to settle scientific questions or to replace politics. But I am concerned to encourage an honest and open debate so that particular interests or ideologies will not prejudice the common good" (n. 188).[9]

Chapter 6: Ecological Education and Spirituality

The final chapter invites everyone to an ecological conversion. The roots of the cultural crisis are deep, and it is not easy to reshape habits and behaviour, but education and training are the key challenges as "change is impossible without motivation and a process of education" (n. 15).

Pope Francis asks us all to "aim for a new lifestyle" (n. 203-208), to "bring healthy pressure to bear on those who wield political, economic and social power" (n. 206).[10] This thoughtfulness calls for a review of our lives and our organisations. Inequalities in our world, our throwaway culture and the gap between rich and poor are

---

[8] Ibid.
[9] Ibid.
[10] Ibid.

interconnected with our understanding of a common home. God is revealing himself to us all the time if we can hear and listen to the water, sand and movement of Earth. We often pray for human need, which is good and noble but not at the cost of Earth. Personal ecological change is not enough; we must also change our organisations. We must dialogue between faiths and cultures, especially with our Indigenous peoples. Ecological education is for everyone so that we learn about our ecosystems. We need to suspend our judgement and really listen to people and Earth; we must listen at a deeper level.

Dr Miriam-Rose Ungunmerr-Baumann's Insights

Dr Miriam-Rose Ungunmerr-Baumann, an Aboriginal elder from Nauiyu (Daly River), shared how to encounter deeply our spirit in relationship with Mother Earth. She spoke of each of us having an inner deep spring within us, which sometimes requires an awakening. "Sit still, be aware and listen – inner deep listening", she said. "Become aware of what's going on around you and how you belong". Ungunmerr-Baumann went further, saying we need to appreciate all things. We need to allow time to listen to Earth, to let it sink in. Aboriginal people do not speak so much as feel. The bush is like a book and Aboriginal people can read the signs. We do not own the land, we belong to the land. We need to be in rhythm with the land. Ungunmerr-Baumann's most poignant point, which she tried to ensure the gathering grasped was to "*slow down* and *connect*". She encouraged us to create space by changing the pace of our lives.[11]

Ungunmerr-Baumann offered some of the most profound words at the forum, so she would qualify to have a large section in this chapter devoted to her insights. However, her sharing embraced a lot of silence, modelling the value of listening – inner deep listening. To capture this in a book is challenging but readers are invited to

[11] For information on Dr Miriam-Rose Ungunmerr-Baumann and her foundation, see www.miriamrosefoundation.org.au/about-us/who-miriamrose.

sit, be present and listen. This type of 'tuning in' experience is often referred to as *Dadirri*. Ungunmerr-Baumann explained that she could not teach us *Dadirri*, because it is your being.[12]

Informed by Ungunmerr-Baumann's presentation, let us consider the following call to reconciliation with both Indigenous peoples and the land of Australia. It is from a report developed for a Jesuit Social Services' initiative on ecological justice, which is presented below:

> Aboriginal and Torres Strait Islander peoples' law and cultures are the oldest in the world and are inextricably linked to relationship with land as familial bonds. The dispossession of ancestral lands and cultural genocide has had devastating intergenerational social consequences. Viewing the circumstances of Aboriginal and Torres Strait Islander people through an ecological lens highlights how social disadvantage and marginalisation are caused by the loss of relationships with country. The forced severing of healthy familial relationships with land has had clearly negative impact on the wellbeing of Indigenous peoples, resulting in disadvantage and marginalisation that is reflected in disproportionately high incarceration rates, deaths in custody, low health indicators, low education rates, poverty and intergenerational trauma. Ecological justice in Australia, and within the community sector, requires recognition of this violence upon a people whose system of law and life was inherently ecological, and where social and environmental relationships were balanced. In Australia reconciliation needs to be with Aboriginal and Torres Strait Islander peoples, but also with the land of Australia that was taken from its original owners, and suffered from ecological distress as a result. Reconciliation with creation calls all Australians to heal the

---

[12] To begin an encounter with *Dadirri*, see www.miriamrosefoundation.org.au/about-dadirri/dadirri-film.

ecological injustices of the past that impact upon the present so we can care for our common home together.[13]

An Organisational Response to Ecological Justice

Jesuit Social Services commenced their journey of understanding
the relevance of ecology for their organisation in 2008. Bronwyn
Lay, Ecological Justice Project Officer, shared with the forum some
of this journey. A key discussion point for Jesuit Social Services
has been what to do with ecological justice when the organisation
is based on human justice. The word ecology was even considered
too complex for some and many within the organisation were not
culturally skilled so they struggled to find language to consider this
new topic or paradigm. Recognition of this triggered the board
and executive to spend time at the 'Bush Hut' considering the way
forward. The Bush Hut, located in Kew, is a heritage-listed house
in Melbourne located on the Yarra River and surrounded by native
bushland. Supported by the board, CEO Julie Edwards has been the
champion in pursuing this new paradigm of community services
delivery.

Jesuit Social Services recognised that there should be a shift
towards a 'just' relationship between humans and nature as one
cannot do one without the other. Furthermore, people have the
right to a habitat rather then than housing, which acknowledges that
humans are social beings and thrive within community settings. What
is often misunderstood is that this community setting must include
flora and fauna to provide a balanced ecosystem to which all earth
beings belong and in which they can grow together.

Laudato Si' (n. 44) states: "We are conscious of the disproportionate and unruly growth of many cities, which have become un-

---

[13] Jesuit Social Services , 2018. *Ecological Justice: Expanding the Conversation*. Melbourne: Jesuit Social Services, 6, accessed at jss.org.au/.

healthy to live in, not only because of pollution caused by toxic emissions but also as a result of urban chaos, poor transportation, and visual pollution and noise".[14] This quote sits perfectly with Lay's key comment above around having a habitat rather than housing. In this era with its challenges of population growth, housing affordability and homelessness, how do we approach the right for the whole Earth community to grow in partnership and balance? Furthermore, as noted above, some of the challenges to be addressed stem from the impact of eco-related issues on the vulnerable.

Ten years into this initiative, there has been a significant cultural shift within Jesuit Social Services. Ecological justice is part of the staff induction program. Many staff now work from an ecological social work model. Lay shared a story about staff on the way back to Melbourne from the Malmsbury Youth Detention Centre in rural Victoria, stopping at an appropriate place and letting the young people out of the vehicle to breath in the bush air. This helped with relationship building between a young person and their case worker and enabled these youth to find some solace in their circumstances through connecting with the natural world. Ecological justice is now easily spoken of at Jesuit Social Services. Figure 1 below is a tool that the organisation uses with staff to further their relationship with our natural world.

---

[14] Pope Francis, 2015, op. cit.

Figure 1: Jesuit Social Services' Ecology Practice Tips[15]

Ecology Practice Tips

PLACE AND IDENTITY

- Include place in assessments and eco maps of important relationships and places for participants.

- Picture a place where you have felt at peace, where you felt safe, where you have good memories, where you belong

- Close your eyes and visualise the place. Re-live the positive feelings it evokes for you. Breathe.

- Practise this so it's second nature when feeling stressed or anxious.

CARE FOR YOURSELF

- Exercise releases endorphins, our feel-good hormones. Encourage participants to dance, run, skip and walk.

- Learn relaxation techniques, and encourage meditation and mindfulness. Take big belly breaths, in and out.

- Take a mini break by picturing a calm place, while focusing on your breath.

- Plan ahead to stay calm – breathe deeply as you imagine calmly managing a typically stressful scene.

AWARENESS OF NATURE

- Spend time in nature – even looking out a window or at photos of nature can reduce stress.

- Walk with participants around their community – take time to notice the trees, sky and weather.

- Take time to be in the moment – when picking up participants on day of release from prison, celebrate, and see and feel the sun and air. These moments can be recalled at times of stress.

TALKING IN NATURE

- Use nature for difficult or reflective conversations with participants – take a walk, drive somewhere to sit and look, feel and hear your natural surroundings.

- Natural environments promote calmness and wellbeing – take a participant to a local green space and encourage conversation about what's around you.

- Use the Bush Hut for professional or family meetings.

- Give plants as presents.

Brought to you by the Practice Ecology Workshop at Jesuit Social Services – helping you make a strong personal and communal commitment to healing a broken world.

If you're keen to join a Practice Ecology Workshop, we'd love you to take part. Please check the Training Calendar for upcoming dates, or email Julie Boffa (julie.boffa@jss.org.au)

[15] Reproduced with the kind permission of Jesuit Social Services. For information on the Ecology Practice Tips, see jss.org.au.

A Case Study of Eco-Social Justice – Utility Prices and the Cost of Living

As an illustration of the impact of eco-social justice issues on the vulnerable, Gavin Dufty, Manager for Policy and Research with the St Vincent De Paul Society in Victoria, spoke at the forum about his work with the Society on researching utility prices and the cost of living.

The web of life has significant and complex systems operating within it. Many of these are human-made and one current focus is the right to access affordable energy. Affordable electricity, financing alternative power sources such as solar energy, and differences in provider schemes within each state and across the country are some of the parameters concerning what is now a significant political issue. The St Vincent de Paul Society has been active in this space, because, through its emergency relief provisions, it has recognised that access to electricity is a significant issue for many of its clients. Significantly, the St Vincent de Paul Society has observed that most people whose electricity is disconnected for non-payment of bills have children – these parents prioritise purchase of food for their family, triggering other problems such as electricity disconnection. Further, in their uncertain situation, these families often also face major social issues such as educational disadvantage, family violence, poor health, homelessness, exposure to violence, addiction issues and engagement with child protection.

Individuals and organisations have critical roles to play in caring for our common home. In particular, the Catholic Social Services sector can be influential in turning the tide so we flourish in a more sustainable world. To do this we must understand and engage with our social constructions, the political agendas and the market forces swirling around us. Proactively, the St Vincent de Paul Society has done this through a tariff-tracking project titled *The NEM – Time to Shed Some Light on This Market.*

The rationale for tracking changes to domestic energy prices has been to document price changes, analyse market developments and inform the broader community about bill impacts and potential savings to be made.

In our view, there is still a limited knowledge and understanding in the community of the various energy tariffs available, how they are changing, and how tariff changes impact on households' energy bills and energy affordability more broadly.

Only by improving this awareness and understanding can we ensure that the regulatory framework (for example, in relation to price information and disclosure) is adequate and promote a competitive retail market. Furthermore, this increased knowledge will allow for close monitoring of the impact price and tariff changes have on households' bills, and the affordability of this essential service.[16]

The NEM report details how energy prices are changing and the uneven price environment across the nation. Thus, Figure 2 below shows that regulated and standing offer prices (the base-rate) increased significantly in most jurisdictions over 2016/2017. Looking at longer-term changes, the chart also shows the increasing differences in electricity prices between jurisdictions. While South Australia had the highest prices in July 2009 and July 2017, and the Australian Capital Territory had the lowest, the difference between the annual bill for South Australian and Australian Capital Territory households (with this consumption level) was just $350 in 2009 compared to approximately $1,360 a year later.[17]

---

[16] Gavin Dufty and May Mauseth Johnston, 2017. *The NEM: Time to Shed Some Light on This Market.* Melbourne: Alviss Consulting and St Vincent De Paul Society, 5. The full report can be accessed at www.vinnies.org.au/.

[17] Ibid., 9.

Figure 2: Changes to Electricity Prices in Australia July 2009 to July 2017 as Estimated Annual Bills[18]

Chart 1 Changes to electricity prices in Australia July 2009 to July 2017 as estimated annual bills (nominal, inc GST) for electricity regulated/standing offers, 6,000kWh per annum, single rate

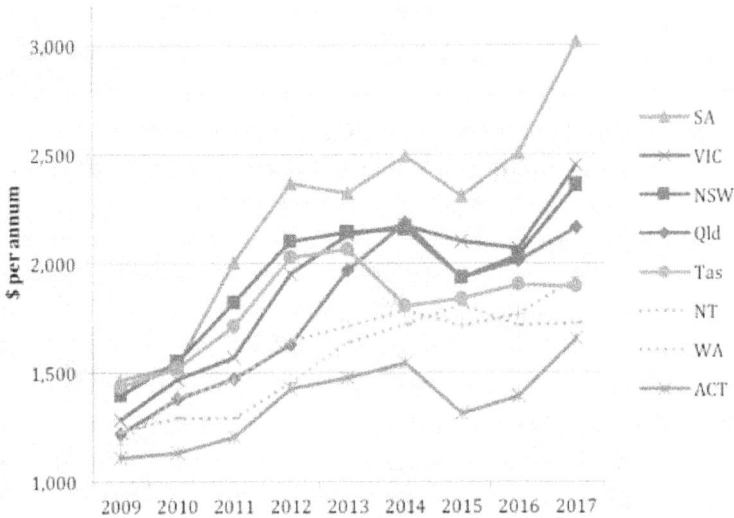

The report advises: "Electricity bills are made up of several components, including generation costs (wholesale market), network costs (distribution and transmission), 'green schemes' and costs associated with other public policy initiatives, and retail costs".[19] Within this complexity lies a number of issues of equity.

Households that invest in a solar system and batteries should receive differential electricity bills compared to those who do not. However, in an environment with ongoing increases in electricity prices, the take-up of solar power and batteries will, in all likelihood, continue to increase and the impact that this will have on those who

---

[18] Ibid., 10; diagram reproduced with the kind permission of the St Vincent de Paul Society Victoria.

[19] Ibid., 12.

cannot invest in such measures requires serious consideration. What is a reasonable return on investments such as roof-top solar panels and batteries? Do only direct users of the grid pay or will we need a 'grid levy' paid by all?[20]

As more consumers take up options such as solar power and batteries, there is a smaller cohort of people to fund the infrastructure (power poles, power stations and power lines) and ongoing maintenance of these assets. Renters are a significant part of this group. So, it is often those who cannot afford their own home and are renting, who are paying for this infrastructure. These population groups, in most situations, live from pay to pay. This seems to present an unfair balance where those that can afford solar power are 'leaving' the financing of infrastructure, which they still rely on as a back-up, to those that have a low disposable income and do not have access to alternative options such as solar power. How can we share the expense of maintaining our infrastructure more equitably?

There is a significant price-spread between electricity market offers in competitive markets. This price dispersion in itself is not necessarily bad. The negative impact of this price dispersion occurs when consumers are unable to identify better offers and therefore pay more than necessary.[21] Furthermore, consumers need to understand product differentiation clearly and easily with basic illustrations describing how bills can be lowered, enabling the consumer to make more informed choices. Barriers, such as the capacity to read English, the social confidence to visit a store and ask questions, or having access to a phone, the internet or transport to visit stores, are daily issues that prevent many people from accessing lower priced electricity. So, once again those who do not have limitations

---

[20] Ibid., 40.
[21] Ibid., 41.

in engaging in Australian society are privileged above those that have different levels of restrictions and preventers.[22]

Engaging with utility pricing, markets and the political nature of this area can create a force field restricting us from a heart-centred approach. However, Pope Francis is calling us to do just that, engage with cerebral matters from an ecological/heart-centred approach. The challenge is for us to explore how equity is paramount when considering sharing a resource such as electricity with all members of society. Furthermore, how can we all access adequate levels of energy without destroying our planet, without it harming our Mother Earth? Our Aboriginal brothers and sisters have reminded us that we do not own Earth, we belong to it. To engage with this particular issue of energy access, but also its related social issues, we must be formed in our thinking. We need to engage with our political partners in soulful conversation. To make a loud-enough noise to gain some traction, we must unite as a sector – mirroring a holistic ecosystem – so that we can collectively and effectively share our Earth-based opinions and recommendations.

Moving Forward

The Catholic Social Services sector is vast, and there is much work to do in our social service agencies.

Parishes too are an important part of our ecosystem, and some are already very committed to ecological conversion. In the lead up to the forum, some of them expressed the desire for conversations moving beyond further ways to recycle to seeking input and support around how to change hearts and lifestyles. This is an encouraging example of individuals and organisations embracing the call to be more progressive and intentional with Pope Francis' *Laudato Si'*. Further, thinking practically, some parishes also want to move from a

---

[22] The St Vincent De Paul Society has made resources available to help educate consumers about their electricity bills. These can be found at www.vinnies.org.au/page/Our_Impact/Incomes_Support_Cost_of_Living/Energy/.

situation of each developing its own resources to looking at having a central point for shared resources.

In the spirit of being proactive and sharing some productive ways of moving forward, the following actions are offered to groups of all shapes and sizes:

- watching Catholic Earthcare Australia's video: *Laudato Si' – An Urgent Appeal for Action,*[23]
- celebrating the World Day of Prayer for the Care of Creation, which Pope Francis has introduced on 1 September each year and the Season of Creation, which commences on that day,[24]
- starting a garden in at your home, school, parish or office and connecting with "our common home",
- considering where your investments are placed and inviting your organisation to start divesting from fossil fuels,
- gathering parishes to reflect further and discuss collective actions.

Pope Francis's issuing of *Laudato Si'* on "care for our common home" has been a blessing for us all. It has provided us with an opportunity to become more connected with our earth, with our Indigenous peoples, with our community, with the people we serve who are on the margins of society and with our God. This journey starts with our own inner spring and finding ways to nurture it. We have an opportunity to lead within our community agencies where ecological practice can be embedded in our services. As a sector, we have the opportunity to recognise the strength of our own "web of life", and use it to address inequitable systems that not only hurt our brothers and sisters, but also our common home – Mother Earth.

---

[23] The video can be accessed at www.youtube.com/watch?v=IcP5E2trsX4.

[24] For information on the World Day of Prayer for the Care of Creation, see catholic-climatemovement.global/world-day-of-prayer/.

14

Emerging Issues in Not-for-profit Governance

Elizabeth Proust AO

Context

The challenges facing not-for-profit organisations, particularly faith-based agencies, have rapidly been escalating over the past ten years. Service provision regulations, requirements relating to charitable status, organisational size, financial viability and sustainability, changing government funding models, mergers and amalgamations, the competitive fund-raising environment, and the professionalisation of boards, are just some of the issues that are more frequently being addressed by governing boards.

Add two major concerns for Catholic not-for-profit organisations – the Royal Commission on Institutional Responses to Child Sexual Abuse (Royal Commission)[1] and the need constantly to re-examine the meaning and application of 'mission' – and the issues facing boards of governance seem almost insurmountable.

The pace of change is unlikely to ease, so what further challenges to governance will there be in the future? How can organisations 'governance-proof' themselves and be proactive in understanding and addressing future concerns?

Elizabeth Proust AO is a highly regarded company director and currently Chair of the Australian Institute of Company Directors. She has held chief executive positions in government and corporate

---

[1] For information on the Royal Commission into Institutional Responses to Child Sexual Abuse, see www.childabuseroyalcommission.gov.au/.

sectors over many decades, and was Vice Chair of the Catholic Church's Truth Justice and Healing Council.

At the 2018 Catholic Social Services national conference, Proust led a workshop on 'Emerging Issues in Not-for-profit Governance' which explored governance issues for the not-for-profit sector, including the role of the Australian Charities and Not-for-Profits Commission (ACNC).

Proust's expanded opening address is reproduced below together with a summary of the discussion from the floor about governance issues with which workshop participants are currently dealing.

Emerging Issues in Not-for-profit Governance

When I consider the emerging issues in not-for-profit governance, I feel there are three particular areas on which not-for-profit boards should be reflecting this year. It is these three that I would like to canvass with you:

- the issue of culture and trust, not only of major importance to not-for-profits but for many types of our major institutions,
- the role of not-for-profits and advocacy, particularly for charities with Deductible Gift Recipient (DGR) status, and
- the need for not-for-profits to make a profit.

Trust and Culture

The 2017 Edelman Trust Barometer[2] found that 53 per cent of respondents believe the current overall system, that is the key institutions of government, business, media and not-for-profits, has failed them. They believe the 'system' is unfair and offers little hope

---

[2] For information on the 2017 Edelman Trust Barometer, see www.edelman.com/trust2017/.

for the future. Indeed, only 15 per cent believe the current way of doing things is working. An assumption amongst many is that this fall in trust is isolated to the social pillars of government, business and the media. But the not-for-profit sector has not escaped unscathed.

The report found that barely half of Australians, at 52 per cent, have trust in the not-for-profit sector. While this is a better result than trust in government which declined from 45 per cent to 37 per cent and trust in the media which fell 10 points to 32 per cent, it still represents a decline in trust of five points for the not-for-profit sector compared to 2016.

The trust of the community in the not-for-profit sector is not merely 'a nice to have', it is a 'must have'. Trust in the sector – in its reputation, its service delivery – is absolutely vital. The sector relies on community trust for donations, volunteerism and support. It also matters in indirect ways, for example, in supporting the role of the sector in advocating for causes, to which I will refer later.

As community leaders, we need to understand that trust is in decline and act with that in mind. There are no simple answers but ignoring valid concerns and fears will only worsen the credibility and trustworthiness of the organisations we lead. It imposes on us the need to be creative and consistent in the way we listen to, and respond to, other stakeholders, and in a way that builds and strengthens trust in our sector.

Many of you will no doubt have seen negative press about the practices of fund-raisers. Misspent money, dubious employment arrangements and aggressive face-to-face solicitations – sometimes referred to as charity 'muggers' or 'chuggers' – are undermining the community's trust and confidence in the sector. It is one thing to consider the immediate need for funds. But, if we are to act as long-term custodians, it is incumbent on us – on boards and directors – to ensure and to demonstrate a level of ethical behaviour that gives confidence to the broader community.

Linked to the issue of trust is the issue of culture. The concepts are often conflated, particularly in the media, and I will try not to do that here. Obviously though when matters of poor culture become public they further diminish trust. Culture, to me, is a key driver of how people behave when no-one is watching and is a central force in the formation of an organisation's ethics.

The Australian Institute of Company Directors (AICD) *2017 NPF Governance and Performance Study*[3] showed how critically important a strong culture is, but it also indicated how poorly that culture was being monitored in many organisations. It found that while not-for-profit directors overwhelmingly believed their organisations had good culture, few were taking proactive steps in managing culture.

Most directors gave a resounding endorsement of their organisation as a place to work, with more than 70 per cent saying they would be very likely to recommend their organisation to friends and family. At the same time though, fewer than half (45 per cent) of the directors surveyed said the culture of their organisation was clearly defined and formally embedded in their systems and policies.

Even among the group of directors who said that their organisation's culture had been clearly defined and formally embedded, most said that oversight at the board level was minimal. Indeed, of this group:

- 36 per cent reported that culture had not formally been part of their agenda for 12 months,

- 29 per cent said that their board did not receive reports, or set organisational key performance indicators (KPIs), based on culture, and

[3] Australian Institute of Company Directors (AICD), 2017. *2017 NFP Governance and Performance Study: Building Long-term Strength.* Sydney: AICD, accessed at aicd.company-directors.com.au/advocacy.

- nearly half (46 per cent) said that culture had been discussed at the board level at least five times in the last 12 months but, importantly, only when it arose in regard to other matters.

Overall, more than half of directors surveyed said that culture was not formally part of the board agenda in the last 12 months, while 48 per cent said that they had not received any reports on organisational culture in the same time period.

These results show that in the not-for-profit sector there are many boards that are not actively overseeing and monitoring culture. If 2017 showed anything, it was that organisational culture must be a key concern for boards. While many of the cultural issues that made the headlines related to harassment and unsafe workplaces in the corporate sector, there is nothing to stop such destructive cultures appearing in the not-for-profit space.

Indeed, the desire to continue working towards a greater good could have the harmful effect of causing an employee or volunteer to put up with an unhealthy or poor culture. In other respects, a poor culture could result in people turning a blind eye to someone committing fraud, of which unfortunately we also saw too many cases in recent years in the not-for-profit sector.

The AICD teaches that in setting the tone from the top, directors must lead, support and encourage an appropriate culture for their organisations. They also need to create a culture of disclosure, where bad news travels to the top and employees feel empowered to come forward if something is sour.

Given the significance of culture to an organisation's success, a good culture must be driven and supported by the leadership of those who govern. The board, which sits at the apex of organisational governance, must play a critical role in defining and monitoring culture. Like other areas of governance, such as strategy, understanding the organisation's culture, and bringing about change to that culture if needed, has to be an ongoing process where the board and management work together in a shared responsibility.

The most recent AICD *Director Sentiment Index*[4] revealed that the vast majority of directors (92 per cent) are putting in either substantial or some effort to change culture within their organisation. Directors are tackling this issue in a variety of ways:

- capturing data on key cultural indications,
- communicating the ethical positions of their organisations to staff, and
- ensuring it is a regular item on their board and audit committee agenda.

I believe this shows evidence of a move towards a greater focus on culture by boards, both within and outside of the not-for-profit sector, than we have seen in the past.

Charities and Advocacy

An emerging issue, indeed a potential threat, to the not-for-profit sector in 2018 is the Federal Government's focus on the undertaking of advocacy by charities. This is along with the broader review of the Australian Charities and Not-for-profits Commission (ACNC).

Advocacy has been an important part of the work of the charity sector since its earliest days. However, the Treasury's consultation on Tax Deductible Gift Recipient Reform in the latter half of 2017 looked at a number of potential regulatory options, such as mandating a maximum percentage of a charity's resources that could be devoted to advocacy activities if it were to maintain DGR status.[5]

---

[4] AICD, 2017. *Director Sentiment Index: Second Half 2017*. Sydney: AICD, accessed at aicd. companydirectors.com.au/advocacy.

[5] For information on the Tax Deductible Gift Recipient Reform consultation, see treasury.gov.au/consultation/tax-deductible-gift-recipient-reform-opportunities.

The AICD does not support requiring additional information from charities about their advocacy activities. We strongly believe that this would create a significant regulatory burden without public benefit. Indeed, information about how a charity pursues its charitable purpose, including through any advocacy activities, is already required through the ACNC Annual Information Statement. This information is likely to be sufficient for the purposes of determining whether an entity is maintaining its entitlement to access DGR status.

Advocacy is both a legitimate charitable purpose under charity law as well as an important part of the contribution made by the not-for-profit sector to the community. The AICD is concerned that proposals to impose limitations or additional reporting burdens regarding advocacy activities may diminish the capacity of the sector to perform its important role in public life. The advocacy role of not-for-profits is an essential part of Australian civil society. Public debate and public policy making would suffer immensely without the expertise, knowledge and perspective of our not-for-profit and charity sector.

The experience of those who work hand in hand with disadvantaged communities or on the front lines of our most pressing social issues is invaluable. Their advocacy role gives voice to the voiceless on matters of public importance and provides crucial insights to the media and decision makers. The role and right of charities to continue their important advocacy role, without facing financial hardship or overly complex regulatory hurdles, must be protected.

Financial Stability – Not-for-profits Need to Make Profit

"Not for profit organisations do need to make profit". Susan Pascoe, former Commissioner of the ACNC, made this comment at the launch of the 2016 NFP Governance and Performance Study, *Profit is Not a Dirty Word.* For a not-for-profit organisation, profit is the foundation of building the long-term confidence needed for the organisation to achieve its purpose. As Pascoe also noted, "Not for profits can and do make profits. But a not-for-profit's profit is retained by the organisation and applied to achieving its mission, rather than distributed to individuals for their private benefit".[6]

One of the recurring themes that emerges from the annual NFP Governance and Performance Study is the misconception around the need for not-for-profits to be financially strong, and the continuing evidence that approximately half of all not-for-profits are not financially strong.

Because of this continued theme, the 2016 study focused specifically on the topic of financial performance. That year, over 1,800 directors from a diverse range of not-for-profit organisations participated in the study, making it the largest survey of not-for-profit governance in Australia. What the survey found was that:

- about two-thirds of directors (64 per cent) reported that, on average, their organisation made a profit in the last three years,
- one in five (20 per cent) reported breaking even, and
- 14 per cent reported making a loss.

Their outlook for the coming year was less positive:

- 59 per cent of surveyed directors reported their organisation will make a profit, one quarter will break even, and
- 17 per cent expected to make a loss.

Significantly, of the directors that reported making a profit, a quarter reported profits of less than three per cent, an amount that would barely cover inflation. That is alarming because what those results told us was that directors were saying the capacity of their

[6] For details of the study's launch, see aicd.companydirectors.com.au/membership/the-boardroom-report/volume-14-issue-8/profit-is-not-a-dirty-word.

organisation to meet their purpose will, in real terms, shrink moving forward. Not-for-profits can survive a loss in a single year, or even for a few years, but unless they have a reliable benefactor, over the long-term, they must make a profit to survive.

What these data indicate is that although some not-for-profits are making a profit, the profit is often insufficient for long-term survival. If profit does not exceed inflation, an organisation is effectively making a loss and will need to draw down on assets to continue to operate in the longer term. Boards and directors need seriously to consider their roles and drive the cultural change necessary to support the long-term financial strength of their organisations.

Not-for-profits making a profit can be a challenging concept for government and the broader community but, without long-term financial strength, the sector will not be able to deliver vital services or its mission. This is most starkly the case in the disability care sector, which is facing a profound shift in its funding model from one that has traditionally been block-funded by government to one that is now expected to generate revenue from clients. This development has major implications, not just on cash flow but also on the whole business model of needing to market services and to make them attractive over those of other service providers.

All not-for-profit directors do need to consider their fundamental role as stewards for the long-term health and sustainability of their organisations, and a core part of that duty is ensuring the financial stability – not just in this year's accounts – but that there is future financial stability including the capacity to reinvest and enhance the organisation and its resources.

Conclusion

There is no doubt that the whole area of corporate governance is changing. For many organisations in the not-for-profit sector, it must feel like they are facing a tsunami of change. While this may be the case, there are also amazing opportunities to harness this change to achieve great outcomes for the organisations and their beneficiaries, and to deliver on their respective missions.

This will require directors with the right skills and dedication to match the passion they have for the cause. Without such skills on boards, the coming change may wipe out some great organisations.

Workshop Discussion

The issues that arose from participants at the workshop expanded on the themes discussed by Elizabeth Proust, and also highlighted other governance matters being dealt with by not-for-profit boards. The following summarises some of the main themes of discussion from the workshop.

Culture

The topic of the board's responsibility for culture raised a particular issue about the difficulty for boards of being in a position to understand and measure the culture of the organisation. How can a board be expected to understand the culture of an organisation when a board member may be at a meeting once a month whereas management is there day-in and day-out? Board members are often not in a position to see practical behaviour in their organisation, and are often reliant on management to 'read' and understand the culture and report to the board.

Among the many tools that could be used to understand culture, staff engagement surveys help boards to recognise 'hot spots'. These reports can be presented as 'traffic light' reports and include verbatim comments from staff. This issue also goes to the point of how a board sees its responsibility. Is it only monitoring the 'bottom line', signing off on accounts, or does the board see its responsibility in a broader light? What 'walking around' does the board do?

It was also recognised that measuring culture is difficult for an organisation. Therefore, the skills set of a board encompassing professionals who understand human resource dynamics, diversity, etc., is very important and can contribute to the board's understanding in the area of culture.

Catholic Identity and Mission

Catholic identity, mission and governance were raised by several participants, particularly highlighting the difficulty of promoting mission in an organisation when often many staff members have no background as Catholics at all. Sharing the mission and the vision of the organisation becomes critical for organisations and boards must be prepared to lead this.

A further current challenge can be the reputational damage to which some Catholic organisations might be exposed because of the Royal Commission. However, it was also noted that strong Catholic identity and mission can be capitalised on and support a strong culture in organisations, as well as Catholic mission and identity being a point of difference from non-faith-based or for-profit organisations.

On the issue of governance and mission, the AICD Company Directors Corporate Governance Framework[7] outlines the practices (skills, attributes and expertise) that comprise good director practice. One participant felt that no matter how small or large, AICD governance guidelines should apply to all not-for-profit organisations, to ensure that board members understand that they are signing on to best practice models of governance. The difference for faith-based boards is that directors also sign up to the mission of the organisation, with its elements of respect, the dignity of all, and compassion. So, boards need to understand best practice guidelines *and* understand mission.

---

[7] AICD 'Company Directors Corporate Governance Framework', accessed at www.companydirectors.com.au/director-resource-centre/corporate-governance-framework.

Transition to New Governance Models

Some of the issues raised by participants related to models of governance – often specific to Catholic organisations – under which boards are governing. For example, some Catholic-based organisations operate under charters that may not reflect current governance best practice. Further, some bishops or religious institute leaders who have carriage of responsibility for such organisations have no experience or understanding of governance best practice, because this is not their area of expertise.

It was noted too that many organisations have made the transition from the previous boards of management to new types of governance that, while more sophisticated, may come with many implications. For example, the creation of ministerial public juridic persons (PJPs), at the instigation of religious institutes so that the laity can continue the congregation's works, can also lead to blurring of the lines of accountability. The danger is that there might be duplication of decision-making at the levels of PJP trustees and board directors, or some decisions might 'fall through the cracks', so trustees and boards must work out such governance arrangements carefully.

The future of unincorporated associations as a model of governance was raised, and while it was accepted that there is still a place for unincorporated associations, this type of governance is declining. Most such bodies are subject to both federal and state laws, which adds complexity, in addition to the fact that some are advisory, and some have no fiduciary responsibilities, and therefore the 'blurring' of accountabilities also exists here.

Similarly, a federated model, where organisations have state boards and an over-riding national board, can be complicated, as can models of governance which have either staff or geographic representation on boards. While none of these might be seen to be particularly best practice, the important point is that there must be clarity around board responsibilities and accountabilities.

The Wider Not-for-profit Environment

Other issues of importance in the current not-for-profit environment were brought up as 'watch this space' for boards to monitor. Governments for some time have been outsourcing what previously were core government services such as child care. With the introduction of the National Disability Insurance Scheme (NDIS), there are major challenges for the not-for-profit sector because, in effect, governments are expecting more services for less cost.

The danger of this type of model is that it moves the risk from the government to the not-for-profit sector. We may see that the gap in funding is pushed onto the organisation, meaning that those entities will need to 'dip' into their reserves to retain services, or alternatively those services risk becoming second-rate. This development may become an unacceptable situation for some organisations in the future and they might choose to take a stand and withdraw their services.

A further challenge in the 'watch this space' context is the future of the Australian Charities and Not-for-profits Commission under the new Commissioner, Dr Gary Johns. There is no certainty in which direction the ACNC might head but, under the past Commissioner, Susan Pascoe, there was a positive relationship with the AICD. Not-for-profits make up 40 per cent of the director membership of the AICD and the latter sees a responsibility to monitor and comment on issues affecting the sector. Three years ago, an AICD not-for-profit forum was formed covering geographical areas, sectors and size, and it is hoped this group will continue to have traction with government.

Thirdly, there will be ongoing impact on Catholic not-for-profits in relation to the recommendations of the Royal Commission. The safety of children is paramount, and the impact particularly in relation to professional standards and working with children, with the additional responsibility and compliance requirements, will be ongoing.

Concluding Comments from Elizabeth Proust

The whole area of corporate governance, not just for the corporate sector but the not-for-profit sector too, is evolving. We are seeing significant and sometimes ideological changes being made by funding bodies, government or regulators, and the erosion of trust in the four sectors of government, business, media and not-for-profits at a level that has not been seen here and overseas in the past ten years.

Put these factors together, and overlay that with the impact of the Royal Commission, then the levels of trust and suspicion are such that it will be harder in the future for not-for-profit organisations. Certainly, dedication to your organisation and its mission will be important factors in steering through those difficulties, but none of these developments are short-term trends that will evaporate. I think the demands of government, increased accountability, and lack of trust, mean that board directors need to be alive to many more things than they faced in the past.

So, with more accountability, more onerous responsibility, and often less funds, this space requires dedicated people who not only understand their own organisations and the sector but also understand the community and the global factors at work, which will change and disrupt what we are doing. Some of these factors, like those relating to the Royal Commission, may be self-inflicted for organisations, while many others are outside their ability to control. I believe that it is up to umbrella bodies like Catholic Social Services Australia and the AICD, and your own boards, to be alive to the changes, and to advocate to government, because the changes with us now and emerging are very significant and the impact of change is unlikely to abate any time in the foreseeable future.

15

Priorities in Governance of Catholic Organisations

Gabrielle McMullen AM and Des Powell AM

The Church has a three-fold nature of "proclaiming the word of God, celebrating the sacraments, and exercising the ministry of charity". Each of the Church's social service, education, health and aged care ministries exemplifies the Church's "ministry of charity", which is indispensable to the nature of the Church.[1] In "exercising the ministry of charity", these ministries continue the mission of Jesus, responding to the invitation to be His presence to those served. Thus, in their calling to ministries of governance and stewardship, board directors and trustees of Catholic agencies have a further dimension to their responsibilities beyond those of their counterparts in non-faith-based entities.

This chapter focuses on the governance and stewardship of Catholic ministries. It complements the previous chapter of this volume entitled 'Emerging Issues in Not-for-profit Governance', which addressed the civic context in relation to governance in the not-for-profit sector. In considering the roles of board director and trustee of Catholic organisations, the chapter identifies these as the ministries of governance and stewardship, respectively. From this perspective, formation for mission emerges as an essential element in undertaking the roles. The chapter then goes on to explore more deeply the identity of a Catholic organisation, with reflections and

---

[1] Pope Benedict XVI, 2005. Encyclical Letter: *Deus Caritas Est*, n. 25, accessed at w2.vatican.va/.

case studies relating to authenticity, and a mission-centred focus on managing risk relating to the mission-business nexus, succession planning and board practice.

Governance and Stewardship as Ministry

The Ministry of Stewardship

Catholic social service, education, health and aged care agencies have been established by a variety of Church entities – dioceses, parishes, religious institutes and *ministerial* public juridic persons, each of which is defined in Church or Canon Law as a public juridic person (PJP).[2] A PJP is a legal entity under canon law that allows ministries to function in the name of the Catholic Church. Those ultimately responsible for dioceses, parishes, religious institutes and ministerial PJPs are the bishop, parish priest, congregational leader and trustees, respectively.

In recent years, religious institutes have instigated the creation of ministerial PJPs, a pioneering model of sponsorship and of lay leadership for their ministries to ensure their continuation as works of the Catholic Church. Thus, the ministerial PJPs provide for long-term continuation and development of the ministries. Most importantly, in continuing Church ministries and the works of the instigating religious institute, a PJP serves the needs of the disadvantaged and marginalised. At any given time, a group of trustees is 'missioned' to sponsor a PJP's ministries. Unlike the other models of stewardship undertaken by bishops, parish priests and congregational leaders, the trustees of ministerial PJPs follow a collegial model of stewardship.

---

[2] A *juridic person* is the Church's canonical equivalent of a corporation and is set up for one or more specific purposes. Each juridic person functions through designated physical persons (e.g. trustees) who serve as its representative according to its approved statutes. A *ministerial* PJP represents the Church in the same way that religious institutes do. Such entities are called *public* juridic persons because their ministries are formally sanctioned by a Church authority and carried out publicly under its auspices. *Ministerial* PJPs have the role and responsibilities of stewardship of ministries, enabling the ministries to relate directly to the Church; Gabrielle McMullen, 2017. "One Mission, Many Ministries", *Mary Aikenhead Ministries Journeys*, 10(4), 1-2.

Thus, in their role, trustees exercise the *ministry of stewardship* (as do by bishops, priests and congregational leaders in the other contexts). The trustees' role is a 'calling' to what is technically titled 'canonical stewardship' and the trustees (canonical stewards) have both Church (canonical) and civil responsibility for the ministries entrusted to them. In exercising their ministry of stewardship, trustees delegate to incorporated and other entities the governance of specific ministries.

The Ministry of Governance

The *ministry of governance* is exercised by the board directors of Catholic agencies. In governing as directors of Catholic ministries, they develop a strategic direction to ensure that the facilities flourish, exemplify contemporary best practice, and crucially remain faithful to continuing the mission of Jesus. Directors need to 'interiorise' their ministry's mission, vision and values[3] and ensure that the mission is "the senior partner driving and permeating *all* decisions in the business side of facilities".[4]

Effective ministry of governance and stewardship is underpinned by a responsiveness to the "signs of the times"[5] to ensure that the ministries are developed and adapted to meet the needs of the contemporary Church and society. Thus, board directors and trustees oversee the evolution of the ministries whilst exercising vigilance to ensure harmony with their heritage and discernment about their 'refounding'[6] to ensure that they continue to serve the mission of Jesus. These roles for lay members of the Church affirm Vatican II's "vocation of the laity":

---

[3] Gerald Arbuckle, 2016. *Intentional Faith Communities in Catholic Education: Challenge and Response*. Strathfield, NSW: St Pauls Publications, 212.

[4] Gerald Arbuckle, 2007. *Crafting Catholic Identity in Postmodern Australia*. Canberra: Catholic Health Australian, 84.

[5] Pope Paul VI, 1965. *Pastoral Constitution on the Church in the Modern World: Gaudium et Spes*, n. 4, accessed at www.vatican.va.

[6] Gerald Arbuckle, 2013. *Catholic Identity or Identities? – Refounding Ministries in Chaotic Times*. Collegeville, MN: Liturgical Press.

modern conditions demand that their apostolate be broad-
ened and intensified … making the laity ever more conscious
of their own responsibility and encouraging them to serve
Christ and the Church in all circumstances.[7]

Some 50 years after the Council, this vision is flourishing in lay
people accepting and performing the roles of board director and
trustee of Catholic agencies (and in taking on many other Church
ministries including as executives and in pastoral and service roles).

Formation for Ministry

As highlighted above, in addition to their civil and corporate responsibilities, board directors and trustees of faith-based agencies carry
significant responsibilities on behalf of the Church. Critical to the
future of Church ministries and effective succession planning is:

> the degree to which these lay leaders are appropriately
> recruited, formed and supported to fulfil their wide-ranging
> responsibilities. Formation encompasses the variety of ways
> people are assisted to grow in the knowledge, skills, self-
> awareness and disposition necessary to fully appreciate and
> serve the vision and purpose of the Catholic mission and
> ministry.[8]

Without a significant commitment to, and investment in, formation
for the stewardship, governance and leadership roles of Catholic
ministries, their vision, ethos and culture risk:

> being assimilated into the contemporary cultural milieu
> … Should such mission and cultural drift occur, Catholic
> services would cease to be authentic and prophetic witnesses

---

[7] Pope Paul VI, 1965. *Decree on the Apostolate of the Laity: Apostolicam Actuositatem*, n. 1, accessed at www.vatican.va.

[8] Catholic Health Australia (CHA), 2013. *Governance and Leadership of the Mission: Towards a 10-Year Plan*. A discussion paper prepared for the conference, 'Stewards of the Mission', 15-16 April. Canberra: CHA, 3, accessed at www.cha.org.au/.

Priorities in Governance of Catholic Organisations

on behalf of the Church to the Gospel vision and so lose their fundamental mandate and their reason for existence.[9]

Board directors and trustees need to be qualified to take responsibility for both the civic and canonical aspects of their role and then, through induction and ongoing formation, be supported to:

be accountable for mission, as well as actively discern what is contrary to the mission. To be effective, leaders will need the confidence and commitment to communicate effectively within and beyond their organisations and foster relationships within their local Church.[10]

In the following section, we explore and deepen understanding of the ministries of governance and stewardship through the consideration of case studies. The three thematic sections below consider issues faced by many contemporary ministries. They seek to relate to situations which may be typical of readers' own environments. The specific themes addressed are:

- deeper understanding of the identity of a Catholic ministry,
- authenticity of a Catholic ministry,
- managing risk.

Des Powell, who was Chair of Edmund Rice Education Australia (EREA) from 2005-2012 and since 2015 has been Chair of MacKillop Family Services, brings his observations and experiences in those roles to the case studies relating to each theme.

Deeper Understanding of the Identity of a Catholic Ministry

The essential factor in being effective in governance and leadership roles within the Church is to have a deep understanding of the identity

[9] Ibid., 6.
[10] Ibid.

233

of the organisation. This is core to ensuring the decisions taken truly reflect the mission intent. While such roles are very much a personal journey, the board chair and members have clear responsibilities to realise mission intent. Significantly, we can often bring to our ministries the critical element of reflective practice. Further, formation and governance forums and participation in immersion experiences and pilgrimages deepen our understanding of mission and reflective practice, and can also impact upon the individual in a very personal way.

There is, as well, a wealth of resources which assist in understanding a ministry's Catholic identity. These can include foundation or theological statements from the establishing Church agency or religious institute, statements from assemblies, chapters and other critical events, and agency charters if they exist. An understanding of Catholic Social Teaching principles is also a key point of reference.

EREA Charter for Schools in the Edmund Rice Tradition

The first example of deepening insight into Catholic identity relates to the *EREA Charter for Schools in the Edmund Rice Tradition* which articulates the essence of those education ministries.[11] It is more than 200 years since Edmund Rice commenced his first school for boys in Waterford, Ireland, 150 years since Br Ambrose Treacy cfc stepped onto the dock at Station Pier in Melbourne and started the Christian Brothers Australian network of schools, and twelve years since the commencement of Edmund Rice Education Australia (EREA). The charter was one of the key foundation documents developed prior to the formation of EREA to document expectations of Catholic schools operating in the tradition of Edmund Rice.

A few years into EREA's operation and with the new entity well established, a process was put in place to review the charter and this

---

[11] *EREA Charter for Schools in the Edmund Rice Tradition*, accessed at www.erea.edu.au/about-us/the-charter.

included seeking feedback from all key stakeholders. This process led to a revised charter as a means to deepen understanding of EREA's 'touchstones' – namely liberating education, inclusive community, Gospel spirituality, justice and solidarity – and to guide EREA into the future.

The charter, together with EREA's three documents on Foundations, Formation and Renewal, describes the ministry's distinct, though not unique, identity as Edmund Rice Education Australia. It provides a practical expression of this identity and so is of crucial use in decision-making, planning and review.

The renewed charter continues to use the four touchstones to describe the culture of a Catholic school in the Edmund Rice tradition that is striving for authenticity. These touchstones provide ideals demonstrably linked with the charism which underpins the ministry in EREA schools and educational endeavours. They help define the direction and goals as, following Blessed Edmund's vision, EREA continues to reflect and to seek to make the Gospel a living reality in its communities.[12]

Catherine McAuley's 'Sucipe'[13]

Here we recount an example of an experience which Des Powell found stimulating in deepening his understanding of the ministry of governance, namely Catherine McAuley's *Sucipe*:

> While on a Mercy Leadership programme in Dublin, I had been impacted in conversations with Sisters of Mercy by their humility, their earthliness and great sense of serving those most in need. During the programme we were asked to go to the heritage centre library and read some of the letters and prayers Catherine wrote as the founder of the Sisters of

---

[12] Ibid.

[13] *Susipe* (Latin – receive) is the name given to a prayer by Catherine McAuley, as explained in this section.

Mercy. It was there that I came across her *Suscipe*, in essence a letter written prior to her death, often referred to as her act of resignation -

My God, I am yours for time and eternity.

Teach me to cast myself entirely

into the arms of your loving Providence

with a lively, unlimited confidence in your compassionate, tender pity.

Grant, O merciful Redeemer,

That whatever you ordain, or permit may be acceptable to me.

Take from my heart all painful anxiety;

let nothing sadden me but sin, nothing delight me but the hope of coming to the possession of You

my God and my all, all in your everlasting kingdom. Amen.

For me, this experience reinforced the notion that faith in God above all else is central to the Congregation and clearly the cornerstone of the faith of the Sisters of Mercy. But here we are in 2018 and with lay leadership and a different society from Ireland in the 1830s. It leads one to think how we make decisions in our ministries – with ultimate trust and faith in God?

I saw this as personally insightful in thinking about how we lay people need fully to appreciate the faith of the founders' ministries that we now steward. In doing so, are we conscious of whether each decision taken is consistent with the Gospel?

Authenticity of a Catholic Ministry

A critical consideration for Church agencies is how to assess whether their organisations are effective Catholic ministries. It could be likened to mission 'accreditation', given many Catholic agencies undergo other forms of accreditation relating to their service delivery of education, health, aged care and/or community care ministries.

EREA School Renewal

The first example to illustrate a range of ways mission 'accreditation' could occur is from the EREA context and its approach to education as set out in the EREA *Charter for Schools in the Edmund Rice Tradition.* Since its inception EREA has required its schools to participate in a five-year renewal programme. School Renewal in Edmund Rice Schools is a life-giving process by which a school community is helped to reflect critically on its nature as a Catholic school in the Edmund Rice tradition and to identify ways for continuous improvement. The objective of renewal is positive change for the school community.[14]

Renewal is activated within the context of the Gospel and the charism of Blessed Edmund Rice as expressed in Church and EREA identity documents, particularly the *Charter for Catholic Schools in the Edmund Rice Tradition.* The core aspects of identity, expressed in the four touchstones of the charter, form the lens through which the school is invited to look at its policies, structures, practices, culture and relationships. The outcomes of the renewal journey are used by the EREA Board in the process for the school being accredited as an authentic Catholic school in the Edmund Rice tradition.

School renewal is not a process of inspection or checking adherence to curriculum or legislative requirements. These areas are monitored through school registration processes managed by other bodies. School renewal focuses on authenticity of Catholicity and charism, with schools focussing on how they see the charter being a lived reality within the school.

Schools are supported in renewal by the EREA Identity Directorate which briefs the school community through the school leadership team and board, and provides an external panel to validate the reflection process undertaken by the school. The

---

[14] *School Renewal in Edmund Rice Schools,* accessed at www.erea.edu.au/our-schools/school-renewal.

panel writes a renewal report, incorporating recommendations including regarding accreditation as a Catholic school in the Edmund Rice tradition, to the EREA Executive Director and Board. Two crucial phases follow. The first is holding a special event at the school to receive the renewal report and celebrate the renewal journey undertaken and ongoing accreditation. The second is implementation of the outcomes of the renewal process by incorporating recommendations into ongoing school planning and reporting processes.[15]

MacKillop Family Services Research Project

A recent project at MacKillop Family Services (MFS)[16] offers a second example of 'taking the mission temperature'. As part of the MFS strategic planning process in 2017, it was important to do some research into how its staff, clients and other stakeholders experienced MFS services. Did MFS activities still reflect the ministries' intended mission, and did they demonstrate the core values of the founding religious institutes, the Sisters of Mercy, the Christian Brothers and the Sisters of St Joseph?

The MFS Board's approach was to do research across the organisation as to the link between the services' values and MFS behaviours and to assess what characteristics were noticed in the way the Board, leaders and staff work. The process undertaken included extensive data collection and the analysis of that data against a framework of the founder's heritage for each of the three Congregations, the role of Mary MacKillop in the organisation, the foundation values of MFS, and the history of MFS over its first 20 years. Significantly, the research confirmed faithfulness to the

---

[15] Ibid.

[16] MacKillop Family Services was formed in 1997 by the Sisters of Mercy, the Christian Brothers and the Sisters of St Joseph and is a leading provider of integrated services to children, young people and families. For information on MacKillop Family Services, see www.mackillop.org.au/history.

founders' vision for MFS, and board, leader and staff 'behaviours' aligned with the mission and values of the organisation.

The two examples presented above demonstrate that there are different ways to assess the authenticity of a Catholic ministry. The important point is that such assessment happens and is embedded in the agency's planning processes.

Managing Risk for Mission Effectiveness

Importantly, managing risk in a Catholic agency is not simply a matter of stepping out in faith! Assessment of risk must be an undertaking based on the agreed strategic direction, with proper appraisal as to the accountabilities, costs and organisational capabilities and conducted with some rigour and due process.

The environment today means many agencies work with government. It is mandatory that they have a formal risk framework and ensure their boards are supported by Quality, Audit and Risk, and Ethos and Ethics committees in focusing the board directors on the processes and systems for which they have responsibility. Boards also need to consider how internal and external audits can assist in attesting to the effectiveness of their systems and processes.

Three examples of managing risk to ensure mission effectiveness are now considered.

The Mission-Business Nexus

A common issue is how Catholic agencies bring mission into financial considerations. Two examples are provided where mission and identity have influenced financial decisions.

The first is MacKillop Family Service's (MFS) funding of its Heritage Centre which provides an essential link back in time to past clients of the services of the three founding religious institutes.[17]

---

[17] For information on the Heritage Centre, see www.mackillop.org.au/heritage-and-information-service.

The Heritage Centre has over 700 contacts each year for family connections and other reasons. It is a focal point of the MFS commitment to those who have used the services in the past. While it is a significant cost centre in terms of space and staff resources, reducing its services would never be considered as a means of cost-cutting. Rather, given the high level of expectations of maintaining contact and information appropriately into the future for clients, the service will need to grow, with its funding increased. Therefore, a proportion of MFS income from investments is allocated annually to this Centre due to its centrality to the MFS mission.

As a second example of the mission-business nexus, we consider the EREA schools' co-responsibility funding policy. This requires a contribution by all schools to agreed common good objectives as part of mission. It is collected via an annual levy of which an agreed proportion is allocated for new and emerging mission matters, including funding of flexible learning initiatives for those most at the margins and for other projects similarly aimed at addressing disadvantage. The process is institutionalised into the EREA budget framework.

Succession Planning

Another key area of mitigating risk is appropriate board succession planning. By way of example and building on a previous initiative in 2010, MacKillop Family Service (MFS) addressed board succession planning in 2015 by advertising externally for members which created a high rate of expressions of interest from New South Wales and Victoria.

The initiative involved the MFS Members (Trustees) and Board Chair firstly agreeing on the process, which started with identifying the skills and characteristics required in light of the turnover that was about to occur through retirement of existing board members. The external advertising through congregations, ministries and *The*

Catholic Weekly website resulted in over 60 expressions of interest. Information sessions were then held in both states, where the MFS story was told, roles and responsibilities were outlined, as were expectations of the time commitment. Following that step, applicants were asked to indicate if they wished to go to the next stage. Panels made up of Trustees and Board members were then established for considering applications for Board and committee roles.

It was a time-consuming effort over five months and required considerable resource support, specially to explore with the candidates their own sense of faith and its compatibility with MFS values. However, the result was three new Board and six committee members, who brought a broad mix of skills, diversity of backgrounds and age, and in some senses new life to MFS governance. Three years later, some of those committee members have now 'graduated' to Board membership. Of the nine who formed a new link with MFS, all are still involved.

Board Practice Manual

A further useful tool for minimising risk is a board practice manual for the reference of board members and recruiting new directors. Thus, MFS utilises the 2017 revised *MacKillop Board Practice Manual* which has the following contents:

- outline of the governance framework in operation,
- roles and responsibilities of the board and its code of conduct,
- relationship to the constitution,
- selection, induction and development of board members,
- specific sections for the roles of chair, deputy chair, committee convenors and congregational nominees,
- committee roles and terms of reference.

The important message of these case studies is that, across the Catholic education, health and aged and community care sectors, there are examples of practices and instruments that can be implemented effectively. Further, there is generally willingness to share resources. Networking with other agencies and their trustees and boards is a means of discovering how you can tackle the important drivers addressed above to ensure effectiveness in the governing of a Catholic agency.

Conclusion

The roles of trustee and board director are critically important for ensuring that Church agencies faithfully continue the ministry of Jesus in the 21st century. Trustees and board directors must guide their ministries to respond to the "signs of the times" so that they are developed and adapted to meet the needs of the contemporary Church and society, while remaining true to their heritage. These respective ministries of stewardship and governance see the laity playing an increasing role in the Church as envisaged by Vatican II.

16

Love of Neighbour – What are Our Parishes Doing?

Bob Dixon

Parish communities are called to reach out in service to those in need. In many ways, they can reach parts of the community that professional service agencies cannot. In this chapter, we look at the range of social service activities carried out by Australian parishes, and consider in some detail a few examples of the services offered by specific parishes.

One source of information about the social service activities carried out in parishes is the National Church Life Survey (NCLS).[1] In 2016, 277 parishes participating in the National Church Life Survey replied to a question about whether the parish provided or ran any of a number of social services or social action activities (see Table 1). Results showed that more than three-quarters of the responding parishes offered emergency relief and material assistance (77 per cent) and carried out some type of visiting (82 per cent), whether it be to visit institutions such as prisons or hospitals, or simply parishioners. More than a third offered counselling or similar services (35 per cent) and were involved in political action or social justice activities (35 per cent). About a quarter of the responding parishes offered aged care services such as Meals on Wheels and support activities for migrants and refugees.

---

[1] The National Church Life Survey is a research project undertaken every five years since 1991 by NCLS Research to collect data on church attenders and local church leaders. It is a joint venture sponsored by a number of Australian churches that provides an evidence base to help churches enhance their vitality and connect with the wider community; see www.ncls.org.au/.

Table 1. Data on Responses to the NCLS Question: "In the past 12 months, did this parish provide or run any of the following social services or social action activities?"

Activity type	Parishes that ran this activity in the past year (%)
Emergency relief/material assistance	77
Visiting (e.g. prisons, hospitals, parishioners)	82
Counselling services	35
Political/social justice activities	35
Aged care services such as Meals on Wheels or home help	25
Migrant/refugee support activities	23
Care for the disabled	18
Community development/local resident action groups	15
Accommodation for the aged (nursing homes, aged-care units)	13
Children or youth support	11
Animal welfare/environmental care	11
Services or activities for unemployed people	7
Other welfare/service/action	36
Other accommodation (e.g. crisis accommodation)	15

Source: NCLS 2016, Operations Survey for Catholic parishes. These results are for a total of 277 parishes, made up of 149 parishes that completed and returned Operations Surveys out of 195 selected in a national random sample, and a further 128 parishes that chose to take part in the survey. Results from the two groups were combined in this table for reasons to do with sampling adequacy and data quality. This means that the results apply accurately to the 277 parishes that responded to the Operations Survey but cannot be assumed to apply accurately to all 1,323 parishes in Australia. This limitation does not apply to the results for Mass attenders that appear in the following tables.

Around one in every seven parishes provided some form of care for the disabled or accommodation for the aged or infirm, and a similar number were engaged in community development or local resident action groups. Just over ten per cent of parishes reported that they offered children or youth support services, and animal welfare and environmental activities, but only seven per cent reported offering services or activities for unemployed people.

All of these 277 parishes carried out at least one and usually several of the listed activities, or reported that they carried out or provided activities and services other than those listed. Ironically, however, although all Catholic parishes are active in at least a small way, and often a big way, in the provision of social services, only a relatively small proportion of the people who go to Mass in the parish contribute to the provision of those services.

Table 2. Data on Responses to the NCLS Question: "Do you regularly take part in any parish activities reaching out to the wider community (e.g. community service, social justice, welfare, outreach, evangelisation)? (Mark ALL that apply)"

Activity type	Mass attenders (%)
Yes, in outreach or evangelisation activities	7.3
Yes, in community service, social justice or welfare activities of this parish	19.1
Our parish has no such activities	9.6
I am not involved	67.3
Total	**103.2**

NCLS 2016. N = 23,725. The total exceeds 100 per cent because respondents could select more than one option.

In the 2016 NCLS, Mass attenders in a random sample of 191 parishes were asked about their participation in the activities of their parish that reach out to the wider community. Table 2 shows that just 19 per cent of Mass attenders have any involvement in their parish's community service, social justice or welfare activities. Two-thirds (67 per cent) said they were not involved and a further 10 per cent said that their parish had no activities of this type. Since Table 1 suggests that the provision of some type of social service activity appears to be virtually universal among parishes, and since their fellow attenders at the same parish rarely agreed with them, it appears that those in the last group are simply uninformed about their parish's activities.

Mass attenders who are involved in parish activities reaching out to the wider community – whether the activities be related to evangelisation (such as the RCIA, Rite of Christian Initiation of Adults) or of a social justice or community welfare nature – are also more likely than their fellow attenders to be involved in all types of groups that are not connected to the parish. Seventy-two per cent of those who are not involved in parish activities are also not involved in other types of community groups, whereas three-quarters of those who are involved in parish outreach of some type are also involved in community service or social action groups outside the parish. This is particularly noticeable for such activities outside the parish, where those who are involved in their parish's activities are more than four times as likely as those who are not to be involved in non-parish community service or care activities (50 per cent compared to 11 per cent) and social action (13 per cent compared to three per cent). What we do not know is if active parishioners are inspired to get involved in wider community activities, or whether people who are involved in wider community activities are also likely to become involved in their parish's activities, or whether people join both parish and non-parish community welfare and social justice groups because of some third factor that cannot be identified from these results.

Although the data show that many Mass attenders are not involved in community welfare or social justice activities either in their parish or in the wider community, this is not to imply that they take no action of a social justice or community welfare nature. Table 3 shows that Mass attenders who have some involvement in parish or non-parish community service or social justice activities and those who have no such involvement do carry out informal acts of service and charity on a casual, personal basis. Nevertheless, those who are involved in community welfare or social justice types of activity, whether they be parish-based or in the wider community, are more likely to have carried out informal acts of service than those who are not so involved. Moreover, less than two per cent of those who are active in any field of community welfare or social service have not carried out any of the listed informal acts of service in the past twelve months, whereas the corresponding figure is almost six per cent among those who are not involved in parish or community-based services or activities. It seems, then, that the desire to be of service can be detected in multiple aspects of a person's life: those who are active in parish-based community welfare and social justice activities are also more likely to be involved in non-parish-related activities of the same nature and to carry out a range of informal acts of service than those who are not involved in parish-based activities.

Examples of Social Service Activities in Parishes

The NCLS data about the sort of social service activities that parishes conduct are necessarily grouped into general categories such as those shown in Table 1. To see the details of actual activities, we have to look at specific parishes, something that we can do with the help of the Building Stronger Parishes project. The focus of the Building Stronger Parishes project[2] was on the exploration of successful

---

[2] For information on the Building Stronger Parishes project, see www.buildingstronger-parishes.catholic.org.au/.

Table 3. Percentage Who Have Done Any of the Following Informal Acts of Service in the Previous 12 Months by Involvement in Parish or Non-Parish Community Welfare or Social Justice Activities

Informal acts of service	Involved in parish or non-parish community welfare/social justice (%)	Not involved in parish or non-parish community welfare/social justice (%)
Lent or gave money to someone outside your family	56.3	45.3
Cared for someone who was very sick	39.5	28.7
Helped someone through a personal crisis (not sickness)	46.4	33.6
Visited someone in hospital	59.0	44.3
Given some of your possessions to someone in need	46.5	34.3
Tried to stop someone abusing alcohol or drugs	12.7	9.9
Donated money to charity	83.5	73.2
Contacted a parliamentarian or councillor about a public issue	20.8	8.3
None of the above	1.5	5.8
Total	**366.2**	**283.4**

NCLS 2016. N = 20,656. The total exceeds 100 per cent because respondents could select more than one option.

initiatives in parishes around Australia, with an emphasis on how these parishes have used their available skills and resources to develop programs or activities to overcome certain challenges. Fieldwork for this project involved a visit by members of the project research team to twenty parishes around Australia between 2010 and 2013. In what follows, we shall refer to these as the 'BSP parishes'.

All twenty of the BSP parishes had developed successful programs or initiatives in some dimension of parish life. Here we mention just a few of the many successful programs or activities that numerous BSP had developed in the social service area. These parishes were conscious of their cultural context and tailored their efforts to suit.

Providing Food to Those in Need

Providing food to those in need is a service offered by many parishes. This can be a large-scale service such as that offered through Sacred Heart Mission in St Kilda, which grew out of an initiative of St Kilda West parish in the Archdiocese of Melbourne. But it can also be small-scale and still make a difference. Numerous BSP parishes found unique ways of adapting this idea to meet the needs of their community and provide food to needy people. For example, Albany Creek parish in the Archdiocese of Brisbane has a group that hands out food cooked by parishioners to anywhere from 20 to 100 homeless people every Saturday night. Mount Isa parish (Diocese of Townsville) has a volunteer kitchen service run on a roster basis that provides meals for the prisoners in the local watch house. Shepparton parish (Diocese of Sandhurst) set up a soup kitchen in partnership with a local Muslim man; volunteers from the parish run it several times a week. In another variation of this idea, Cororooke parish (Diocese of Ballarat) has an informal food bank, with meals cooked by parishioners, that are made available to families suffering bereavements or with sick children.

Empowering Women

Many BSP parishes found ways to empower women and bring them together. These groups and initiatives took on different forms in different parishes. Perhaps the most direct approach was the "Mum's Cottage" project initiated by Sugarloaf parish in the Diocese of

Maitland-Newcastle. Mum's Cottage is a centre where young mothers can drop in and find some company to talk to or share problems with. It has ecumenical dimensions as well; although a project of the Catholic parish, the centre is situated in a Uniting Church building. The centre offers counselling, advocacy, and a host of other services and activities to all mothers in the community, not just Catholics.[3]

Myall Coast Parish, also in the Maitland-Newcastle Diocese, has several women's groups that have been highly successful in engaging and empowering women of all ages. These include the "Yummies for Mummies" playgroup that assists young mothers in the community to establish social networks within a relaxed and supportive environment, and the "Wrap with Love" knitting group that meets fortnightly in an atmosphere of fun and friendship to make colourful wraps and blankets that are distributed through aid agencies within Australia and throughout the world.[4]

There were many other social service type activities run by BSP parishes that could be listed here, but space precludes us from doing so. Instead, we will turn to two particular parishes that have been active in providing important but different types of social services.

South Yarra Parish

South Yarra Catholic parish,[5] consisting of St Joseph's and St Thomas Aquinas Churches, is located in the very heart of one of Melbourne's major urban revival areas. It stretches from Prahran and Windsor, with the eccentricities of Chapel Street and its stylish restaurant and cafes, to the new apartment buildings popping up along the Yarra River to accommodate the young professionals who want to live close to their city centre offices.

---

[3] For information on Mum's Cottage, see www.mumscottage.org.au/.

[4] The Myall parish website provides further details; see www.myallcoastcatholicparish. org.au/.

[5] The South Yarra Catholic parish website provides further details; see parishofsouth-yarra.org.au/.

South Yarra has it all, with easy access and a variety of services, but it also has a large community of marginalised and disadvantaged people who are either homeless or who live in high-rise public housing. The area is in desperate need of concentrated emergency relief support and this has been the case for some years.

The Augustinian priests who staff the parish have always looked for different ways to support the needy, and some early attempts, more than 20 years ago, included placing a refrigerator on the priory veranda from which those in need could take food and bread, and also making available a room in the outside laundry building, where sleeping rough at least meant a clean room with a bathroom attached.

Things began to change in 1998 when a group gathered in the Botanical Hotel to discuss how to make things better and to do something positive about homelessness in the area. Thus, the St Joseph's South Yarra Emergency Housing Association was established with the organisation registered as a not-for-profit, with DGR (Deductible Gift Recipient) and tax exemption status, so very important when raising money. The group wanted to work to overcome poverty in the community and to provide those in need with emergency housing while they waited for their public housing applications to be processed. At first, the group worked on organising the facilities previously managed by the priests, but then the St Joseph's Parish Primary School was closed due to the reduction in the number of students and a new era commenced.

The Association took the opportunity to create an emergency housing centre, and from 2002, when the school was closed, until 2008, it was able to establish 12 fully furnished self-contained transitional housing units plus one crisis unit. It was a mammoth effort and many members of the organisation put a lot of time into bringing this idea to fruition. However, this effort was not without pain and even though the Association was able to raise the funding for the refit of the old school building, operating the units and the additional outreach services was putting a big strain on the finances of the priests and the parish. As with many parishes, Mass attendances were dwindling, as was revenue from the parishioners, and finding additional funds to support the outreach services was becoming very difficult.

Once more, a group met, probably at the Botanical Hotel again, and a new plan was formed. The Association would change its name to accommodate all the outreach services provided by the parish and, as a registered not-for-profit, this new organisation would be able to support the parish by renting the building, paying for the goods distributed and paying a service fee to the parish for the administrative services provided by the parish team. The outreach services have been maintained, but the costs of operation are now not the responsibility of the priests or the parishioners of the South Yarra parish.

The new organisation, St Joseph's Outreach Services Inc. (SJOS), immediately started to create new initiatives and provide new opportunities to ensure the sustainability of the project, which now included the 12 transitional housing units, the crisis centre, a Food Store and a Bread Bank. As SJOS pays a service fee to the parish, the residents of the SJOS units are all encouraged to use the facilities of the parish environs, whether it be the new community garden where fresh produce for the Food Store is grown, or the family playground located in the gardens of the Parish Centre.

SJOS is now associated with HomeGround Real Estate Agency,[6] a division of Launch Housing. This relationship offers SJOS the services of a part-time support worker who works with the residents and their case workers to help them find the best long-term

---

[6] Details of the HomeGround Real Estate Agency can be accessed at www.home-groundrealestate.com.au/.

permanent public housing option available. Forced into emergency crisis accommodation by domestic violence, a financial crisis, family break-up, loss of employment and/or health issues, these formerly homeless people often stay in the SJOS units for a transitional period only. This gives them time and security in which to apply for public housing, as well as to deal with other problems in their lives. SJOS also provides a designated unit, supported by the Brigidine Asylum Seeker Support Group, to accommodate asylum seeker families and refugees.

The SJOS team of over 50 volunteers maintains these units as well as the Food Store, through which food parcels are distributed. SJOS collaborates with SecondBite to provide fresh produce every Sunday, and the Food Store, open three days every week, provides a 10-item food parcel to those in need on a monthly basis. Three times every week, volunteers also collect bread for freezing from local bakeries to support the 24-hour Bread Bank, from which people can take a supply of bread and rolls for their family needs.

The Association's core values are SHELTER | OPPORTUNITY | SUPPORT and they drive the outreach services provided. Just as people come to SJOS from many different cultural and ethnic backgrounds, they also come for many different reasons. The SJOS volunteers are the backbone of the organisation and they work diligently to assist many who are homeless and disadvantaged through a period of difficulty. These volunteers provide a 'can do' spirit at all times in order to ensure that the services are always available, providing friendly assistance and a happy face. SJOS is meeting the challenge of providing outreach services outside of the financial confines of the parish, while allowing those in the parish, plus others from surrounding areas, to participate in a comprehensive and sustainable range of outreach services for the marginalised and disadvantaged in the community. It is true "love thy neighbour" spirit.

Montmorency Parish

St Francis Xavier's Parish, Montmorency,[7] is a middle-class parish in the north-eastern part of Melbourne. It has a weekend Mass attendance of about 450 people, and two parish primary schools, Holy Trinity (with an enrolment of around 400 children) and St Francis Xavier (330 children). There is some good energy and some good life around the place, and the parish has developed an extensive range of social service activities.

Philippines Outreach

The parish has a long-standing involvement with the Philippines that started with one couple, who had adopted three Filipino children and established an extraordinary network of connections with various communities, and who suggested that the parish run a social immersion visit to the Philippines. The idea took off and the parish is now up to about its twelfth or thirteenth immersion visit. Over 100 parishioners have visited the Philippines, including some Grade 6 children from the schools. The parish's main project is the support of two schools in Cebu. Parishioners sponsor many of the children from these schools to assist them in their education, and the parish's two schools, Holy Trinity and St Francis Xavier, have also provided sponsorship and held fund-raising events in order to send educational supplies to the schools in Cebu. Working through an agency called Kadasig Aid and Development, the parish has also assisted the Cebu community in very many other ways – for example, through the provision of solar lights to supplement a very limited electricity supply, purchasing goats and pigs to help support families, helping the community to purchase land for housing, and sending clothes, educational supplies and medical supplies such as bandages. The parish also has projects in Manila; these include supporting an

---

[7] The St Francis Xavier's parish website provides further details; see sites.google.com/site/sfx3094/.

orphanage, a nurse who works with burns victims, and Columban Missionary Fr Shay Cullen, the founder of PREDA, an organisation that rescues children from human traffickers and paedophiles.[8]

Sacred Heart Mission

The current parish priest of Montmorency, Fr Terry Kean, was previously the parish priest of West St Kilda parish, the home of Sacred Heart Mission, where three-course meals are served to hundreds of people every day. When he arrived in his new parish, it was suggested to Fr Kean that he might be able to find a small group of parishioners to serve as volunteers at the Mission, perhaps once a month. Within two weeks, 100 people had volunteered! Now, eight years later, there are still 107 volunteers on the list and that means Montmorency parish can provide the Mission with volunteers every Sunday.

Other Projects

After Pope Francis' encyclical *Laudato Si'* came out, the parish was contacted by a woman from one of the Montmorency community groups who asked if there were any plans to hold a conversation on the encyclical and, if so, whether local community groups including other churches could join in, as she believed it was an encyclical for everyone and not just for the Catholic community. Her suggestion was taken up by the parish's excellent social justice group and led to the formation of a group called the Community Coalition for Caring for our Common Home, made up of representatives from a wide range of community groups in Montmorency and surrounding suburbs. The group has held two seminars and formed a group to study *Laudato Si'*.

The parish has made a contribution to the Eltham Refugee Project, conducted by CatholicCare Melbourne and St Vincent's

---

[8] For information on the PREDA Foundation, see www.preda.org/.

Health Australia, by completely furnishing and equipping four units in a 24-unit residential centre now occupied by refugees from Syria and Iraq, a contribution made possible by the very generous donations of parishioners. Another collection in the parish resulted in 223 good quality warm coats being delivered to the Salvation Army for distribution to asylum seekers and refugees.

These are just some of a long list of social service programs and activities that Montmorency parish sponsors or is involved in. In all these activities, parishioners have observed how much they themselves have learnt and benefited from the experience of contributing their time and energy in the service of others.

Conclusion

Research carried out through the National Church Life Survey (NCLS) has found that almost all Catholic parishes provide some type of social service, with many parishes providing diverse services to parishioners and to a range of different groups within the local community. Many of these activities depend on the effort and enthusiasm of parish leaders, especially the parish priest, and are supported by only a relatively small number (19 per cent) of the Mass attenders in the parish.

NCLS results also show that those parishioners who are involved in parish-based community welfare and social justice activities are also more likely to be involved in non-parish-related activities of the same nature and more likely to carry out a range of informal acts of service than those who are not involved in parish-based activities. This is evidence in support of the impression that it always seems to be the same people who get involved in social service type activities, regardless of whether those are parish-based or non-parish-based, or simply informal acts of charity and service.

While NCLS results can show us a broad picture of the type of social service activities carried out by parishes, they do not provide much detail about the activities and services themselves. For that we have to turn to sources like the Building Stronger Parishes research and other accounts from individual parishes like those from South Yarra and Montmorency. We see that successful initiatives are often inspired by the enthusiasm and vision of one person or a group of people. These initiatives expand and develop when other people also become enthused, when they are supported (but not necessarily driven) by the parish priest and other parish leaders, and when they become structured in some way, for example, by having a definite location or program. Often, too, successful initiatives involve not just providing services *to* someone, but providing services *with* someone, as in the case of ecumenical programs offered in collaboration with other churches, or services provided in association with local government or other community groups.

At a time when Mass attendances are, in general, declining and attenders are ageing, it will become more and more difficult for parishes to offer effective social service programs and activities. There is an opportunity here, then, for Catholic social service agencies to connect with parishes in order to offer support and expertise. Very few of the parishes that took part in the Building Stronger Parishes project reported that any of their social service activities were conducted in association with a Catholic social services agency. Yet there is much to be gained from strengthened collaboration between parishes and Catholic social service agencies; such collaboration can deepen and broaden the work of the Church in reaching out to vulnerable and marginalised members of the community.

17

Hearing Healing Hope – A Reflection

Paul Bongiorno AM

There was no escaping the brutal context of this year's national conference of Catholic Social Services. No matter the good work that the Church's many agencies and volunteers in parishes do, they have all been tarnished by the overwhelming evidence of failure accumulated by the Royal Commission into Institutional Responses to Child Sexual Abuse.

The conference organisers chose to put the detailed discussion of the Royal Commission on the last morning of the conference. My first reaction was that this was putting the cart before the horse. But I was wrong. The five-year unfolding of tragic woe was not news to any of the 250 or so participants who turned up. What they needed was a strengthening of their faith. It was the eminent theologian Hans Küng who posed the question: "Can the Catholic Church save itself?" His answer in light of the election of Jorge Mario Bergoglio as Pope Francis was: "Yes".

It is "yes" if the Church faces up to the reality of its own structural distortions of the Gospel it is charged to announce. The Royal Commission set up by a Prime Minister who professed atheism was initially dismissed as a resurrection of old anti-Catholic bigotry and sectarian suspicion. Instead, it became a clarion call to 'metanoia', a change of heart, a conversion to the truth of our own appalling inadequacy. We all knew this was coming in the Friday session of the conference and Commissioner Robert Fitzgerald did not pull his punches. A committed and informed Catholic himself, he reminded us all that the "evidence of failure was overwhelming".

Fitzgerald, however, was no Savonarola, the Renaissance monk burned at the stake in Florence for his demanding a Christian renewal of the Church after condemning the hierarchy. No, he said, "Part of the Church does get it. Does understand it and is committed to child safety". He said the "Church has two aisles. Your side of the aisle and the other side". He stopped short of nominating who they are, the Commission's report leaves no doubt – they were bishops, priests and religious superiors who turned a blind eye, who covered up and who were captured by institutional loyalties, ambitions and ignorance of the harm they were doing.

The Commission has sixteen far reaching recommendations for the Catholic Church specifically and they do go to cultural and practical changes which at their root can only be implemented if the Australian bishops argue the case strongly to the Pope. The experience of many delegates is that this is a bridge too far. After more than thirty years of rampant clericalism and a dampening of the reform and renewal spirit unleashed at Vatican II, many have lost hope.

That is where the contributions of Phil Glendenning in his opening keynote address and the briefing from Lana Turvey-Collins were a powerful antidote.

Glendenning refused to allow scepticism or even cynicism to paralyse him. He said, "Cynicism is an eloquent form of surrender". From a room full of people who do exercise and show leadership already, he encouraged perseverance: "I believe that this post-Royal Commission time offers a real opportunity for liberation and redemption for the Church in Australia. The truth sets us free, and this ugly truth had been hidden for too long".

Turvey-Collins' task was harder. She had to convince delegates that a new age of transparency and consultation was upon us. She has been appointed by the bishops to co-ordinate and facilitate participation in the 2020 Plenary Council. At face value, Canon Law makes it primarily a bishops' and clerics' affair with the laity – male and female – an afterthought. In itself, this is hardly the sort of body capable of meeting the challenges of a root and branch response to the renewal of the Australian Church. It looks more like "physician heal thyself".

But Turvey-Collins is undaunted. She assured us that "anything can be talked about" in the nationwide consultation leading up to the synod. She warned those inclined to hold back "if we don't engage, no change will come about". She spoke of the *"sensus fidei"*, the Catholic doctrine that says the 'sense' or understanding of all the baptised shapes the belief of the Church. She did caution that not everybody will get everything they want. Those aching for change can only hope that the collegial attitude of Pope Francis will inspire our bishops. More to the point, we should pray that this Pope lives long enough to sustain this atmosphere of openness and accountability.

The forum on 'Economics for a Flourishing Society' had the conference looking beyond the Church walls. Catholic social justice teaching, based as it is on the Gospel option for the poor, is the motivating idea for the Church's social services. Senior Director of Strategic Operations and Economic Policy at Catholic Social Services Australia, Joe Zabar, firmly rejected any downplaying of Australia as an unequal society. He rejected the now unfashionable idea that if you look after the rich the benefits will trickle down to the poor. In this he was firmly on the side of Pope Francis, if not of our current Government – a point he made strongly with a series of rhetorical questions like, "How is it that we require students to carry the burden for undertaking tertiary studies, while allowing multinational companies to construct their financial affairs to pay little or no tax in Australia? Or permit the Government to provide business tax relief while implementing cuts to welfare payments and supports?"

Zabar and Federal Labor MP Clare O'Neil met determined push back from John Roskam, Executive Director of the Institute of Public

Affairs. Roskam said the "most equal societies are the poorest". Real inequality, he said, is between "those in jobs and those out of jobs". He quoted economist Milton Friedman dismissing concerns over the adequacy of the minimum wage by having a more competitive market for jobs.

Of course, this world view does little to address issues like Indigenous dispossession, boat people's indefinite detention, domestic violence, inter-generational poverty or disability, both mental and physical. As Gledenning reminded the conference, "You won't hear the Gospel at the centre, go to the fringes". And that is where Catholic social services agencies are already going. In doing so, the men and women, both professional and volunteer, who staff or run Catholic agencies give meaning to the saying often attributed to St Francis of Assisi: "Preach the Gospel and sometimes use words".

The conference did not shirk facing up to the challenge, the Church and Australia faces, but in coming together delegates were able to take heart from their fellow labourers in the vineyard of the Lord.

18

Liturgies, Spirituality and Mission

Denis Fitzgerald

Responding to the Gospel call to love of neighbour was at the heart of the *Hearing, Healing, Hope* conference and this response is, for many, a spiritual undertaking.

In light of this, a pattern of prayer and reflection was, as on previous occasions, built into the structure of the conference and its documentation: A smoking ceremony and associated welcome and reflection commenced the initial session of the conference on the evening of 21 February; each of the following two days started with a liturgy; the conference Mass on the Thursday drew together many of the themes and aspirations of the gathering; the conference dinner that evening, built around the fourth Mary MacKillop Oration, was an opportunity to consider the faith-related dimensions of hearing, healing and hope from another perspective; and a closing liturgy on the Friday focused on closure as a stage towards future directions.

Once again, on this occasion, the integration of the spiritual into the gathering sought both to inform our work, and to provide a lived experience that participants could draw on back in their workplaces. Feedback on this integration was very positive. And because of this connection of mission and spirituality in the conference as a whole, prayer and spiritual grounding were also a feature of a number of the specific presentations.

Fr Andy Hamilton SJ is a poet and theologian at the service of the community. The conference organisers turned to Fr Andy to capture in words the sentiments and intentions behind the theme of *Hearing, Healing, Hope*. Fr Andy composed a Conference Prayer that exceeded expectations, with each line highlighting some aspect of our multi-faceted mission:

> God of hearing, God of healing, God of hope,
> tune our ears to hear the cry of the abandoned,
> delight our eyes with the glory of your world, our home,
> gentle our hands to embrace one another
> and dress the wounds of those mugged at the roadside.
>
> We call to mind St Mary MacKillop and our other prophets,
> who taught ragged children,
> who cared for the penniless sick,
> and spoke for the silenced.
>
> May the seed of the Gospel germinate within us,
> may it flower in thanksgiving and forgiveness,
> give grain for the harvest of justice,
> and leave seed for a sustainable world.
>
> God of hearing, God of healing, God of hope,
> may we, who gather here, walk in Jesus' way.

The conference proceeded in that spirit, as a gathering of a pilgrim people seeking to respond to the call of the Gospel in a complex and sometimes challenging environment.

In his keynote address Phil Glendenning spoke a lot about hearing, and about hope, and he summed up the challenges facing many in our community:

> It is easy to become cynical when we consider the state of
> the world and, with the notable exception of Pope Francis,

the state of the world's leadership. But I have always held
that cynicism is just an elegant form of surrender, and the
one thing we must not do in the light of challenges we face
is surrender.

Glendenning then articulated a challenge for the Catholic Church
in Australia, to "stand up for, and be seen to stand up for, the weakest,
the poorest and those who are most vulnerable because of their
race, ethnicity, beliefs or health", failing which "we would be a sad
replication of the Church Jesus wants us to be".

Fr Andy's prayer and Phil Glendenning's exhortation both formed
part of the fabric of the conference, the former being recited several
times during the three days, and Glendenning's call being picked up
by many subsequent speakers.

In his encyclical letter *Laudato Si' – Care for our Common Home*, Pope
Francis called on us to "hear both the cry of the earth and the cry of
the poor".[1] This twin theme was picked up in various parts of the
conference and emerges in various chapters of this book. It was also
a feature of the conference liturgies.

Fr Andy's conference prayer reflected on this linkage, with its plea
that God "delight our eyes with the glory of your world, our home"
and its call that the seed of the Gospel:

give grain for the harvest of justice,
and leave seed for a sustainable world.

The Aboriginal spirit that was woven through all the conference
liturgies reinforced this connection, as exemplified in Aunty Betty
Pike's prayer, used in the opening liturgy:

May we listen with great care to the heartbeat of this land
and to its people who cared for it so well and for so long.

---

[1] Pope Francis, 2015. Encyclical Letter, *Laudato Si' – Care for our Common Home*, n. 49,
accessed at w2.vatican.va.

May the peace these people and their land have always enjoyed continue to be strengthened and preserved by all who wish to come and be part of this country and its 'Ancient Dreaming'.[2]

The conference Mass brought conference participants together in a spirit of prayerful reflection on hearing, healing and hope. A reading from *Romans*, Chapter 8 told of the centrality of hope, as we join with all creation in awaiting the fullness of our redemption; and the Gospel reading, from *Luke*, Chapter 14, related the teaching of the banquet, to which we should invite "the poor, the crippled, the lame, and the blind".

Fr Joe Caddy's reflection on these texts led to the heart of the conference and of the commitment of participants to service and work for justice:

As a Church we are called to listen deeply to stories of vulnerability. Those voices are the voices of God in the cries of the poor, those on the margins, who are expendable and of little economic benefit, who are disposable: our Earth – the land and seas and air so delicately hanging in the balance and under such pressure ... How can we transform these pleas into the groans of new birth, into the promise and hope of a new heaven and a new Earth?

Jesus proposes an approach to our social order that starts with the most vulnerable; that is completely other-centred ... It calls for courage in the face of power to put into play this dynamic – it's not about trickle down, looking after the powerful first – it is renewal and resurrection from the bottom – from the grave to new life.

What if we try that? As a Church we can encourage such views, we can walk in solidarity with the poor and the most

[2] Elizabeth Pike, *Opening Prayer*, accessed at www.natsicc.org.au/resources_liturgy.php.

vulnerable and enter respectfully into dialogue with the
diversity of voices and views in our society.

Sr Kerrie Cusack rsj responded to the Mary MacKillop Oration,
delivered by Geraldine Doogue at the conference dinner,[3] and
in doing so she reflected prayerfully on the conference themes. Sr
Kerrie's starting point was service:

> I need to acknowledge firstly that it is the very practical
> work of Catholic social services and its allied entities such
> as MacKillop Family Services that give credibility to Pope
> Francis' image of the Church as the field hospital.

And, even as that service continues, the Church is beset by
challenges:

> The Church's long history of caring for our most vulnerable
> people continues to be valued while the integrity of its
> ministers and all of us, by consequence, is threatened and
> diminishing.
>
> What are the lessons for us as a Church and Catholic social
> services in our damaged and humbled communities? How
> might we move forward humbly and with confidence in a
> God we cannot see?

In addressing these issues, Sr Kerrie was offering her own response
to the gathering, humbly offering her own journey for others to reflect
on as they engage personally with the challenges of the times.

Mary MacKillop was no stranger to adversity, and Sr Kerrie shared
with the gathering the guidance that Mary MacKillop had provided in
her actions and her writings:

> [She] tells us of her overwhelming sense of God's presence
> and of the calmness that overshadowed her after her

---

[3] See pages 69-81 in this volume.

excommunication: 'I saw that God would provide the means, would guide me on the way, and would provide a friend to do for me what I could not do myself'.

'Do have courage. We must all willingly and with constancy suffer all that God sends for our good'.

This was a spirituality of hope, within which Sr Kerrie saw a clear pathway on which to move forward: "To you people here tonight, I say your work is God's work and God will see it truly finished".

Sr Kerrie linked this spirituality of hope to the need for hearing and for healing. She spoke of a need to reach out to ask people for their help to move us beyond this current "dark place"; and to apply Mary MacKillop's maxim that "We must teach more by example than by word". The times, she reflected, call for radical change, as Pope Francis expressed it:

> I dream of a "missionary option", that is a missionary impulse capable of transforming everything, so that the Church's customs, ways of doing things, times and schedules, language and structures can be suitably channelled for the evangelisation of today's world rather than for her self-preservation.[4]

Love of neighbour was at the heart of the *Hearing, Healing, Hope* conference, and most of the issues discussed there were, as this book reflects, related to the people we are called to serve. This discussion, and the collective response for which it calls, arises in a spiritual context, and is sustained for many as part of a shared faith commitment. The liturgies and other overtly spiritual aspects of the conference helped our reflection on the elements of hearing, healing and hope; and provided many participants with food for thought in relation to the integration of liturgy and spirituality with the work of their own organisations.

---

[4] Pope Francis, 2013. Apostolic Exhortation, *Evangelii Gaudium: The Joy of the Gospel*, n. 27, accessed at w2.vatican.va.

19

Bringing Healing and Hope to the World

Gabrielle McMullen AM

Introduction

The closing forum of the Catholic Social Services conference focused on 'Bringing Healing and Hope to the World'. It offered an opportunity to reflect on the previous elements of the conference and contextualise their learnings in participants' ministries. The session invited participants to "grapple together with some of the challenges that face us as a sector, as a church, as a community in this challenging and changing environment of Australia". Fr Frank Brennan SJ facilitated the forum, commencing with a reflection on the conference speakers' input and the insights emanating from the open discussions. He expressed the view:

> I think we've been wrestling with the question: How do we listen to and heal our First Peoples, the last peoples to arrive – the refugees and asylum seekers, those who are left out by government, and survivors of abuse? … The Gospel is not heard at the centre, we need to go to the edges. And each of us in our workplace, we know on the good days that we are privileged to be at the edges. On the bad days, we curse that we are at the edges, that we are always at the edges.

Brennan continued, "As a Church we are not the same, and we cannot remain the same" and our ministries, situated in the contemporary Australia, have to get the "right mix … between the government, the market and the community. Absent ourselves from the community focus, then notions of government and market take over, not just in society". He noted "the respectful space" of the conference and participants' "shared values ... a united passion", which enabled fruitful conversation despite different perspectives and which manifest that we are "on board for any measures to counter inequality and to foster opportunity". He expressed gratitude:

> that within this safe space, we can be attentive to the evidence, the expertise, the listening, the commitment to healing and the abiding hope. It's here within our ranks, looking around this room and reflecting on those with whom we work and those whom we serve ...
>
> So, called to be the people of God, let's turn hearing into getting it, healing into new life, and hope into love, mercy and justice for all ... The wisdom and experience in the room helps us to listen and heal First Peoples, the last people to arrive, those who are left out by government or the market, and those who are the survivors of abuse. This wisdom and experience provides the hope for us to be the Church of the Gospel, rather the church of a bygone clerical era.

Quoting Seamus Heaney's 'The Cure at Troy', Brennan concluded:

> Once in a lifetime
> The longed-for tidal wave
> Of justice can rise up
> And hope and history rhyme.

Wisdom in the Room

Following Brennan's introductory remarks, conference participants in table groups were invited to consider two questions, provide their insights to the forum, and submit written input:

> What is an example of an initiative in your sector that effectively responds to the "signs of the times"?[1]

---

[1] Pope Paul VI, 1965. *Pastoral Constitution on the Church in the Modern World: Gaudium et Spes*, n. 4, accessed at www.vatican.va.

What have we done, or do we plan to do, to address the
contemporary Church's negative 'brand'?

In addressing these questions, the dialogical nature of the forum
enabled participants to hear about, and engage with, the activities
of Catholic agencies across the nation. The discussions opened up
to attendees both established practices and emerging developments
across the Catholic sector, which are effectively meeting the needs
of those on the margins. The forum offered a source of hope
and inspiration to take back to individual agencies, as they imagine
their future. As one participant wrote, "It brought the outputs of
the conference to a reflection on shared practice and new insights".
From participants' feedback both to the forum and in the written
submissions, some key themes emerged.

Developing and Supporting Staff and Volunteers

The most resounding theme was the need to support and develop staff
and volunteers working in Catholic ministries – "they are our greatest
resource". It was suggested that, in an authentic Catholic ministry,
"everyone leads". This focus reinforces how important it is to ensure
that staff and volunteers understand and support the ministry's
mission and values, and to foster a "genuine heart engagement with
the organisational mission" – in other words, to embed Catholicity
strongly in Church agencies.

Importantly, staff and volunteers, Catholic or not, must feel
welcome and enabled to flourish. A focus on the wellbeing of staff
was emphasised, including managers spending more time engaging
with staff and "checking in on how they are going", building
relationships, creating a reflective culture, and providing for ongoing
staff formation and professional development. Staff working on
the periphery are particularly in need of support – "when you work
with the marginalised, you will be marginalised". This focus on staff

wellbeing is of particular importance at times of adverse publicity for the ministry and/or the Church.

Participants advocated for more transparency around processes, decision-making and rationale as elements of building trust. Workplaces should be a safe place for all staff (and for clients) to be able to ask questions and have them answered, to bring issues from "dark places ... into the open". There was a focus on improved communication with and between staff, including providing opportunities for open dialogue. Integrity in the workplace was identified as the basis for ensuring integrity in the services offered. In looking at improved processes suggestions included giving clients a voice in the employee recruitment process, both staff cultural training and staff cultural diversity, and 'professionalising' volunteers.

Getting younger people involved and developing leadership potential were seen as critically important for the future of Catholic ministries. Significantly, the strategy to support emerging leaders participate in the Catholic Social Services conference has led to further development of this focus by Catholic Social Services Victoria. Other strategies identified were mentoring new staff, with a particular focus on leadership for mission, and leaders working side-by-side with staff "so they are assisted to continue what they do with pride".

Agencies Working Collaboratively

Feedback encouraged agencies, especially Catholic ministries, to collaborate more with one another, sharing expertise, and building strengths in service delivery rather than competing with one another: "Collaborations across ministries and sectors are critical in moving forward". One table group wrote: "There is so much expertise under the Catholic banner, but we are not connecting with each other". Collaborative opportunities named were brokering partnerships, preparing joint submissions for funding, corporate purchasing and other processes "to do it better and make funds go further".

Working collectively, where appropriate, was seen as particularly important in rural areas and as a means of offering clients wide-ranging and integrated services. Particular examples given of developing respectful relationships which have brought together complementary expertise included the St Vincent de Paul Society's Matthew's Offering with St Vincent's Hospital Melbourne, which cares for country people requiring medical services in Melbourne and their families back home,[2] CatholicCare Melbourne working with the Brighton Lifesaving Club to offer a water safety program for refugees, applying Montessori principles to the care of the elderly,[3] an agency working with the Royal Automobile Club of Victoria to assist clients gain a driver's licence, and Edmund Rice Services partnering with a housing estate developer "to put measures in place to try and prevent many of the social issues ... coming through our growth corridors". Brennan captured the spirit of partnership as follows:

> we need to foster connectedness, and to partner with each other as Catholic social service providers, sharing our best practice as we have today, and sharing those new ideas which are suffused with hope, because by sharing these ideas, suffused with hope, we can go back to the margins with renewed passion, with renewed energy, with renewed vision, and we can continue our work of the Kingdom breaking in here and now.

Learning from Experience

The forum highlighted the challenging contemporary environment in which our ministries serve – it is highly regulated and rapidly changing; there are growing inequalities and for-profit bodies seeking 'business'; and the reputation of the Church means that 'branding' is an issue

---

[2] Matthew's Offering was featured in the following newsletter: www.vinnies.org.au/icms_docs/282092_Societynews_-_2018_January-February.pdf.

[3] For information about the work of Montessori Ageing Support Services, a division of Montessori Australia, see www.massa.org.au.

for Catholic agencies. Despite these challenges, the forum noted the willingness of the sector to take risks to serve those at the margins, and to learn from initiatives which are not 'optimal' and to develop "new models of care which suit our clients". A powerful example of this is Catholic agencies investing their own resources in engaging with the National Disability Insurance Scheme (NDIS) to establish it on a sound basis, in the context of inadequate government funding, in order to serve the needs of people with disability.

The sector needs a capacity to review gaps in services for those on the margins and, in particular, to develop integrated services which will address their needs holistically, and which may best be achieved through strategic partnerships. Further, the sector must invest resources in research and evaluation to obtain evidence of program effectiveness or otherwise, and to identify improvements or alternative offerings.

The forum noted the effective "handing on of the governance of many ministries from religious and clergy to lay people", who now have "a strong and professional, and committed voice in the Church" in this sector. However, while noting that the wider Church could learn from the effective governance of these Church agencies, the latter were challenged to look further at internal governance to increase transparency. The key role of boards in setting culture was noted and the need for boards to undertake a periodic review of the Catholicity of a ministry.

Responding to the "Signs of the Times"

Forum participants valued the opportunity to hear of others' experiences and learn from them and then potentially to "research and develop solutions at the local level". Being innovative and flexible is critical to serving at the margins and addressing changing client needs. In this context, ministries need to evolve, potentially letting go of some services to address new needs or looking at new ways of tackling embedded disadvantage. While noting "myriad needs", forum participants suggested areas of future focus as:

- implementing and leading in safeguarding practices for children and vulnerable people,
- finding new ways to work with Indigenous peoples,
- addressing domestic and family violence and the "increasingly complex needs of families",
- increased services for the aged, including for aged prisoners and homeless,
- addressing human trafficking and forced marriage,
- services for young people "who fall through the cracks".

Such developments focus on inclusive, community-focused care with a commitment to services to people regardless of sexuality. Agencies need to look at how appropriate facilities are for those of other backgrounds, such as Indigenous Australians, those with disability, and those from other cultures, adapting their spaces to meet current and new needs. A strength of Church agencies was seen as "the organic nature of our services; adapting to individual need is of great importance. This is Jesus' approach".

New areas of need continue to emerge in Australian society. Resources need to be invested in evaluating the effectiveness of services and making improvements, and in identifying service gaps and seeking to meet these, including through partnering with other agencies.

A stronger focus on advocacy should be a cornerstone of future development and be informed by "listening to the voices of children, youth and adults, the people we serve" and by "having dialogue with survivors of abuse" in order "to make a meaningful contribution that is respectful". "We are not good at listening, [but rather] telling them what they need; we need more humility"; we need to be "companions" to engage and assist those on the margins. Advocacy should have a particular focus on "assisting those who are not represented". One table group stated:

> It's just really about getting back to the individual, listening to individuals, and helping people take control of their own lives and helping and walking with them, so that we are the broken working with the broken, not those that are handing out care, but people who are walking with other people.

On the role of advocacy influencing public policy, Brennan emphasised the "need to work together to produce evidence and research, which informs public opinion, and assists lawmakers to develop just and compassionate social and economic policies that will improve the lives of the poor and vulnerable in Australia".

Good News Stories

The forum identified many "good news stories" and the need to "showcase what we do", ensuring that it is known that we are 'open'. The view was expressed on a number of occasions that we should be promoting the good work that Catholic social services and other Church ministries do, as they realise the Church of the Gospel. We need to be willing "to stand up and say we are Catholic" and by "walking the talk of being a Catholic organisation", overcome the Church's negative brand to ensure our Catholic agencies are able to reach out inclusively to the marginalised.

While the Royal Commission into Institutional Responses to Child Sexual Abuse showed that the Church failed so often in the past, we can move forward with hope, "living the Gospel, not as the powerful but as the broken". We need to "use the language of compassion and not direction", to "focus on the person in need and not the circumstances" and to support both staff and clients to flourish – "helping our clients flourish is why we exist". Participants highlighted: "Our client experience is one of the best"; we need tools to spread this positive message and to "bring some balance into the Catholic brand"; we have to change the situation that "we don't talk up Catholic social justice".

Highlighting that Catholic ministries are the Church, it was agreed that it would be "valuable to share the Church in action, especially in its work with the most vulnerable". Pope Francis was seen as a source of inspiration to those in Church ministries at the margins, and they relate well to his powerful message: "Go smell the sheep".

Conclusion

The 'Bringing Healing and Hope to the World' forum with its "examples of renewal and energy shared" was a hope-filled occasion: "it was good to hear about some of the positive actions which are happening across Australia". It was a "opportunity to 'account for the hope within us' on hearing all that is happening", which is of the Church of the Gospel; "the springs of hope are manifold".

In our roles in Catholic social services and other Church ministries, we are privileged to be continuing the mission of Jesus. Of the essence "is always going back to who we're doing it for, the faces of the people that we encounter on a daily basis".

Brennan offered a concluding reflection as the forum drew to a close, highlighting "how much is going on":

> Isn't this our Church at its best? Here we are sharing best practice, and new ideas suffused with hope in our service of people at the margins, which really is the Kingdom breaking in here and now ... the works that we perform day in and day out, the ministries that we perform, the hope that we share, speak to us of that Gospel, speaks to us of the Church at its best.

Contributors

Fiona Basile, Freelance Writer and Photographer

Fiona Basile is a freelance writer and photographer based in Melbourne. She regularly provides writing and photography content for Catholic Social Services Victoria, agencies of the Catholic Archdiocese of Melbourne including the Life, Marriage and Family Office and Media and Communications Office, as well as local Catholic orders and parishes, and other community and commercially-based clients. Fiona contributes a monthly article to *Melbourne Catholic*, the official journal of the Archdiocese, focussing on parish life, mission and outreach and she is the author of *Shhh … God is in the Silence*, a children's book that was recently published by Loyola Press in the United States. Fiona is in the process of writing a second book while contributing to other book projects.

Paul Bongiorno AM, Veteran Journalist and Columnist

Paul Bongiorno writes weekly columns for *The Saturday Paper* and other publications. He is a regular commentator on ABC Radio National and Contributing Editor for Network 10. He has been a journalist for 40 years and in that time has won four national Walkey Awards for journalistic excellence. For the past 30 years he has been a member of the Federal Parliamentary press gallery and for 17 of them he was Ten's Bureau Chief and host of the national political program *Meet The Press*. Before that he covered Queensland State politics for ten years at Channel Ten Brisbane. Paul has a master's degree (STL) in Theology from the Pontifical Urban University, Rome.

Fr Frank Brennan SJ AO, Chief Executive Officer, Catholic Social Services Australia

Frank Brennan is a Jesuit priest and Chief Executive Officer of

Catholic Social Services Australia. He is also superior of the Jesuit community at Xavier House in Canberra. He has been Professor of Law at Australian Catholic University and Adjunct Professor at the Australian Centre for Christianity and Culture, the Australian National University College of Law and the National Centre for Indigenous Studies. He has also served as the National Director of Human Rights and Social Justice for Jesuit Social Services.

Archbishop Mark Coleridge, Archbishop of Brisbane

Elected in May 2018 as Chair of the Australian Catholic Bishops Conference, Mark Coleridge has been Archbishop of Brisbane since 2012, having previously served as Archbishop of Canberra and Goulburn and Auxiliary Bishop in the Archdiocese of Melbourne. Born in Melbourne, and educated in both South Australia and Victoria, Archbishop Mark was ordained a priest in 1974, and worked in parish ministry before undertaking scripture studies in Rome and Jerusalem. His academic career culminated in his appointment as Master of Catholic Theological College, Melbourne, which was followed by four years in the Vatican Secretariat of State. In 2004, he was appointed a member of the Pontifical Council for Culture and Chair of the Roman Missal Editorial Committee of the International Committee for English in the Liturgy. He was subsequently named Chair of the International Commission for the Preparation of an English-language Lectionary.

Dr Bob Dixon, Former Director, Pastoral Research Office

Bob Dixon was Director of the Pastoral Research Office (PRO) of the Australian Catholic Bishops Conference from 1996 until his retirement in 2016. He is the author or co-author of numerous publications about the demography of the Australian Catholic population, aspects of Catholic belief and practice, and Catholic parishes. He holds honorary appointments at Australian Catholic

Contributors

University and the University of Divinity. He and his wife Cath are longstanding members of St Anthony's Parish in Noble Park. One of the significant projects conducted by the PRO during Bob's time as Director was the Building Stronger Parishes project, an in-depth study of 20 vital parishes around Australia that has the capacity to inspire other parishes with ideas and insights by which they can approach the future.

Geraldine Doogue AO, Journalist and Broadcaster

Geraldine Doogue is an Australian journalist and broadcaster known for her reporting on religious and social affairs. She has worked extensively in print, television and radio, including for *The Australian*, ABC's Nationwide, 2UE, Channel 10 news and as presenter of ABC TV's *Compass* program. She played a major role in ABC TV's coverage of the Gulf War in 1991. In 1992 Geraldine began presenting *Life Matters* on ABC Radio National, which covered the full gamut of social issues in everyday life. Geraldine has an interest in the relationship between Islam and the Western world, co-producing *Tomorrow's Islam* in 2003 with Peter Kirkwood. In 2005 the pair co-authored a book *Tomorrow's Islam: Uniting Age-old Beliefs and a Modern World*. Geraldine continues to tackle a wide range of subjects in her ongoing role as presenter of the ABC Radio National program *Saturday Extra* and ABC TV's *Compass*.

Darlene Dreise, Mission Executive, St Vincent's Health Australia (Toowoomba)

Darlene Dreise is a highly skilled, experienced educator originally from Cairns but now living in Toowoomba. With Torres Strait Islander and Chinese heritage, the lived experience of diversity and the importance of inclusiveness have been hallmarks of her approach to relating with and educating others over a career spanning 25 years. Darlene's academic achievements include the completion of a

279

Bachelor of Teaching (ACU), Bachelor of Education (JCU), Master of Learning Innovation (QUT) and Graduate Certificate in Leadership and Catholic Culture (ACU). She respectfully acknowledges that these achievements have been made possible by the efforts of her Aboriginal and Torres Strait Islander forebears, the prioritisation of educational opportunities by her parents and the ongoing support of her husband and extended family.

Denis Fitzgerald, Executive Director, Catholic Social Services Victoria

As Executive Director of Catholic Social Services Victoria for the past 10 years, Denis Fitzgerald has worked with member organisations in public policy advocacy, strengthening cooperation within the sector, and reflecting on Catholic identity and its implications for social services. He is a member of a number of Government advisory committees. Denis' qualifications are in philosophy, accounting and public policy. As an Australian Diplomat, Denis served in High Commissions in London and the Solomon Islands, with the World Bank in Washington DC and three years as Australia's High Commissioner to Nauru. He has also advised the Victorian Government on taxation law and consumer protection, and administered programs in these areas.

Adrian Foley, Coordinator, Welcome the Asylum Seeker Parish Support Program

Adrian Foley grew up in Western Victoria. He worked in Cobden for a livestock company before working with several Commonwealth and Victorian Public Service departments, retiring in 2003. Grandfather of seven, Adrian has contributed in a range of volunteer roles to Catholic Social Services Victoria and the Catholic Prison Ministry since 2006. In 2014 Adrian helped establish the Welcome the Asylum Seeker Parish Support Program, and more recently the Parishes as

Centres of Service program. He aims to support parishes in their outreach ministries to people in need, and to build parish capacity for service.

Phil Glendenning AM, Director, Edmund Rice Centre

Phil Glendenning was one of the original co-founders of Australians for Native Title and Reconciliation (ANTaR) and for 10 years National President. He has served on the Australian Council for Social Service, various committees of the Australian Council for Overseas Aid and the Centre for an Ethical Society. Phil also led the research team for the *Deported To Danger* series, which monitored the safety of rejected asylum seekers in 22 countries, and resulted in the internationally screened documentary, *A Well Founded Fear*.

Maria Harries AM, PhD, GAICD, Chairperson, Catholic Social Services Australia Board

Maria Harries is Adjunct Professor at the Curtin University School of Occupational Therapy and Social Work and a Senior Honorary Research Fellow in the School of Population Health at The University of Western Australia. She runs her own consulting practice, continues her research work and is a research supervisor with a number of PhD students. She also works with a number of state and national organisations involved with people who have experienced 'care'. Maria was the inaugural Chairperson of MercyCare WA. She has held many leadership positions within the mental health and broader social services sector in Western Australia and nationally. In addition to her 'portfolio of other retirement commitments', in 2014 Maria assumed the role of Chairperson of Catholic Social Services Australia.

Ingrid Hatfield, formerly of Catholic Social Services Australia

Ingrid Hatfield is an experienced policy analyst and relationship builder, with a passion for the development of social policy which improves people's lives and promotes flourishing communities. She has worked in the values-led social services sector for over eight years, most recently as Project and Research Officer with Catholic Social Services Australia. As part of this role, Ingrid facilitated the re-establishment of the CSSA National Disability Insurance Scheme network group, supporting the sharing of best practice in disability service delivery in the new NDIS environment, and collaboration to advocate for policy and system change. Ingrid has a background in psychology and community development.

Dr May Lam, Director of Research at Marist180 and Coordinator of the Australian Catholic Housing Alliance

Dr May Lam has a background in education as a secondary teacher and university lecturer. For the past 25 years she has worked in policy, research and other programs for unemployed disadvantaged people, with particular interests in youth transitions, government services contracting and social innovation design. May has worked at the community sector industry peak body Jobs Australia (1992-2004) and served as its Deputy CEO and Policy Manager (2011-2013). In the UK May worked for the employment services company Ingeus and the Department of Work and Pensions (2005-2008). More recent roles in policy and strategy have been at the Brotherhood of St Laurence, Social Traders, and the National Employment Services Association. May was Chair of Writers Victoria (2013-2016) and is currently on the Board of Youth Development Australia. She has a BA, DipEd, Grad Dip Librarianship, MEd and PhD from the University of Melbourne.

Aaron Lane

Aaron Lane is Lecturer in the Graduate School of Business and Law at RMIT University, and Adjunct Legal Fellow at the Institute of Public Affairs (IPA). He contributes to the IPA's Dignity of Work research project and has provided expert evidence to several parliamentary inquiries. His academic research focuses on the relationship between regulation and innovation. Aaron graduated with a Bachelor of Commerce and a Bachelor of Laws (Honours) from Deakin University. He completed a Graduate Diploma of Legal Practice with the College of Law and was admitted to the Supreme Court of Victoria in 2012. He also holds a Graduate Diploma of Theology and a Master of Arts from the University of Divinity, graduating as Vice-Chancellor's Scholar.

Professor Gabrielle McMullen AM, Emeritus Professor, Australian Catholic University

Professor Gabrielle McMullen AM joined the Faculty of Medicine at Monash University and was appointed Dean of the University's Catholic residence, Mannix College, in 1981. She was then Rector of Australian Catholic University's Ballarat campus from 1995-2000 and its Pro- and Deputy Vice-Chancellor (Academic) until early 2011. Gabrielle has been a Trustee of Mary Aikenhead Ministries (2011-2017) and since 2015 one of the lay appointees to the Stewardship Council of the Missionary Sisters of Service. She is a member of the Council of the University of Divinity and the Council of the Divine Word University in Madang, Papua New Guinea. She has served on a wide range of boards across the Catholic sector.

Dr Robyn Miller, Chief Executive Officer, MacKillop Family Services

Dr Robyn Miller is a social worker and family therapist with over 30 years' experience in the community sector, local government and child protection. She was a senior clinician and teacher for 14 years at the Bouverie Family Therapy Centre, La Trobe University, and part of an innovative team working with families who had experienced trauma and sexual abuse. Robyn has practised in the public and private sectors as a therapist, clinical supervisor, consultant and lecturer and was a member of the Victorian Child Death Review Committee for 10 years. She was the recipient of the inaugural Robin Clark memorial PhD scholarship in 2004 and the statewide award for Inspirational Leadership in Victoria in 2010. From 2006-2015 Robyn provided professional leadership as the Chief Practitioner within the Department of Human Services in Victoria. She has also worked as a consultant with the Royal Commission into Institutional Responses to Child Sexual Abuse. In August 2017 Dr Miller was appointed a Director of Catholic Professional Standards.

Mark Monahan, Executive Officer, Edmund Rice Services (Mt Atkinson)

Prior to his current role, Mark Monahan was the Executive Officer of Edmund Rice Camps for nine years. He has a degree in Recreation Leadership and a Master of Social Work. He is a board member of the Australian Camps Association. Mark is married and has three children aged 9, 8 and 4 and loves living on the surf coast at Ocean Grove. He works from an holistic point of view drawing on his personal life experiences, ongoing studies, work experience and day-to-day interactions within the community and being a husband and parent.

Clare O'Neil MP, Member for Hotham Victoria

Clare O'Neil is the Federal Member for Hotham and the Shadow Minister for Justice. She was first elected in 2013 and re-elected in 2016. Clare understands the Australian economy and its impact on everyday Australians. Before entering Parliament, she studied with some of the world's most famous economists. She has also sat in boardrooms and worked in workplaces in mining, manufacturing, telecommunications and retail. Clare studied a Bachelor of Arts and Bachelor of Laws, both with Honours, at Monash University in Clayton. She was then awarded a Fulbright Scholarship to study a Master of Public Policy at Harvard University in the United States.

She lived in Boston and New York, where she spent time working in the New York Stock Exchange. At 23, Clare became the youngest female mayor in Australian history, just twelve months after being elected to represent the people of Springvale South on the City of Greater Dandenong Council. Today, she represents these same constituents, but in the Federal Parliament. Clare has also lived and worked in North East Arnhem Land, supporting local Indigenous women to establish small businesses.

Des Powell AM, Chair, MacKillop Family Services

Des Powell has held a range of senior executive management roles in both the private and public sectors in Australia and Asia. He operated his own consultancy business between 2000 and 2015 and has held a number of key governance appointments. He currently is a Commissioner for the Victorian Gambling and Liquor Commission, Chair of Federation Training, a Director of Barwon Water and a Director of the Victorian Regional Channels Authority. Previously he has held numerous positions at Federal and State level including Director of the Victorian Ports Corporation (Melbourne) with six years as Deputy Chair, and former Commissioner and Deputy Chair of the National Transport Commission. Des was the inaugural Chair of Edmund Rice Education Australia from 2006 to 2012. He is currently Chair of MacKillop Family Services. In June 2014 Des was appointed as a Member of the Order of Australia (AM) in the Queen's Birthday Honours list for his significant contribution to business, commerce and the community.

Elizabeth Proust AO, Chair, Australian Institute of Company Directors

Elizabeth Proust has held leadership roles in the private and public sectors in Australia for more than 30 years. She has worked in local, State and Federal Government, the oil industry and in banking. She has held senior positions in the Victorian Government and was Chief Executive Officer of the City of Melbourne. Elizabeth is currently Chair of Nestle (Australia), the Bank of Melbourne, and the Australian Institute of Company Directors and a Director of Lend Lease Corporation. She was also Deputy Chair of the Catholic Church's Truth Justice and Healing Council. Elizabeth has a Law degree (University of Melbourne) and a Bachelor of Arts (Honours) (La Trobe University).

John Roskam, Executive Director, Institute of Public Affairs

John Roskam has been the Executive Director of the free market think tank, the Institute of Public Affairs (IPA), since 2005. Before joining the IPA he taught political theory at the University of Melbourne. He was previously the Executive Director of The Menzies Research Centre in Canberra, has been a senior adviser and chief of staff to Federal and State education ministers, and was the manager of government and corporate affairs for a global mining company. His publications include *Australia's Education Choices* (with Professor Brian Caldwell), *Terrorism and Poverty in Blaming Ourselves, Liberalism and Social Welfare in Liberalism and the Australian Federation*, and "The Liberal Party and the Great Split" in *The Split Fifty Years Later*. His fortnightly column appears in *The Australian Financial Review*. He is a member of the Editorial Board of *The Australian Journal of Public Administration* and Connor Court Publishing, and the Advisory Board of The Centre for Advanced Journalism at the University of Melbourne. He is a Fellow of the Institute of Public Administration, Australia in Victoria, and is an Honorary Fellow of Campion College.

Patrice Scales

Patrice Scales is a communications practitioner and strategist by profession, and has held senior management positions in the public, private and not-for-profit sector for over 30 years. She has a Bachelor of Arts and Master of Arts (Communications), and from 2003-2016 worked as a management and communications consultant across the not-for-profit sector. Her commitment to social justice was nurtured through her early family life, and as a full-time worker for the Young Christian Workers. Patrice has been on the board of several Catholic social service organisations and was Chair of Catholic Social Services Victoria from 2012-2016. She currently serves on the National Council of Caritas Australia and in other advisory roles.

Joe Zabar, Deputy CEO, Catholic Social Services Australia

In his role with Catholic Social Services Australia, Joe Zabar seeks to advance policies that improve social services to, and the wellbeing of, the disadvantaged and vulnerable in our community. He does this by developing and advocating for policy reforms which address economic inequality and income adequacy, and improve the sustainability of social services provision. Joe has more than 25 years of experience spanning the government and non-for-profit sectors in areas such as advocacy, policy, marketing and fund-raising, human resources and business management.

Acknowledgements

Editors and readers alike are indebted to many people and organisations for their contribution to the writing and the development of this book: this level of cooperation exemplifies the collaboration, dialogue and shared sense of purpose that is a feature of Catholic social services in Australia and the many parts of the Church and society with which they work.

Most of the material in the book is based on presentations at the Catholic Social Services conference entitled *Hearing, Healing, Hope*, held on 21-23 February 2018 at the Catholic Leadership Centre in Melbourne. It has all been revised for publication, and some of it – such as Archbishop Mark Coleridge's *Preface*, the *Introduction*, and Paul Bongiorno's reflective chapter – have been written in light of discussion at the conference. We are in the debt of all these contributors.

Deep thanks is owed to the many authors, most of whom themselves presented at the conference, and to those presenters whose work was incorporated into chapters that have been written by others. A special mention can be made of those who coordinated chapters, and worked with a number of others to integrate a range of material on a particular topic into a coherent body. Fiona Basile, Bob Dixon, Adrian Foley, Maria Harries, Ingrid Hatfield, May Lam and Mark Monahan joined the editors in contributing in this way – thank you.

The cooperation and professional work of Anthony Cappello, Michael Gilchrist and their colleagues at Connor Court Publishing greatly facilitated the development of the book. This is the third book that has been developed in such a way. We are blessed with such publishers.

The conference out of which the book emerged was organised

by Catholic Social Services Victoria in partnership with Catholic Social Services Australia. We are grateful to the participants in the conference from across Australia, who contributed to the discussion of the ideas that were presented. The Steering Committee for the conference was chaired by Denis Fitzgerald and included Sue Cattermole, Tiffany Davis, Peter Hudson, Paul Jensen, Gabrielle McMullen, Mark Monahan and Peter Richardson; with, at various times, Fiona Basile, Lucia Brick, Lil Bryant-Johnston, Kylie Burgess and Joe Zabar. Committee members all contributed to the event in many ways.

Lucia Brick again led staff and volunteers in conference administration, supported in particularly by Huong Nguyen and staff of the Catholic Leadership Centre.

High quality communications support for all stages of the conference was provided by Fiona Basile of Catholic Social Services Victoria, Lil Bryant-Johnston of Catholic Social Services Australia, Tiffany Davis from the Archbishop of Melbourne's Office for Evangelisation, and colleagues from *Melbourne Catholic* and *Eureka Street*, which was the official media partner for the conference. This work significantly facilitated the development of the book.

Sponsors were one of the underpinnings of the conference, in that they made it financially feasible for the participation of presenters and others who added to the dialogue and overall experience; and they thus made this book feasible too. We thank:

- Australian Catholic University
- Cabrini Health
- Catholic Church Insurances
- Catholic Education Melbourne
- Catholic Super
- CatholicCare Greater Melbourne, Geelong, Gippsland

- CatholicCare Sandhurst
- Christian Brothers Oceania Province
- Sisters of St Joseph of the Sacred Heart
- Villa Maria Catholic Homes

The editors, on behalf of Catholic Social Services Victoria and Catholic Social Services Australia, express their thanks to all those mentioned here for their part in bringing this book to fruition, and thus contributing to advancing the Gospel-inspired work of service and work for justice of the Church in Australia.

www.ingramcontent.com/pod-product-compliance
Lightning Source LLC
Chambersburg PA
CBHW071838270326
41929CB00013B/2037